The Pharmaceutical Industry
and Dependency
in the Third World

The Pharmaceutical Industry and Dependency in the Third World

Gary Gereffi

WITHDRAWN

Princeton University Press
Princeton, New Jersey

To my parents, Emily and Nicky Gereffi,
with love and appreciation
for all they have done for their children

Contents

CONTENTS

List of Tables

LIST OF TABLES

Acknowledgments

THIS book spans seven years, several institutional affiliations, and numerous personal friendships. It is a pleasure to be able to acknowledge some of these here. My initial research on the Mexican steroid hormone industry was carried out in 1975 and 1976 on a Foreign Area Fellowship from the Social Science Research Council and the American Council of Learned Societies. While in Mexico I worked at El Colegio de México, which generously afforded me its research facilities and a stimulating intellectual environment. Although my Ph.D. in sociology was awarded by Yale University in 1980, the Center for International Affairs (CFIA) at Harvard University was kind enough to host me as a visiting scholar from 1977 to 1980. In addition, in 1977 the CFIA provided me with a grant from its Transnational Relations Program, funded by the Rockefeller Foundation. For the unusual personal magnanimity that made this institutional hospitality possible, I would like to thank especially Jorge Domínguez, Samuel P. Huntington, and Raymond Vernon. In 1979 Vernon also made available to me a small grant from his Multinational Enterprise Project at the Harvard Business School.

From 1976 until 1980 I was fortunate enough to be a member of the Continuing Working Group on Multinational Corporations in Latin America, which was sponsored by the Social Science Research Council and the American Council of Learned Societies. Thanks go to Peter Evans, Louis Wolf Goodman, and Alfred Stepan for founding the group, although the intense and richly thought-provoking intellectual exchanges that characterized our meetings were thoroughly a collective product involving all of the group's regular members. These included Douglas C. Bennett, Rhys Jenkins,

ACKNOWLEDGMENTS

David Martin, David Moore, Richard Newfarmer, Kenneth Sharpe, Phillip Shepherd, Peter West, and Van Whiting, Jr. Much of the material on the international pharmaceutical industry contained in the last two chapters of this book was gathered while I served as a consultant to the United Nations Centre on Transnational Corporations in New York beginning in 1977. My initial work there culminated in the publication of the UN Centre's sales document, "Transnational Corporations and the Pharmaceutical Industry" (1979). My appreciation goes to Jacob de Vos van Steenwijk, Arthur Domike, Barbara Durr, the late Alberto Jimenez, and Ahmed Rhazaoui for their collaboration and leadership with regard to the Centre's pharmaceutical studies.

Many other individuals have helped me as both friends and colleagues in this undertaking. Wendell Bell, Louis Wolf Goodman, Juan Linz, and Alfred Stepan of Yale University were not only constant sources of support during my graduate school years but they also communicated to me the challenge and excitement of doing cross-national social scientific inquiry. Raymond Vernon has been equally vigorous as a friend and a constructive critic, and I thank him for both. Douglas Bennett, Steven E. Sanderson, Kenneth Sharpe, and Barbara Stallings all read the final version of this manuscript in its entirety and provided me with excellent comments that undoubtedly have made this a better book. Sandy Thatcher of Princeton University Press has shown unfailing good judgment, patience, and enthusiasm at all stages of the editorial process, and it is now clear to me why he is widely regarded as an outstanding social science editor. Cathy Thatcher made the copy-editing process more painless and efficient than I ever thought it could be.

I am especially grateful to the many, many people I spoke with or interviewed in the course of my research for this project in Mexico and elsewhere. Whatever I have learned about the pharmaceutical industry, I owe in large part to them. For typing the last draft of this book, at times above and beyond the call of duty, Louise Rochelle deserves and has my thanks.

ACKNOWLEDGMENTS

Finally my deepest appreciation and gratitude go to my wife Pela and also to our daughter Emily. Pela more than anyone else has lived with this book from beginning to end and throughout the venture has been a constant source of support and encouragement to me.

PART ONE

HISTORICAL-STRUCTURAL DEPENDENCY ANALYSIS: THEORY AND METHOD

CHAPTER ONE

Dependency Theory and
Third World Development

THE study of third world development is in a state of crisis. The crisis has been generated by the sharp contrast between two competing explanations of underdevelopment, known broadly as modernization theory and dependency theory.[1] The central question posed by each approach is the same: How does one account for the stark divergence between the success of those few Western nations called modern and the extreme backwardness that has characterized most of the rest of the world? Despite this common concern the modernization and dependency perspectives differ in their origins, assumptions, and major conclusions. The principal areas of contention can be briefly highlighted.

Modernization theory arose after World War II in the wake of the emerging nationalist and revolutionary movements in the third world that resulted in decolonization and the creation of many new political regimes. The new societies formed by this process quickly assumed an important place in the consciousness of U.S. elites both inside and outside the government as a potential arena of cold war conflict. Government agencies and private foundations encouraged and facilitated research on countries in Africa, Asia, the Middle East, and Latin America in order to identify and propose remedies for some of their most pressing developmental needs as well

[1] I will use the terms theory, perspective, and approach interchangeably in discussing the modernization and dependency literatures. Because the notions of modernization and dependency have been used in so many ways, any attempt at definitional precision at the most general level seems fruitless. Within each perspective, however, it is important to identify a variety of more specific theories and explanations.

3

as to increase the flow of information concerning these societies in the United States. Primarily through the efforts of North American social scientists in a variety of disciplines—economics (Rostow, 1960; Hoselitz, 1960), political science (Almond and Coleman, 1960; Rustow, 1967), sociology (Lerner, 1958; Inkeles, 1969), psychology (McClelland, 1961; Hagen, 1962), and history (Black, 1966)—modernization theory became the dominant form of development analysis in the 1950s and 1960s.

Intellectually, the idea of modernization grew out of the traditional-modern dichotomy so prominent in nineteenth-century social thought.[2] The classic bipolar models of social change of the nineteenth century were adapted in the mid-twentieth century by the American sociologist Talcott Parsons (1951) into a scheme of "pattern variables,"[3] which be-

[2] Among the best-known formulations of the polar social categories of tradition and modernity are Sir Henry Maine's (1861) distinction between societies based on status and those based on contract, Ferdinand Toennies' (1887) contrast between *Gemeinschaft* (community) and *Gesellschaft* (society), Emile Durkheim's (1893) focus on mechanic versus organic solidarity, Herbert Spencer's (1850) evolution from undifferentiated homogeneity to differentiated heterogeneity, Karl Marx's (1867) theory of the transformation of feudal-agricultural societies into capitalist-industrial ones, and Max Weber's (1922) discussion of traditional and rational forms of authority. In every instance the direction of change was toward that set of features which supposedly characterized Western Europe alone.

[3] Parsons' pattern variable scheme is an attempt to break the time-honored polarity of tradition and modernity into a series of more specific and exhaustive value orientations or "dilemmas of choice" for social action: ascription vs. achievement, affectivity vs. affective neutrality, collectivity-orientation vs. self-orientation, diffuseness vs. specificity, and particularism vs. universalism. Writers of the structural-functionalist school began to employ this pattern variable scheme as an ideal-typical construct of development, with an entire society seen as moving from a position near one end of a continuum involving the traditional poles of these dichotomies toward the other end of the continuum. For Bert Hoselitz (1960), for example, underdeveloped (traditional) societies are those in which roles are ascribed, functionally diffuse, and oriented toward narrow particularistic goals; developed (modern) societies are characterized by achievement criteria, clearly delineated specific roles, and universalistic norms. A more ample listing of variables associated with the traditional and modern poles is given in Valenzuela and Valenzuela (1978: 537–538).

came the basis for much of his structural-functionalist theorizing. Structural-functionalism, in turn, spawned two distinct theories of national development: the theory of industrial society,[4] which drew upon the experiences of the advanced countries, and modernization theory, which addressed the nations of the third world.

The basic assumption of modernization studies has been that the institutions and values of the United States, at least in their idealized forms, represent an appropriate model that other less fortunate societies should emulate. Underdevelopment is conceived of as an original state characterized by traditionalism; development thus consists in abandoning these features and adopting those of the advanced nations. This change occurs, according to the modernization perspective, via "diffusion." Both material benefits (capital and technology) and cultural patterns (institutions and values) are diffused or spread from the developed to the underdeveloped countries and within each underdeveloped nation from the modern to the traditional sectors. The material inputs are to

[4] The theory of industrial society, associated with a diverse group of authors including Ralf Dahrendorf (1957), Clark Kerr et al. (1960), and Raymond Aron (1962), asserts that the fundamental distinction in the modern world is between traditional agrarian society and urban industrial society. The unitary character of industrial society is determined by particular technologies and by the social relationships and groups that they generate. A rash of "post-industrial" theorizing concerned with the impact of technology on modern rather than traditional or transitional society emerged in the late 1960s and 1970s with such scholars as Alain Touraine (1969), Zbigniew Brzezinski (1970), and Daniel Bell (1973). By and large, however, the works of the latter group maintain the assumptions of the theory of industrial society and the bipolar model of social change on which it is based. First, post-industrial society is supposed to be superseding industrial society in the same unilinear fashion that the latter developed out of traditional society. Second, society is thought to derive its central features from economic and social factors, not from political ones; the state, in other words, is assumed to be subordinate to society. Third, industrial and post-industrial society theorists predict that in the long run the similarities inherent in the course of economic change will bring about a convergence of social systems and an erasing of differences that derive from distinct pasts. More specifically, the United States is viewed as having replaced Britain in offering to the industrialized world an image of its future.

5

be transmitted mainly through foreign investment and aid; cultural patterns such as democratic attitudes and modern entrepreneurship should be diffused through education and the mass media. The anticipated result is the elimination of those internal obstacles that prevented the underdeveloped societies from following the path already set by the advanced nations.

By the mid-1960s the correctness of these views was being called into question in Latin America and elsewhere. Poor economic performance in many third world areas appeared to be at odds with the benefits espoused by adherents of the modernization approach. The early optimism of the 1950s rapidly gave way to disillusionment: there was continued widespread economic stagnation in Latin America even though foreign investment and aid had been greatly increased, as called for by the theory. During the 1960s, the overall economic gap between the wealthiest and the poorest countries of the world actually grew wider rather than narrower.[5]

In an effort to explain this lack of progress, an alternative interpretation that became known as the dependency perspective was elaborated in various Latin American intellectual circles in the 1960s. By the mid-1970s this approach had gained extensive attention in international organizations, government planning agencies, and the North American and European academic communities and was being touted widely as the "new paradigm" for development studies.

Dependency theory is the progeny of diverse intellectual currents. Within Latin America the seminal work was by Fernando Henrique Cardoso and Enzo Faletto, *Dependency and Development in Latin America* (1969). Because this book was not available in English translation until 1979, much of the North American and British "consumption of dependency theory" (Cardoso, 1977) has relied heavily on the writings of

[5] For some evidence of this widening gap see Dos Santos (1969: 163–165) and Portes (1976: 56–59).

Andre Gunder Frank (1967*a*, 1969, 1972).[6] Frank not only provided one of the earliest and most devastating critiques of post-war modernization theories (Frank, 1967*b*) but, like Cardoso and Faletto (1969), he took as his theoretical point of departure the structuralist doctrines of the United Nations Economic Commission for Latin America (ECLA). Frank, a staunch Marxist, and the more eclectic Cardoso both formulated dependency analyses that, although at odds in a number of respects, served the same double purpose: they were a response to the perceived failure of national development through the import-substituting industrialization strategy recommended by ECLA,[7] and at the same time they offered an alternative to the ahistorical and apolitical structural-functionalist assumptions of modernization approaches. These two men were thus key figures in marking the emergence of the new dependency paradigm in the late 1960s.

The starting point for the dependency approach is a rejection of the notion, implicit in the modernization literature, that European and U.S. development and third world underdevelopment are isolated phenomena or separate stages in the history of mankind; on the contrary, dependency adherents regard them as integral parts of a single historical process, the global expansion of capitalism. Rather than being a backward state prior to capitalism, underdevelopment is thus considered a necessary consequence of its evolution. The dependency approach views nations as inserted into a capitalist world economy characterized by a functional division of labor in which there are "central" and "peripheral" economic regions. Countries of the center are industrially ad-

[6] The efforts of English-speaking interpreters or popularizers of dependency theory (e.g., Bodenheimer, 1970, 1971; Chilcote and Edelstein, 1974; Chilcote, 1974) have also been significant in the United States.

[7] Under the leadership of Raúl Prebisch, ECLA had already opposed orthodox economic development theories that justified the nonindustrialization of Latin America in view of the comparative advantages that might be obtained with agricultural and mineral production for export (see Prebisch, 1950).

7

vanced and viewed as capable of developing dynamically in accordance with their internal needs; they are the main beneficiaries of global links. The periphery has a less autonomous type of development conditioned by the requirements of the center's expansion. Dependency analysis attempts to understand, and evaluate, the developmental implications of peripheral capitalism.

A given "situation of dependency" is defined not only in terms of external constraining factors but also includes internal features of the peripheral society, such as its class structure, its system of economic production, and its political processes. The potential for social change in these countries is analyzed largely in terms of the roles played by key social actors, most notably transnational corporations, the state, the national private business sector, and urban and rural labor. The road to development usually suggested, implicitly or explicitly, by the dependency approach is liberation from external control and from the internal structure of inequality that this is said to promote.[8]

This book concentrates on the process and problems of dependent development in third world countries. The very selection of this topic has theoretical implications. "Dependency" implies a situation of external reliance by third world nations on flows of goods and capital (foreign investment, foreign loans, and foreign aid), usually coming from center countries of the capitalist world economy. "Dependent development" is a special instance of dependency that refers to cases where capital accumulation and diversified industrialization are occurring in a peripheral country, despite the fact that this economic growth is externally conditioned in significant ways.[9] With respect to internal class relations, Peter Evans (1979a: 32, 52) adds that a triple alliance which in-

---

[8] In contrast, modernization theory recommends that ties between central and peripheral countries in the capitalist world economy be strengthened (by diffusion) rather than cut if the development of the periphery is to proceed.

[9] Wallerstein (1974a, 1974b, 1976) argues that the more advanced nations characterized by dependent development occupy their own distinct

cludes transnational corporations (TNCs), the state, and the local industrial bourgeoisie is a necessary condition for dependent capitalist development, even though the relative dominance of any one of these actors may vary from industry to industry, by country, or over time.

In the study of capitalist development in the periphery, dependency theory is far more useful than the modernization approach.[10] To begin with, the appropriate unit of analysis is not the nation-state, as modernization theory would have it, but rather the relationships between nation-states, social classes, and the world system. It is no longer sufficient to view social development as the unfolding of endogenous forces within a society, with external factors regarded merely as an environment to which the society adapts. In the contemporary world where close and intricate interdependencies and tensions span the globe, few if any societies are the isolated, internally unfolding systems emphasized by the modernization model.[11]

---

position within the international system, which he calls the "semiperiphery." For a detailed examination of this proposition with regard to Brazil and Mexico see Evans and Gereffi (1980, 1982) and Gereffi and Evans (1981). A more general discussion of the relationship between Wallerstein's world system approach and the dependency approach is given in Evans (1979b).

[10] As Portes (1980) points out, one should not lose sight of the fact that modernization theory made a significant intellectual contribution when it appeared. With their focus on cultural factors (value orientations, religious and lay ideologies, etc.) as determinants of social change, modernizationists liberated sociological analysis of nonindustrial societies from earlier biologically grounded theories of evolution that attributed the existence of inequality among nations to immutable racial differences.

[11] To be more specific, modernization theory assumes that the primary impetus to change in those countries that developed early (the United States and the advanced nations of Western Europe) stemmed from endogenous cultural and institutional transformations. Conversely, the principal change agent in late developing societies are exogenous stimuli (new ideas, values, techniques, organizations, and capital) that lead to the rejection of traditional ways of thinking and acting. Despite this radical difference in context the modernization perspective has held that underdeveloped nations must in some way replicate the path followed by the early

In addition, if development and underdevelopment are indeed opposite faces of the same coin—the expansion of capitalism on a world scale—then it follows that the development of a society is profoundly influenced by the historical-structural conditions that underlie its insertion into the global system. This basic dependency postulate is in sharp contrast to the common modernization practice of periodization according to developmental as opposed to historical stages, whereby societies are located at different points on an evolutionary scale running from tradition through one or more transitional stages of social organization to modernity.[12] This developmental history approach subordinates the historian's past (the actual comparison of societies) to a developmental past (the fitting of particular events into longer-term patterns of "progressive" change).[13]

---

modernizers and that being "modern" means being like the West (see Gusfield, 1967; Tipps, 1973; Portes, 1973; Valenzuela and Valenzuela, 1978).

[12] Walt Rostow (1960) and Cyril Black (1966), both modernization writers, established sets of universal stages through which all national societies were expected to pass on their way to modernity: for Rostow these were five stages of economic growth and for Black four phases of modernization. Similarly, Dankwart Rustow (1967) argues that there are three key requirements of political modernization—identity, authority, and equality—that together form the political basis of the modern nation-state; and the Social Science Research Council (SSRC) Committee on Comparative Politics led by Gabriel Almond identified five crises that all societies have to confront in the process of political modernization: identity, legitimacy, penetration, participation, and distribution (Huntington, 1971: 312–313). What all of these periodization schemes share is both an evolutionary framework that is bounded by the dichotomous concepts of "tradition" and "modernity" and a focus on society or the nation-state as their basic unit of analysis. The one significant difference among them relates to the ordering of the stages outlined: Rostow and Black assert that the order in which societies must pass through their stages is invariant, while both Rustow and the SSRC Committee on Comparative Politics claim that a key characteristic that distinguishes societies from one another is precisely the variety of sequences in which their "requirements" or necessary "crises," respectively, may be dealt with.

[13] For a discussion of the differences between "conventional" and "developmental" history and their relation to the use of the comparative

Finally, modernization research has tended to be very *multi*disciplinary in nature. Scholars in economics, sociology, political science, psychology, and history have focused on specialized aspects of the modernization process in an unconnected fashion. The dependency perspective, on the other hand, has had from its beginnings a markedly *inter*disciplinary character that serves to integrate the social sciences in a comprehensive analysis of development (Cardoso and Faletto, 1969).

In short, my preference for the dependency approach to development studies reflects my belief that the problems of underdevelopment in the third world can best be understood if one adopts a global rather than national framework for analysis, an open-ended rather than evolutionary view of history, and an integrated and interdisciplinary rather than dualistic and multidisciplinary conception of development.

To say that dependency theory provides a better understanding of current third world development problems than does modernization theory does not mean that the dependency perspective is without inconsistencies and possible anomalies of its own. The remainder of this chapter attempts to more fully elaborate the components of dependency theory and to provide the bases of a constructive critique. My discussion of recurring problems or inconsistencies in historical-structural studies of dependency will emphasize three main themes: 1) the issue of nondependency, 2) the political question of how, and under what conditions, various authors believe that dependency can be overcome, and 3) the theoretical eclecticism of dependency analysis.

The Explanatory Framework of Dependency Theory

Historical-structural dependency studies utilize a holistic methodological approach that looks at the structure and

method in nineteenth-century social thought, see Nisbet (1969) and Gereffi (1980: 11–32).

11

change of entire societies, attempts to classify these structures and changes into patterns or stages, and then tries to explain what factors account for differences in the patterns or stages.[14] To understand how these tasks are carried out in the dependency perspective, a closer look at the following elements is necessary.

Units and Level of Analysis

Dependency theory has two distinct units of analysis: the nation-state and social classes. Both are viewed in terms of their manifold relationships to the capitalist world system. The level of analysis in holistic dependency theory is primarily structural,[15] and the basic dependency argument is contextual: given a situation of dependency that is historically and structurally defined, certain processes (not specified by the notion of dependency itself) affect the rate, the direction, and even the possibility of economic expansion or development. The diverse situations outlined in dependency studies are in large part a product of the global expansion of the capitalist system. The factors that explain this global expansion have been explored most systematically in theories of capitalist imperialism[16] and are outside the scope of the dependency model although compatible with it.[17]

[14] Actually, the dependency and modernization literatures both include three very distinct methodological approaches: holistic analysis, correlational analysis, and abstract analytical theory. The resultant six varieties of development literature are reviewed in Gereffi (1980: Chapter 2 and Appendix). The holistic approach is the most popular in both the dependency and modernization theoretical traditions and because of the detailed nature of its empirical research is particularly important as a source of testable hypotheses.

[15] Its structural predilection notwithstanding, the dependency perspective also considers subjective factors in the development process. One of the most interesting topics in this regard is elite ideologies. For good empirical assessments of elite ideologies in Argentina and Brazil see Cardoso (1971) and McDonough (1981).

[16] For an overview of some of these theories see Fieldhouse (1967).

[17] The complementarity between the analyses of imperialism and de-

Objects and Sources of Social Change

The dependency perspective assumes that underdevelopment results at least partially from the structural integration of peripheral nations into the capitalist world economy on terms that are asymmetrical and exploitative in favor of the center countries. To a significant degree, therefore, the object of change (i.e., the obstacle to development) is exogenous to the societal unit: the structural relations of dependency in a world capitalist context. This approach further assumes, however, that dependency is not solely or even primarily an external phenomenon; it also appears as an internal force through the behavior of local groups and social classes whose values and interests coincide (or are perceived to coincide) with those of the foreign actors they support.[18]

pendency is strikingly illustrated in the figure of V. I. Lenin, who contributed not only one of the most important theoretical works on imperialism, *Imperialism, The Highest Stage of Capitalism* (1916), but also wrote what some consider the pioneering classic of dependency studies, *The Development of Capitalism in Russia* (1899), which is the first systematic attempt within the Marxist tradition to provide a concrete analysis of the development of capitalism in a backward nation. Lenin's contribution in this context is extensively discussed in Palma (1978: 889–898) and also in Cardoso (1972a: 83–87). In the contemporary period the theoretical writings of Paul Baran (1957) were an indispensable bridge between the "Eurocentric" or "metropolitan" focus of the classic theories of imperialism and the dependency perspective's concern with the consequences of imperialism for the countries of the periphery. Baran's model of how the penetration of international capitalism would lead toward stagnation in the periphery heavily influenced the thinking of Andre Gunder Frank and several other dependency theorists. For a useful discussion of Baran's work see Evans (1979a: 19–22).

[18] The idea that dependency is a phenomenon that can only be understood through the systematic interaction of its "internal" and "external" aspects is stressed even by those writers such as A. G. Frank whose focus is most heavily on the latter (i.e., the global characteristics of capitalism):

> For the generation of structural underdevelopment, more important still than the drain of economic surplus from the satellite after its incorporation as such into the world capitalist system, is the impregnation of the satellite's domestic economy with the same capitalist structure and its fundamental contradictions. (Frank, 1967a: 10)

In parallel fashion the sources of change (i.e., the stimuli to development) are both exogenous and endogenous. At the world system level changes in the nature and strength of center-periphery linkages presumably will have an effect on development outcomes in third world countries. At the local level development can be stimulated through the action of the state, domestic elites, or social classes designed to realign dependency relations over time.

Descriptive and Value Asymmetries

The dependency perspective is highly historical when taking into account diverse kinds of dependent situations, yet it tends to be very abstract or vague when considering the opposite type of situations. These are usually taken, implicitly or explicitly, to be either increased "autonomy" within a continued capitalist path of development or "socialism," envisaged as a radical break from the capitalist mode of production. The use of history by dependency analysts is generally in the conventional or historiographic mode rather than the developmental history mode since their focus is on detailing concrete situations or types of dependency and trends of change in an open-ended and nonevolutionary framework devoid of necessary stages. Doctrinaire Marxists who identify with the dependency outlook are an exception to this rule be-

---

Cardoso and Faletto, whose analysis is far more sensitive to varied internal structures of dependency than Frank's, emphasize the same point:

> We conceive the relationship between external and internal forces as forming a complex whole whose structural links are not based on mere external forms of exploitation and coercion, but are rooted in coincidences of interests between local dominant classes and international ones, and, on the other side, are challenged by local dominated groups and classes. (Cardoso and Faletto, 1979: xvi)

This interaction between the internal and external aspects of dependency unfortunately was overlooked by Smith (1979), who in his stereotyped critique of the literature identifies only Baran, Frank, and Wallerstein as principal dependency theorists whom he chastizes for ignoring local histories.

14

cause they believe that capitalism will inevitably give way to socialism.[19]

Along with the descriptive asymmetry in the dependency approach there is also a value asymmetry. Dependency analysts almost always favor the lessening or (if possible) elimination of dependency rather than its continuance. Said differently, dependency studies document with greatest detail the condition they reject (dependency).[20]

Historical Periodization

One of the most important aspects of dependency analysis is historical periodization. The function of periodization in holistic studies is to cut history into stages or periods unified by like structural relations, thus establishing a framework within which propositions and interpretations are most meaningful. The analytical cuts made in dependency research are of two sorts: at the world system level structurally distinct periods in the historical transformation of global capitalism are identified, with a focus on the nature and strength of the links between peripheral and central economies, and at the national level various historical forms of class domination of the productive process are highlighted and related to the larger scheme. Dependency authors differ considerably, however, in their relative emphases on the external and internal dimensions of dependency and consequently in their evaluation of the determinism or openness that characterizes the capitalist system.

At one extreme is Andre Gunder Frank, whose work is singularly insensitive to variations between types of dependency

[19] There is a degree of historical openness even in this position, however, because Marxists as a whole do not agree that any contemporary socialist society is the model toward which all underdeveloped countries are, or should be, moving. For an outline of three distinct socialist exemplars see Heilbroner (1980: 87–88).

[20] Conversely, modernizationists elaborate most thoroughly the condition they accept (modernity).

relations in a world capitalist context. For Frank, the development of the core capitalist economies *requires* the underdevelopment of the periphery, which at a regional level leads to the conclusion that it is capitalism in Latin America that has precluded and continues to preclude development (see Halperin-Donghi, 1982; Palma, 1978: 900; Booth, 1975: 69). The one source of variation that is significant for Frank—the strength or weakness of metropolis-satellite ties—is used to support the above claims:

> ... the satellites experience their greatest economic development and especially their most classically capitalist industrial development if and when their ties to their metropolis are weakest. This hypothesis is almost diametrically opposed to the generally accepted thesis that development in the underdeveloped countries follows from the greatest degree of contact with and diffusion from the metropolitan developed countries. ... A corollary of [this] hypothesis is that when the metropolis recovers from its crisis and re-establishes the trade and investment ties which fully re-incorporate the satellites into the system, or when the metropolis expands to incorporate previously isolated regions into the worldwide system, the previous development and industrialization of these regions is choked off or channeled into directions which are not self-perpetuating and promising. (Frank, 1969: 9–11)

According to Frank, these hypotheses are confirmed by evidence of marked autonomous industrialization and growth in Latin America in precisely those periods of temporary isolation caused by major crises in the world metropolis—the European (and especially Spanish) depression of the seventeenth century, the Napoleonic Wars, World War I, the Great Depression of the 1930s, and World War II—or of geographic and economic isolation prior to a region's full integration into the mercantilist and capitalist system (Frank, 1969: 10–13). Because Frank believes the weakening of the

DEPENDENCY THEORY

metropolis-satellite network can take place only for reasons external to the satellite economies and is of a necessarily transient nature, it follows that there is no real possibility of sustained development within the system. The stark alternative thus posed by Frank is breaking completely with the metropolis-satellite network through socialist revolution or continuing to "underdevelop" within it (Palma, 1978: 899).

Theotonio Dos Santos holds an intermediate position among dependency authors with regard to the periodization and development debate. Unlike Frank, Dos Santos distinguishes different types of relations of capitalist dependency at the international level: colonial, financial-industrial, and technological-industrial. Furthermore, in place of a uniform process of satellization Dos Santos argues that each of these types of international dependency relations generates a different kind of internal structure of dependency in peripheral countries. Like Frank, however, Dos Santos establishes the priority of external over internal structures, thus losing the notion of movement produced through the dynamic contradictions between these structures. The sense of antecedent causation and inert consequences is clear in Dos Santos's formal—and hence static and unhistorical—definition of dependency:

> By dependence we mean a situation in which the economy of certain countries is conditioned by the development and expansion of another economy to which the former is subjected. The relation of interdependence between two or more economies, and between these and world trade, assumes the form of dependence when some countries (the dominant ones) can expand and can be self-sustaining, while other countries (the dependent ones) can do this only as a reflection of that expansion, which can have either a positive or a negative effect on their immediate development. (Dos Santos, 1970: 231)

Dos Santos, along with Frank and a number of other dependency analysts, tends to fall into a "stagnationist trap" by assuming that, in a context of dependency, capitalism loses its historically progressive character and can only generate underdevelopment (Palma, 1978: 901–903).[21] Once again the political outlook is that Latin America is at a crossroad between socialism and fascism (Dos Santos, 1972).

Within the dependency spectrum Cardoso and Faletto (1969) mark the extreme that is most sensitive to local as well as international variations in dependency relations and to the independent significance of internal structures even in an approach that highlights external conditioning. Whereas Cardoso and Faletto agree with Dos Santos that both international and local dependency relations should be periodized in order to reflect the changing forms of modern-day capitalism, Dos Santos establishes a strict one-to-one correspondence between global and local dependency structures for a given period, while Cardoso and Faletto insist that multiple situations of dependency may, and in fact do, coexist in Latin America within each phase in the transformation of the world capitalist system. Thus, during the period of externally oriented development in Latin America (1850–1930), Cardoso and Faletto argue that there were two distinct situations of national dependency[22]: the situation of national control of the export system and the situation of foreign-controlled export enclave economies (with two subtypes, the plantation enclave and the mining enclave).[23] Following World War II, the situation

---

[21] Palma (1978: 904) calls the stagnationist group of dependency theorists, including Frank, Dos Santos, Marini, Caputo and Pizarro, and Hinkelammert, "contemporary Narodniks," in reference to the late nineteenth-century coterie of Russian intellectuals who argued (against Lenin, among others) that from an economic point of view capitalism was probably not a viable system for a backward country such as Russia and that capitalist development was not necessary for the attainment of socialism in Russia.

[22] Both situations were "dependent" because the stimulus to production came almost entirely from external demand and because the marketing of the exports was conditioned by prices, quotas, and so forth set by the financial and commercial sectors of the central economies.

[23] The plantation enclave employs much labor and may need little capi-

known as the internationalization of the internal market or associated-dependent development based on large investments by manufacturing TNCs producing for domestic consumption crystallized in several of the larger Latin American countries,[24] and by the 1970s the situation of diversified export promotion (including manufactured exports) had emerged in Brazil and Mexico, also under TNC control. Over time, a number of individual Latin American nations have passed through several of these situations of dependency,[25] and a cross-sectional look at the region today indicates that in one country or another most of the situations mentioned above still continue to exist. This multiplicity of local dependency structures implies a far more variegated set of political options than the Manichean dichotomies brandished by Frank and Dos Santos.[26]

---

tal, while the mining enclave uses little labor and requires a large capital input. There was an added element of dependency in the case of enclaves because local output could not expand without foreign technology and capital.

[24] In terms of diversification of industrial production the levels of development attained by this strategy were high, but the level of dependency was high also. The new flow of direct investment capital came overwhelmingly from a small number of large TNCs, and the external public debt of these nations grew rapidly. Crucial decisions about economic growth became concentrated more and more in the hands of foreigners.

[25] Since 1880 Brazil and Mexico, for example, have gone through four parallel shifts in dependency situations (see Evans and Gereffi, 1980, 1982; Gereffi and Evans, 1981).

[26] The degree to which Cardoso and Faletto depart from the mechanical determination of internal by external structures, which is so pronounced in the work of both Frank and Dos Santos, is evident in the following statement:

In mechanistic conceptions of history, Latin American economies are perceived as having always been determined by the "capitalist system," as it has developed on a global scale. Fundamental periods of change at the international level, it is contended, marked the significant moments of transformation of Latin American economies. In these interpretations, general characteristics of capitalism replace concrete analyses of specific characteristics of dependent societies. . . . we do not pretend to derive mechanically significant phases

The local situations of dependency outlined by Cardoso and Faletto are structurally distinct in terms of the makeup of ruling or hegemonic domestic coalitions and concomitant patterns of social exclusion. Dependency analysis must also show, however, that these situations lead to different sets of developmental outcomes in peripheral nations. This case is clearly made by Cardoso and Faletto (1969) for the two basic situations of national dependency that occurred during the period of outward expansion in Latin America (1850–1930). Countries that had national control of their export systems (Argentina, Brazil, Uruguay, and Colombia) later manifested more powerful and active local bourgeoisie groups and industrialization policies dominated by private rather than state initiative; countries whose export sectors had been foreign controlled (Mexico, Bolivia, Venezuela, Chile, Peru, and the Central American nations) developed relatively weak domestic entrepreneurial sectors and had more state participation in the early stages of industrialization.

---

of dependent societies only from the "logic of capitalist accumulation."

. . . our approach is both structural and historical: it emphasizes not just the structural conditioning of social life, but also the historical transformation of structures by conflict, social movements, and class struggles. . . . our approach should bring to the forefront both aspects of social structures: the mechanisms of self-perpetuation and the possibilities for change. Social structures impose limits on social processes and reiterate established forms of behavior. However, they also generate contradictions and social tensions, opening the possibilities for social movements and ideologies of change. The analyses have to make explicit not only structural constraints that reinforce the reiterative aspects of the reproduction of society, but have also to delineate chances for change, rooted in the very social interest and ideologies created by the development of a given structure. In this process, subordinated social groups and classes, as well as dominated countries, try to counterattack dominant interests that sustain structures of domination. (Cardoso and Faletto, 1979: xiv–xv, x–xi)

Any discussion of realistic alternatives to dependency at a given historical moment must identify, therefore, not only the structural possibilities for change but also factors affecting political capacity at the local level, including organization, will, and ideologies.

To take a different era, in the situation of associated-dependent development that has characterized the industrialized countries of Latin America such as Argentina, Brazil, and Mexico since 1955, the shift of foreign capital from the extractive into the manufacturing sector has been coupled with a greater measure of national autonomy as the state has expanded its role in economic regulation and the formation of new capital (Cardoso, 1973; Cardoso and Faletto, 1969: 149–176; Evans, 1979a). This has led to a notable increase in local development, especially related to the manufacture and sale of consumer goods for the growing urban upper- and middle-class markets in these countries. Although levels of industrial development have risen for nations in this situation, many of the previously existing dependency links nonetheless have been maintained or redefined (e.g., foreign domination of key industries, technological dependence, increasing foreign indebtedness, TNC control over export networks), thus reinforcing certain patterns of underdevelopment associated with the more classic forms of dependency.

THE ISSUE OF NONDEPENDENCY

Historical-structural dependency studies have systematically drawn attention to the undesirable or malevolent concomitants of dependent capitalist growth in the periphery, and in this respect they have made an important contribution to the development literature.[27] Dependency theorists tend to say

[27] These deformations or structural distortions generated or exacerbated by the expansion of capitalism in the periphery of the world system are multifaceted. In the economic sphere they include a series of limitations on self-sustained growth: a heavy penetration of foreign capital in the form of direct equity investments or foreign debt; the absence of locally owned technology; the absence of intermediate and, especially, capital goods industries to complete the industrialization cycle; and "unequal exchange" in its various forms. From the social point of view dependent capitalism is said to promote the growing marginalization of the mass of the population due to the partial and heterogeneous nature of industrialization in the periphery; the creation or reinforcement of clientele social

very little about situations of nondependency, however. In other words, the dependency perspective tells us much more about what is wrong and why than about what is correct and how to get there. This imbalance has left a highly contested conceptual gap: What is the opposite of dependency? For those who believe that dependency is caused by the economics of capitalism, its opposite, or nondependency, is *socialism*. For those who view dependency as a political-economic problem caused either by simple disparities of power between nations and social classes or by a more complicated process of domination in which external actors pursue their economic interests in an underdeveloped country in shifting alliances with key local groups (including the state), the opposite of dependency is *autonomy*.

These two different meanings of nondependency—socialism and autonomy—correspond to distinct perspectives within the dependency framework that are identified by some writers as the Marxist view and the liberal view, respectively (Chilcote, 1978; Harding, 1976; Cueva, 1976). According to the Marxist view, since dependency is equated with participation in the capitalist world market, nondependency can be achieved only by breaking out of that market. The international capitalist system, however, does not cause underdevelopment directly; it does so indirectly, by generating and reinforcing in Latin America and elsewhere in the third world an infrastructure of dependency. This infrastructure is made up of certain local institutions, social classes, and processes that respond to the interests or needs of the dominant

---

classes whose objectives, actions, and privileged positions are derived from their ties to foreign interests; and large peasant sectors that are undernourished, uneducated, and—given their subordination to big capital and a whole range of intermediaries, and their inadequate land—frequently unproductive beyond a bare subsistence level. On the political front there is the appearance of authoritarian regimes, often controlled by the military, which tend to justify widespread repression (in the short run at least) as one of the main costs of capitalist development in the context of national dependency.

22

powers in the international system rather than to alleged national interests or needs. Because dependency is thus more than mere external domination and has its own internal dynamics, a total rupturing of dependency as an internal condition of development requires not only severing relations with the capitalist world market but also a profound socialist transformation at the national level.[28]

The liberal view of nondependency manifests a concern with the building of autonomous national capitalism within the context of international capitalism.[29] This perspective comes quite close in a number of ways to the political thinking of the ECLA "developmentalists" of the 1950s and 1960s who shared a belief in the "enlightened state" that would reinforce the idea of national development and autonomy by expanding the endogenous content of key decisions and that was oriented toward the good of the oppressed classes through its concrete measures to create an all-encompassing market of consumers. For ECLA it was not necessary to presuppose a socialist revolution; it was assumed that a reform-minded state apparatus in peripheral countries would promote industrialization policies in which foreign capital was controlled but not rejected and in which measures like agrarian reform, redistributive wage policies, and progressive taxation would force the distribution of the benefits from technological advances in favor of workers and rural laborers.

There are certain differences, however, between the dependency view of national autonomy and that of ECLA theorists (see Cardoso, 1977). The "enlightened state" as seen by ECLA became the "repressive-entrepreneurial state" for dependency theorists. In the 1960s and 1970s in much of

---

[28] Among the dependency authors who explicitly adopt this Marxist formulation of nondependency are Amin (1970, 1973a), Bodenheimer (1971), Dos Santos (1972), Frank (1972), Marini (1973), Thomas (1974), Gilbert (1974), and Chilcote (1974).

[29] Liberal dependency theorists, in other words, emphasize autonomy *within* the international capitalist system, while Marxist dependency theorists advocate autonomy *from* the international capitalist system.

Latin America the state tried to build national consensus around a policy of economic growth and social stability. In order to create a good investment climate for big business, social stability was taken to mean labor docility, low wages, and widespread political demobilization, all carried out in a coercive authoritarian context. TNCs in Latin America also changed their strategy during this period: increasing competition among the international oligopolists for the peripheral countries' domestic markets, coupled with a range of new behavioral and ownership controls on TNCs at the local level, reversed many of the old anti-industrialization policies of foreign capital. Transnationals were viewed as capable of playing a more progressive role in capitalist industrialization in the periphery, even by critics from the left.[30] In a growing number of situations the state therefore had both the will and capacity to substantially renegotiate or redefine the terms of national dependency in the direction of greater autonomy and welfare, even though ties with the dominant powers in the capitalist system remained intact.[31]

Frequently the issue of whether nondependency is socialism or autonomy is not made explicit in dependency studies, thus casting doubt upon the very definition of dependency itself. Nowhere is this conceptual ambiguity more striking than in Cardoso and Faletto's *Dependency and Development in Latin America* (1969), certainly one of the most influential documents in the dependency literature. In the preface to the 1979 English edition of their book Cardoso and Faletto make it clear that their focus is on dependency within capitalistic societies and that in the abstract their preferred alternative to dependent development is socialism[32]:

---

[30] The article by Warren (1973) documents the extensive amount of industrialization occurring in at least some peripheral countries.

[31] Those who identify nondependency or reduced dependency with greater local autonomy to pursue capitalist development include Jaguaribe (1969), Sunkel (1969), Evans (1971), O'Donnell and Linck (1973), Moran (1974a, 1978), and Caporaso (1978b).

[32] Cardoso and Faletto (1979: xxiv) admit that "there are forms of de-

A real process of dependent development does exist in some Latin American countries. By development, in this context, we mean "capitalist development." This form of development, in the periphery as well as in the center, produces as it evolves, in a cyclical way, wealth and poverty, accumulation and shortage of capital, employment for some and unemployment for others. . . . It is not realistic to imagine that capitalist development will solve basic problems for the majority of the population. In the end, what has to be discussed as an alternative is not the consolidation of the state and the fulfillment of "autonomous capitalism," but how to supersede them. The important question, then, is how to construct paths toward socialism. (Cardoso and Faletto, 1979: xxiii–xxiv)

Nonetheless, in the original 1969 Spanish-language edition of the book the authors state openly that dependency is primarily a political phenomenon and that its true opposite is autonomy:

"National underdevelopment" is a situation of objective economic subordination to outside nations and enterprises and, at the same time, of partial political attempts to cope with "national interests" through the state and social movements that try to preserve political autonomy. . . . The contradiction between the attempt to cope with the market situation in a politically autonomous way and the de facto situation of dependency character-

pendent relationships between socialist countries, [although] the structural context that permits an understanding of these is quite different from that within capitalist countries and requires specific analyses" (see also Cardoso, 1972b: 17n). This assertion runs contrary to the notion held by some critics that the dependency perspective is based on the premise that dependency is *necessarily* a function of capitalism (see Ray, 1973: 7–10; Packenham, 1978: 4). Some Marxist dependency theorists do indeed adopt this premise, but by no means is its acceptance required by the general approach. For a useful discussion of some of the distinctive structural features of socialist countries in the post-World War II center-periphery system of the world economy see Pinto and Kñakal (1973).

izes what is the specific ambiguity of nations where political sovereignty is expressed by the new state and where economic subordination is reinforced by the international division of labor and by the economic control exerted by former or new imperialist centers. From a sociological viewpoint, here is perhaps the core of the problem of national development in Latin America. (Cardoso and Faletto, 1969: 21)

The emphasis on the political dimensions of dependency is repeated when Cardoso and Faletto (1969: 18) highlight the distinctions between three pairs of concepts: central and peripheral economies, development and underdevelopment, and dependency and autonomy. The ideas of "central" and "peripheral" economies stress unequal positions and functions within the overall structure of world production but "overlook the socio-political factors involved in the situation of dependence." The idea of "underdevelopment" refers to the degree of diversification of the production system in a country but says nothing about the patterns of decision-making control over production and consumption, whether internal (socialism, capitalism, etc.) or external (colonialism, periphery of the world market, etc.). The idea of "dependency" indicates a situation that entails structural links with the world productive system such that what happens internally in a dependent country cannot be fully explained without taking into consideration the links that local groups (classes, states, and enterprises) have with external ones. Dependency analysis, in short, seeks to explain the economic processes of development as social processes; the theoretical point of intersection is politics.

In addition to socialism and autonomy another alternative to dependency is sometimes put forward: *interdependence.* Caporaso (1978*a*, 1978*b*) provides a good discussion of some of the theoretical and methodological implications of the competing conceptualizations of dependency-autonomy and dependence-interdependence. Whereas "dependency" (the absence of actor autonomy) refers to the process of incorporation of underdeveloped countries into the global capitalist system and the structural distortions resulting therefrom, "dependence" (a highly asymmetric form of interdependence) refers to the narrower phenomenon of external reliance on other actors. This suggests fundamentally different analytical frameworks. Dependence-interdependence has a dyadic (actor to actor) focus, in which dependence is a "net" concept measured by looking at the differential between A's reliance on B and B's reliance on A.[33] Dependency-autonomy, on the other hand, represents a unit-environment focus where an actor is viewed in relation to all external influences, or at least to the most important external influences. Ultimately, then, "dependence" is unidimensional in nature (i.e., an attribute of nation-states, enterprises, or other entities assumed to be unitary actors), while "dependency" is a historical syndrome of related concepts (e.g., external penetration, ties between local and foreign capital, uneven integration of various parts of the economy).

Given the confusion that exists in the literature over defining dependency's opposite, how significant is this? What are its concrete implications? The significance is indeed great for the politics of dependency reversal, as the next section will show. There are also important theoretical and methodological implications, however. For one thing, the notion of whether dependency is a dichotomous or continuous variable hinges on the nature of nondependency. If dependency is associated only with capitalism, then the dichotomous alternative from a strict Marxist viewpoint is socialism. An underdeveloped country faces a choice between two "roads": it is dependent and exploited, or it is not—a classic zero-sum game. If the opposite of dependency is autonomy, however, it

---

[33] The reliance of one country on another may involve trade, capital flows, technology transfer, cultural relations, etc.

makes sense to talk about changes that represent differences of degree, such as a relative increase or decrease in the autonomy or capacity for action of certain Latin American states. A view of dependency-autonomy as a continuum does not contradict the emphasis of historical-structural studies on global analysis, nor does it deny the correctness of focusing on concrete situations of dependency. It does allow, however, the possibility of asking whether changes in dependent economies over time have resulted in "more" or "less" autonomy. It implies related questions as well. Autonomy for whom? What are the trade-offs? What are the net effects on social welfare?

The debate over socialism versus autonomy raises another, more serious problem for the dependency approach. If dependency is made solely a function of capitalism, as the Marxists are wont to do, then the relationship between dependency and underdevelopment is likely to become circular. This point has been made most forcefully by Lall, who summarizes dependency as follows:

> In the usage of the *dependencia* school . . . "dependence" is meant to describe certain characteristics (economic as well as social and political) of the economy *as a whole* and is intended to *trace certain processes which are causally linked to its underdevelopment* and which are *expected to adversely affect its development in the future.* (Lall, 1975*b*: 799–800)

The potential circularity is established when the hypothesis that dependency causes underdevelopment is combined with an operational definition of dependency that incorporates many of the distortions or deformations generally considered as underdeveloped, or undeveloped, structures (little or no integration across a society's key productive or exchange sectors, lack of responsiveness of production structures to domestic demand, etc.).

From a theoretical point of view the critical question does not concern the existence of undesirable features of capitalism in underdeveloped countries but rather whether these features add up to a distinctive state of dependency. Lall's argument, with which I am in basic agreement, is that many of the undesirable concomitants of dependent growth are general characteristics of capitalistic growth—in certain stages and in certain circumstances—and are not confined to the present condition of underdeveloped nations. Dependent capitalism does not constitute a unique mode of production, or even a unique phase with its own laws within the capitalist mode of production (Cueva, 1976: 14–15).[34] As a result, the attempt by some scholars in the dependency tradition to arbitrarily pick some salient features of modern capitalism as it affects some third world nations and put them into a distinct category of "dependency" is not only unhelpful but misleading. It neither furthers the efforts of those who want both to preserve the capitalist system and promote equality (goals that, although perhaps incompatible at certain points, at the very least require an understanding of capitalism's continuously evolving dynamics) nor of those who believe a completely different path is feasible for achieving true development (in this case attention should be focused not on the inadequacies of capitalism in the third world but rather on what a country needs to do to break out of the international capitalist system).

The circularity in the relationship between dependency and underdevelopment is broken, however, once the possibility is admitted of significant variations in dependency situations within capitalist and noncapitalist development paths. This requires an emphasis on autonomy rather than socialism as the alternate pole of dependency. Cardoso and Faletto (1969: 18–19, 162), for example, discuss development-under-

---

[34] For an introduction to the broad literature on the modes of production controversy in development studies see Roxborough (1976) and Foster-Carter (1978).

development and dependency-autonomy as crosscutting economic and political dimensions, respectively. Thus, there are cases where development and autonomy have been achieved simultaneously under both socialist (the Soviet Union and China) and capitalist (Japan) regimes. There are also cases, like Argentina, Brazil, and Mexico in Latin America, where a modern industrial structure has developed without the creation of autonomous national decision-making centers (the heavy penetration of foreign capital in these countries means that much of the industrial sector is controlled from abroad). A third category refers to countries that are both underdeveloped and dependent. This is the situation of the majority of third world nations, especially the smaller ones. Finally, there are cases where a national society achieves certain decisional autonomy (e.g., by breaking its ties with a given system of domination without incorporating itself totally into another) without attaining an economic maturity in its production system or income distribution comparable to that in the center countries. Yugoslavia, Algeria, Egypt, and Tanzania are instances of this pattern.

What the above examples show is that the connection between development-underdevelopment (or the degree of diversification and integration of the economic system) and the creation or absence of autonomous decision-making centers is given empirically, and not just logically, within the dependency approach. This is only the first step, however, in demonstrating that the notion of dependency serves a useful analytical purpose. Historical-structural studies must also show that dependent or externally conditioned economic growth has adverse consequences for the development of third world nations that exist over and above the negative aspects of industrialization in general. In other words, dependency studies should be able to sustain the argument that, other things being equal, the effects on national development of increased local autonomy or control are different from (the weak version) or better than (the strong version) the effects deriving from foreign control.

30

DEPENDENCY THEORY

The Politics of Dependency Reversal

If dependency and its consequences are deemed undesirable, what can be done to reverse dependency situations?[35] This question is at the very heart of historical-structural analysis, which begins with the idea that social structures not only condition social life but also are historically transformed by class struggles, social movements, and conflict. At the same time, therefore, as political alliances work to maintain structures of domination, the struggles and redefinitions of interest among classes and groups open the possibility of alternative political futures. When it comes to concrete evaluations of the conditions under which a given situation of dependency might be overcome and who might be the historical agents of this transformation, however, the political thinking in dependency studies turns out to be relatively impoverished.[36]

To the extent that historical-structural dependency studies have broached the issue of the possible agents of dependency reversal, the responses again tend to differ according to one's

---

[35] Some, like Albert Hirschman (1978), believe that the asymmetries in economic relations among nations' implied by dependency often contain the "seeds of their own destruction"—i.e., countervailing, dialectical forces that would transform an asymmetrical relation not into its Hegelian opposite but at least into a relation where the initial asymmetry is considerably reduced or perhaps even eliminated. For example, the asymmetry of attention generated by a large economic disparity between two countries may actually favor the dependent nation if the stronger nation's global involvement dilutes its attention to the pattern of trade or investment dominance while the weaker nation in the relationship concentrates its diplomatic resources in escaping from this overreliance.

[36] Although not extensively analyzed from a dependency viewpoint, there have been a variety of attempts by nations to eliminate or decrease dependency. These include economic autarchy, self-reliance (see Galtung, 1980), regional economic integration (as represented by the Andean Pact countries or the Association of Southeast Asian Nations), and the formation of commodity cartels (such as the Organization of Petroleum Exporting Countries or the Intergovernmental Council of Copper Exporting Countries). These strategies are open to both capitalist and socialist countries.

31

view of nondependency. If the alternative to dependency is socialism, then according to Marxist theory only the exploited masses, and in particular the proletariat, can bring about the required transformation. Undoubtedly, the Cuban Revolution was a key exemplar in the reformulation of Latin American development theories in the 1960s. It was taken by some as the political complement to the dependency thesis because it established socialism as a real political option in Latin America—an option that could eradicate the pernicious effects of class exploitation and international capitalism on the well-being and industrialization of the periphery.

The belief in proletarian revolution as the only alternative to dependency was challenged within the dependency tradition on both intellectual and political grounds. Intellectually, there was a reaction against the narrow determinism of "vulgar" or "mechanistic" Marxism. In opposition to the view that history runs a predetermined or inevitable course, there was instead a tendency to conceive of history as an open-ended process. Drawing heavily from the works of contemporary neo-Marxists (Sartre, Lukacs, and Gramsci) and also from non-Marxist theorists (such as Weber, Dilthey, and Mannheim), a number of dependency scholars began to emphasize the role of ideology, political processes, and conditioning structures that set constraints or limits on human action without determining specific outcomes (Cardoso, 1977: 10–11). With respect to the development policies of peripheral countries this intellectual current did not imply any criticism of the appropriateness of socialism per se as a possible strategy for overcoming dependency. Rather, it was a rejection of that line of thinking which automatically invoked revolution as a *deus ex machina* in the face of entrenched dependency relations and which as a result frequently overestimated the feasibility of installing socialism and underestimated the viability of continued capitalist expansion in the periphery.

Politically, the analysts who repudiated mechanistic interpretations tended to see greater local autonomy as the most

32

likely route to reduced dependency and better development outcomes. The historical agents whose responsibility it would be to bring about this change were not the popular classes, as under socialism, but rather the elites. The composition of the elite coalitions that seemed capable of generating increased autonomy shifted over time, however. Up to the end of the decade of the 1950s in Latin America it was widely believed (with considerable justification) that the large transnational companies from the advanced capitalist countries were not interested in the industrialization of the periphery: their principal objective was the control and eventual export of primary mineral and agricultural products. At this point anti-imperialist struggles and struggles for industrialization were one and the same. During the Depression and World War II years in many Latin American nations, import-substituting industrialization (ISI) became the key strategy for economic development, controlled for the most part by a coalition built around the local bourgeoisie and the state. Once the industrial growth process exhausted the "easy" consumer goods phase of production in the early postwar period, however, the larger countries like Argentina, Brazil, and Mexico were led by balance of payments deficits, foreign indebtedness, and inflation to push for an extension and "deepening" of ISI through the local manufacture of consumer durable products (most notably automobiles) and intermediate and capital goods—all of which were being imported in steadily increasing quantities prior to the mid-1950s. Because advanced ISI required vast investments, complex technology, and a highly skilled managerial organization, a new actor was brought into the developmental alliance: the manufacturing TNCs. The main aim of these companies was no longer the export of primary commodities but rather industrial production to serve the growing internal markets of certain Latin American nations.

Under these conditions the whole question of national autonomy was redefined. It became clear that capitalist development in the periphery, unlike that in the center countries, would not be led by the national bourgeoisie. In the triple alliance that characterizes dependent development the national bourgeoisie associates itself with TNCs as a subordinate and minor partner. The local leadership role in the industrialization process thus passed into the hands of the state, the only institution capable of bargaining with and controlling the TNCs. The state has exercised, and even been able to expand, its power in this situation through two channels: the state bureaucracy, which has sought to prevent TNCs from single-handedly appropriating the most strategic sectors and dynamic branches of the economy, using a wide variety of instruments such as legislation, executive decrees, regulatory bodies, special commissions, and ad hoc bargaining at the administrative level; and state enterprises, which not only supplement the lack of private capital in meeting the basic, high risk, low return investment needs of the peripheral country but also are beginning to move extensively into the profitable, dynamic sectors of the economy as well (e.g., petrochemicals, mining, and direct consumer goods such as food and drugs), where they face, and through joint ventures even link up with, the TNCs.

This pattern of growing state involvement in Latin American economies has led one prominent observer to suggest that a new, highly significant social category may be appearing—a "state bourgeoisie" that, although formally part of the public bureaucracy, is endowed with entrepreneurial capacity which to some degree allows it to achieve a separate basis of power (Cardoso, 1972*b*: 15–17; 1977: 19 and n. 15; 1979: 53). Conceivably this state bourgeoisie may emerge as the social stratum with the best chance to lead dependent countries toward national capitalist development, given that neither the local private bourgeoisie nor various middle-class groups have been able to fill that role successfully. It is doubtful, however, that the existence of a state bourgeoisie will alter, at least in the short run, the elitist and international character of the developmental alliance in key countries such as Argentina, Brazil, and Mexico. Thus, the fundamental contradiction of the dependent development model is likely to remain the same: it has been unable to combine advanced industrialization with either economic equity for the majority of the population in terms of jobs and well-being, or the political freedoms found in Western capitalist democracies.

If elite coalitions have not brought desirable development outcomes in Latin America, and if it is difficult to conceive of "a political passage to socialism by a strictly proletarian route given the structural conditions of industrial capitalism in the periphery" (Cardoso and Faletto, 1979: 213), it is fair to ask what kind of political alternatives, if any, dependency analysts might judge to be both positive (in terms of dependency reversal and welfare) and feasible. Cardoso's own views in this regard are illuminating (see Cardoso, 1973: 175–176; 1974: 13–15; Cardoso and Faletto, 1979: 213–214; and Kahl, 1976: 179–184). Above all else Cardoso appears to value participation by the masses not only in the forms of politics but in the real distribution of income. It is not just a matter of reducing economic dependency, since you can do that and still have regimes that are viewed as undemocratic. The crucial question is how to link the economic benefits of development in the periphery with nonauthoritarian and nontotalitarian politics. To do this, Cardoso believes, means going beyond elitist or statist solutions; it requires popular participation, but in a way that excludes manipulative links with dominant classes and the state as an option. Such links were the basis of the populist alliance, which attempted to tie the masses, middle-class groups, and the national entrepreneurs to the state in the name of the nation. Cardoso would like to see the emergence of an alternative, more genuine model of development, with a free flow of information and less coercion and in which social goals are not sacrificed to national ones.

There is an uneasy tension, not just in Cardoso's work but in the dependency literature as a whole, over the relative importance of nation-states and social classes, and this contributes greatly to the ambiguity regarding the politics of dependency reversal. By and large, the notion of dependency is almost invariably tied to the idea of a territorial nation-state; it is countries, after all, that are spoken of as dependent. This means that policies promoting the reduction or reversal of dependency can easily become, or be used to justify, ideologies supporting nationalism. Cardoso recognizes that this can lead to equivocation:

> "Maybe there are some contradictions in my work; it seems at some places that I'm pleading for national autonomy, but I'm also saying that the nation is losing importance. I'm trying to demonstrate that the trend in the structural situation of the world economy means that the least important frame of reference may be the nation. Yet how far can we go with the idea of dependency without the nation? What would that mean? It's an open question. But I don't want to pose false solutions." (Cited in Kahl, 1976: 178)

The major problem is that the nature of the benefits from dependency reversal and the form their class distribution would take are far from certain. Policies that strengthen the nation-state (i.e., increase its autonomy to act) do not necessarily make development more equal or more free in terms of the popular classes. Dependency analysis, when carried out in a comprehensive fashion, thus must be more than a practical guide for maximizing autonomy. It should make us aware that there are often trade-offs in development between two separate goals: autonomy and social welfare.

THE THEORETICAL ECLECTICISM OF DEPENDENCY ANALYSIS

The central analytical category in most versions of the dependency approach is "situations of dependency."[37] Dependency in this sense is not meant to be a precise *concept* in a theory; it does not by itself explain or account for development.

[37] The most obvious exception here is Andre Gunder Frank, who does not see important changes in dependency situations over time.

Rather, the term dependency delimits a *context* of inquiry within which the likelihood, the rate, and the direction of economic expansion are determined by a variety of processes not encompassed by the notion of dependency itself. The processes typically associated with dependency and the extreme reliance on external flows of goods and capital that it entails involve endogenous political and economic forces as well as external ones. These include the interaction of TNC strategies with the political and economic strategies of local social classes and host country states. The strategies of foreign firms are conditioned by the world economic environment, especially as it impinges on their home states, and by the forces of oligopolistic competition in global industries. The strategies of local groups vis-à-vis TNCs are mainly expressed through the policies and actions of the state apparatus. These are shaped not only by the international context but also by a historically given configuration of class structure, ideology, and local productive base. The local class structure and productive base, in turn, are the outcome of previous relations between foreign capital and local classes.

Because it is primarily contextual in nature, then, the dependency focus tells one what to look for, but it does not specify what one will find upon doing so. The analyst is guided in the latter area by many theories that are quite diverse in scope and origin. The perspective's theoretical coverage is not only partial, therefore, but due to its eclecticism also runs the risk of being inconsistent.

Although there are exceptions,[38] dependency scholars have tended to reject attempts to propose a single "theory of dependency" or "laws of dependent capitalism" since by definition the main features of dependent capitalistic economies are determined by the phases and dynamic trends of capitalism at the world level. If major theoretical contributions are to be made, it is presumed that they will come from a general

[38] Among the Marxists who claim that there are laws of transformation peculiar to dependent (as opposed to classical) capitalism are Dos Santos (1970), Marini (1972, 1973), and Bambirra (1974).

economic theory of capitalism and not from the analysis of dependent situations per se (Cueva, 1976: 14–15; Cardoso and Faletto, 1979: xxiii). By no means, however, is this the only kind of theory relevant to a dependency focus. In addition to a concern with international factors, an analysis of concrete situations of dependency must pay close attention to the nature of class conflicts and alliances at the local level. Yet despite this need to understand domestic social and political forces, the dependency approach has no theory of the state, even though state activities are assumed to affect national development in highly significant ways. Nor does it have a special theory of class formation and class behavior. The key actors in dependency studies, other than the state, are usually the rural oligarchies, the national and international bourgeoisie (the latter most commonly embodied in the TNCs), and in some cases various middle-class groups. When the popular sectors make an appearance, more often than not they are portrayed as passive and manipulated masses, even though their activity (e.g., in strikes or as members of revolutionary coalitions like Allende's *Unidad Popular* in Chile) has been an important aspect of contemporary Latin American politics. Thus, while strong in its analysis of dominant groups and ruling alliances the dependency perspective has generated very few works that focus on the subordinated classes.[39]

There are a number of theories that dependency scholars have employed in discussing the behavior of states and social classes in dependent societies. The problem is that frequently these approaches are not compatible either in their assumptions or in their explanations of concrete events. This is true, for example, of the various theories of the state incorporated in dependency studies. In the *instrumentalist Marxist* view, the state is defined a priori as a dependent entity conditioned at every step by the needs and wishes of ruling classes in the

[39] Dependency studies that have concentrated on the subordinated classes include Erickson and Peppe (1976), Faria (1976), and Spalding (1977).

centers (Miliband, 1969; Hamilton, 1975*a*, 1975*b*). Recent writings on *bureaucratic-authoritarianism,* on the other hand, depart from a strict Marxist model and instead focus on the "inherent association" between the socio-economic crises characteristic of advanced levels of industrialization and the emergence of the bureaucratic-authoritarian state in Latin America (O'Donnell, 1973, 1978; Collier, 1979). There is even more emphasis on the state's capacity in dependent capitalist societies to develop new institutional forms and autonomous policies in the quasi-evolutionary *historical variations* approach derived by some scholars from the work of Alexander Gerschenkron (Bennett and Sharpe, 1980; Bennett et al., 1978). Finally, the state in Latin America has also been studied using a *balance of bargaining power* framework in which the host government and TNCs are assumed to be interest-maximizing, unitary actors engaged in a non-zero-sum struggle over the distribution of benefits that are being generated or could be generated from a particular investment. Often, the focus is on extractive industries and the end result is nationalization (Moran, 1974*a*; Goodsell, 1974; Tugwell, 1975). More recently, the bargaining framework has been used in looking at state-TNC relations in manufacturing industries where a variety of factors including changeable technology and domestic class alliances with foreign firms make nationalization far less likely (Bennett and Sharpe, 1979; Gereffi and Newfarmer, 1982).

With respect to TNCs, there is an equally diverse theoretical literature that scholars have drawn from in analyzing dependency relations. One taxonomy lists six schools of thought on foreign investment and its performance in underdeveloped countries: the Marxist approach, the dependence approach, the nationalist approach, the traditional economic approach, the neo-traditionalist approach, and the business-school approach (Lall, 1974: 43–46; see also Biersteker, 1979: Chapters 1–3).

A single type of theory is not necessarily superior to all others for purposes of dependency analysis. Different sorts of orientations, methodologies, and data are relevant and can be fruitfully combined. What is needed, above all, is a clear understanding by the analyst of the assumptions, strengths, and blind spots of each theory used. Employed intelligently, a plurality of approaches can produce complementary results. When inconsistent perspectives are brought together, however, the outcome is confusion and indeterminacy.

This brings me to one of the most important issues facing any theory: the question of falsifiability. Critics of the dependency approach have claimed that it is unrejectable—i.e., it fails to specify or imply kinds of data that would disconfirm hypotheses (see Packenham, 1974: 45–51; 1978: 27–28; 1982: 137, 143–145). I do not agree. To address this charge fully, however, the question of falsifiability must be posed at two different levels: the level of *structures*, or situations of dependency; and the level of *processes*, or the developmental outcomes associated with each situation.

The notion of situations of dependency is what Reinhard Bendix calls a concept of socio-historical configurations (Bendix, 1963: 533). This type of construct, like most used in comparative sociological studies, is of intermediate applicability: it is at a level between what is true of all societies (pure theory) and what is true of one society at one point in time and space (pure history or description). For example, whereas stratification is present in all societies, stratification by "class" is present only in some; or, although the exercise of authority requires subordinate agents everywhere, their organization in a "bureaucracy" is a more specific phenomenon. Similarly, whereas there have always been disparities of power and relations of dominance and dependence between nations and social classes, these disparities and relations adopt a particular form in situations of capitalist dependency. The socio-historical configurations delineated by comparative sociological studies are often clarified through the elaboration of paired concepts: "bureaucracy" is better understood when contrasted with a nonbureaucratic, "patrimonial" type of government; stratification by "class" becomes an improved analytical tool when it is contrasted with alternative types of stratification; and "dependency" gains in meaning once the nature of "nondependency" (autonomy or socialism) is made explicit. Finally, since no social structure is static, a further task in comparative sociology is "to analyze the transformation a given structure undergoes without losing its distinguishing characteristics" (Bendix, 1963: 538). In the dependency literature this refers to the identification of changing forms or emerging new situations of dependency.

In terms of falsification, are there criteria at the structural level that allow socio-historical configurations such as bureaucracy, slavery, capitalism, situations of dependency,[40] etc. to be rejected or confirmed? Strictly speaking, the answer is no. Socio-historical constructs cannot be meaningfully characterized as "true" or "false" since they are not unidimensional indicators; they are composite concepts defined by a cluster of attributes. There is still a scholarly standard, however, by which these constructs can be evaluated: their utility in scientific research. In place of validity, in other words, a more appropriate criterion is reliability. The relevant question becomes: To what extent do given socio-historical configurations effectively distinguish and allow one to compare important recurring patterns of behavior across a variety of societies? Judged on these grounds, the notion of situations of dependency has proven its worth. It has highlighted a range of significant patterns of dependency across time and space, emphasizing the complex linkages between internal and external interests—and social, political, and economic ones—related to the expansion of capitalism on the periphery of the world system.

At the level of processes, which refers to the developmental outcomes associated with a given historical-structural situation of dependency, normal falsifiability criteria *are* applicable. Here dependency hypotheses can confront and be

[40] A close intellectual forerunner to the term "situations of dependency" in the sociological literature is the "colonial situation" concept introduced by Balandier (1955: Chapter 1).

rejected by data, even when multiple theories and methodologies are used. Theodore Moran (1978) provides an excellent review of how nondependency studies can contribute to testing hypotheses taken from the dependency literature about the impact of TNCs on the host (or dependent) country. At their most general level Moran's (1978: 80) dependency propositions are as follows: first, that the benefits of foreign investment are poorly (or unfairly) distributed between the TNCs and the host; second, that foreign investment causes economic distortions in the local economy; and third, that foreign investment causes political distortions in the host society. Each of these propositions, in turn, is broken down into a series of testable hypotheses. The second proposition, for instance, is converted into four specific allegations:

> ... first, that multinational corporations "preempt" the development of an indigenous economic base by squeezing out local entrepreneurs in the most "dynamic" sectors of the host country economy; second, that multinational corporations employ "inappropriate" capital-intensive technologies when they move in, adding to host country unemployment; third, that multinational corporations worsen the distribution of income in the host country or even produce an absolute loss for the lower 40 percent; fourth, that multinational corporations alter consumer tastes and undermine the culture of the host country. (Moran, 1978: 85)

The political distortions linked to TNCs are also spelled out:

> Foreign investors pervert or subvert host country political processes (1) by co-opting the local elites; and/or (2) by using their influence in their home countries to bring pressure to keep host governments "in line"; and/or (3) by structuring the international system to respond to their multinational needs to the detriment of host authorities. (Moran, 1978: 93)

Thomas Biersteker's (1979) book *Distortion or Development?* is another work that shows it is both feasible and desirable to systematically evaluate dependency propositions vis-à-vis those from contending theoretical perspectives. In particular Biersteker is concerned with the effects of multinational investment on the social structure, patterns of consumption, income distribution, displacement of indigenous production, transfer of technology, and balance of payments of underdeveloped countries. He concludes that the dependency writers who are critical of the TNCs are generally more accurate than the conventional business-school approach to the subject.[41]

In summary, I have argued that at the structural level of socio-historical configurations, where the idea of situations of dependency is located, the question of falsifiability is not relevant. Comparative sociological concepts are not falsified or confirmed but rather are judged as useful or not useful according to whether they illuminate significant areas of social reality (in the fashion of Weberian ideal types). At the level of dependency processes, on the other hand, the falsifiability of hypotheses about the developmental outcomes implied by dependency situations is possible. Contrary to the opinion of some critics, then, the dependency perspective can and does generate testable propositions.

This chapter has attempted thus far to outline the main analytical features of the historical-structural dependency approach to third world development as well as to indicate several potential problem areas. The worth of this perspective can only be evaluated by seeing how well it explains particular cases of development and underdevelopment. Before moving to the cases, though, this theoretical discussion of the dependency approach should be complemented by a methodological overview of how dependency studies have actually been carried out. Industry studies, I will argue, are one of the best ways to exploit the strengths of dependency theory and avoid the pitfalls mentioned above.

---

[41] Biersteker's counterarguments to dependency propositions are largely derived from the work of individuals associated with the Multinational Enterprise Project of the Harvard Business School (see Vernon, 1971, 1976b, 1977).

DEPENDENCY ANALYSIS AND THE STUDY OF INDUSTRIES

Historical-structural dependency studies have employed a variety of research strategies that allow the authors to develop and test propositions with diverse degrees of generality. The strategies differ in terms of their *level of analysis* (the third world as a whole or a particular third world region, a country, an industry, a given situation of dependency, or the combination of an industry in a particular country), their *key variables* (situations of dependency or nation-states), and their use of the *time dimension* (longitudinal or cross-sectional). Table 1.1 outlines five principal research strategies based on these distinctions.

At the most general level of analysis dependency authors may refer in their writings to the evolution of dependency relations in the third world as a whole (Amin, 1970, 1973*a*; Frank, 1978), or in a particular region of the third world such as Latin America (Frank, 1969, 1972; Cardoso and Faletto, 1969; Dos Santos, 1969; Sunkel, 1969, 1973; Furtado, 1970) or Black Africa (Amin, 1973*b*). These works trace the historical-structural changes that lead the overall region, or groups of countries within it, from one situation of dependency to another. Some writers choose to look at specific countries in order to carry out a more detailed dependency analysis: examples include Quijano (1971) and Stepan (1978) on Peru, Furtado (1959) and Evans (1979*a*) on Brazil, Frank (1967*a*) on Chile and Brazil, Leys (1974) on Kenya, and the Latin American case studies[42] in Chilcote and Edelstein (1974). As with the regional studies the emphasis is on the causes and consequences of shifts in dependency situations over time.

A third type of dependency research is concerned with specifying the common features of different countries in the same situation of dependency. Recent works of this kind have concentrated on the situation of associated-dependent devel-

---

[42] The countries included in this volume are Guatemala, Mexico, Argentina, Brazil, Chile, and Cuba.

TABLE 1.1
Five Research Strategies Used
in Historical-Structural Dependency Studies

Constants	Key Variables	Time Dimension	Representative Authors
Blocs of countries (the entire third world or a particular region)	Situations of dependency	Longitudinal	Amin, Cardoso and Faletto, Frank, Dos Santos, Sunkel, Furtado
A country	Situations of dependency	Longitudinal	Quijano, Furtado, Chilcote and Edelstein (Latin American case studies), Leys, Evans, Stepan
A situation of dependency	Countries	Cross-sectional	Cardoso, Evans, Gereffi
An industry	Countries in similar or different situations of dependency	Cross-sectional	Group projects sponsored by the Social Science Research Council (New York) and the Instituto Latinoamericano de Estudios Transnacionales (Mexico City), Jenkins
An industry in a country	Situations of dependency	Longitudinal	Moran, Wionczek, Tugwell, Newfarmer, Gereffi, Bennett and Sharpe

opment or on the similar structures and dynamics of semi-peripheral countries in the third world: Brazil, Mexico, Argentina, India, Egypt, Nigeria, etc. (Cardoso, 1973; Evans, 1979a: Chapter 6; Gereffi and Evans, 1981; Evans and Gereffi, 1982). The relevant group of nations varies for each distinct situation of dependency (Central American and some Caribbean countries would be most appropriate, for example, if one were interested in foreign-controlled plantation export enclaves). This line of investigation leads one to select a cross-sectional sampling of countries, since changes in the international economy make the comparison of cases drawn from disparate time periods unreliable.

The two remaining strategies for dependency research involve a focus on industries. In large part this industry approach was a natural outgrowth of the tremendous importance that TNCs acquired in most third world areas following World War II. To understand the dynamics of capitalist growth in the periphery, it was considered necessary to look at the principal economic factors conditioning TNC behavior, internationally as well as in particular host countries. Industry structure at both the global and local levels and its change over time therefore became a major variable in dependency studies. It was also increasingly clear that third world states themselves act in terms of an industry frame of reference. National development plans generally target particular industries or sectors of an economy for incentives or government controls (including nationalization). The success or failure of these policies cannot be adequately understood without a close look at industry characteristics.

One industry strategy adopted by dependency authors is marked by its primary attention to the structure, functioning, and third world impact of a single worldwide industry such as automobiles, steel, food, or pharmaceutical products.[43] The

[43] Two group projects, one in the United States and one in Latin America, are currently producing a series of important studies utilizing this perspective. The Working Group on Transnational Corporations in Latin America, sponsored by the Social Science Research Council in New

idea is to show how the opportunities and constraints generated by the global industry are dealt with in a variety of national contexts. The second industry strategy utilized in dependency research examines one or more industries in a particular country and highlights the consequences associated with changing situations of dependency. The focus of attention tends to be on TNCs in the industry and their shifting relationship with the host country state, although other national actors like the local private sector, urban labor, or peasants usually enter the picture.

Works dealing with extractive industries, such as copper in Chile (Moran, 1974a), sulphur in Mexico (Wionczek, 1967), and oil in Venezuela (Tugwell, 1975), or with an infrastructural industry like electric power (Wionczek, 1964; Newfarmer, 1980b), begin with an initial situation of almost total foreign control and end with the host country's nationalization of the industry in question. The dependency studies of manufacturing industries, such as drugs in Mexico (Gereffi, 1977, 1978) and Brazil (Bertero, 1973; Evans, 1976), automobiles in Mexico (Bennett and Sharpe, 1979) and Brazil (de Oliveira and Travolo Popoutchi, 1979), and petrochemicals

York, has completed a set of case studies on the following international industries: automobiles, tractors, tires, electrical equipment, steel, pharmaceuticals, food processing, and tobacco (see Newfarmer, 1983). The impact of each industry in a variety of third world (and especially Latin American) countries is examined, with a main objective being to show how the structural sources of the TNCs' economic and noneconomic power often lead to negative consumer and national welfare outcomes in underdeveloped nations in the absence of effective host country policy to the contrary. The second project is coordinated by the Instituto Latinoamericano de Estudios Transnacionales, headquartered in Mexico City, and includes an in-depth structural analysis of the automotive "sectorial complex" in various nations in Latin America such as Mexico, Peru, Venezuela, Argentina, Uruguay, and Brazil. (A prior, very informative dependency study of the automobile industry in several Latin American countries was carried out by Jenkins, 1977.) In both projects the accurate characterization of phases in the evolution of the worldwide industry is a central concern, although the actual nations selected for comparison may represent the same or different situations of dependency.

47

(Evans, 1977) and electrical machinery (Newfarmer, 1980a) in Brazil, outline a more complicated and indeterminate course for TNCs, however. In natural resource industries the bargaining power of the state is lowest at the time of TNC entry because of uncertainties about the amount, quality, and costs of extraction; after the first large investments have been made the balance of power starts to swing steadily in favor of the state as the uncertainties are reduced and the host country moves up a learning curve that leads from monitoring industry behavior to replicating complex corporate functions (see Moran, 1974a: 157–169). In manufacturing industries the situation is often the reverse. The power of the state is likely to be greatest at the beginning, when it can set the conditions for TNC access to the local market. Once the manufacturing enterprises are integrated into the local economy, their bargaining power is enhanced because they can more effectively mobilize domestic allies and reinforce the perceived host country need for their kind of products (often through advertising and the role of product brand names). Furthermore, if the industry is dependent on external sources of technology, the credibility of nationalization as a threat is greatly diminished (Gereffi, 1978; Stepan, 1978: Chapter 7; Bennett and Sharpe, 1979).

This book will employ both the one industry/one country and the worldwide industry strategies for analyzing dependency relations. Chapters 3 through 5 will look in detail at the steroid hormone industry, a key segment of the modern "wonder drugs" industry, as it originated and developed in Mexico over a forty-year period. Chapters 6 and 7 will broaden the focus and shift to a cross-national analysis of the performance of TNCs in the pharmaceutical industry in a variety of countries from Latin America, Africa, and Asia. In each case the dependency of local industries stems from the multifaceted nature of foreign control over them—i.e., foreign ownership, foreign technology, foreign scientists, and reliance on foreign markets. Strategies for lessening or reversing dependency in the pharmaceutical industry of these countries seek to reduce the extent of this external reliance. In the larger countries, vulnerability is generally thought to be reduced through local industrialization efforts directed especially at the production of essential drugs. For smaller nations the first steps toward lessening dependency often involve modifying the conditions under which drug products are imported in order to try to achieve lower prices (e.g., through international tenders and bulk purchasing arrangements) while ensuring acceptable quality and encouraging that priority be given to drugs judged most "appropriate" for local needs. Rarely is complete nationalization of the pharmaceutical industry considered to be a viable option by these countries because transnational firms control the rapidly changing technology that generates a steady stream of new and improved products.

This book, then, will try to combine the merits of both case-study and cross-national analyses of dependency. As a point of departure Chapter 2 will introduce the Mexican case, frame my main hypotheses regarding it, and suggest some concepts and techniques that I hope will add to the overall theoretical and methodological rigor of historical-structural dependency analysis.

PART TWO

A CRUCIAL-CASE TEST OF DEPENDENCY THEORY: THE STEROID HORMONE INDUSTRY IN MEXICO

CHAPTER TWO

Dependency Analysis and the Mexican Steroid Hormone Industry

OVER the last four decades Mexico has sustained one of the highest economic growth rates of any country in the world. The key to this growth, especially since the 1950s, has been industrialization. The dynamism of Mexican industry has, in turn, been due in large part to the massive entry of foreign investment in the form of the transnational corporation.

The TNCs tend to be concentrated in the fastest-growing industries in Mexico, and within these they are usually the leading firms. Their potential power to set guiding policy is increased by the fact that most of these industries are oligopolies; thus, the conduct of a few big sellers largely determines industry performance. This concentration of TNCs in positions of industrial leadership has been the source of great concern in Mexico. The fear is that the development of TNC-dominated industries may serve foreign goals much better than national ones.

The steroid hormone industry in Mexico is a case that combines the elements of rapid growth, an oligopolistic structure, and foreign domination.[1] Steroid hormones are best known

---

[1] Discussion of the Mexican steroid hormone industry in this and the following three chapters draws substantially from my previous treatments of the subject (Gereffi, 1977, 1978, 1980) but also extends and emends them in key areas. My research on this topic includes extensive personal interviews (over fifty in number) with managers and other corporate personnel from the TNCs and the two state-owned enterprises that have operated in Mexico's steroid hormone industry, with government officials, and with a wide range of other industry experts, along with the analysis of secondary data as well as unpublished materials. Most of the research was carried out in Mexico between December 1975 and December 1976, with brief return trips to Mexico in February 1978, January 1980, and the summer of 1982.

today as the active ingredient in birth control pills. In the 1950s these hormones already were called "wonder drugs" because one of them—cortisone—was found to have nearly miraculous anti-inflammatory powers to relieve the painful symptoms of rheumatoid arthritis. As cortisone derivatives with fewer undesirable side effects were discovered, and as oral contraceptives became widely used, the steroid industry grew at an increasingly rapid rate. By 1975 world retail sales of steroid-containing drugs totaled $3 billion, placing them behind only antibiotics and the mood-changing drugs (stimulants and depressants) in their share of the international pharmaceutical market.

For nearly thirty years Mexico has been the world's leading producer of bulk quantities of steroid hormones. This prominent position stems from the achievements of Syntex, a Mexican firm formed in the mid-1940s which discovered that a wide variety of steroids could be produced on a large scale from the roots of a Mexican plant called barbasco. From that time to the present steroid hormones have been one of the country's most important sources of export sales. In 1973 Mexico ranked second only to Hong Kong[2] among all third world and southern European countries in the dollar value of its pharmaceutical exports, estimated at U.S. $45 million (UNIDO, 1978a: 43–44). In 1975 steroids accounted for over 60 percent of all pharmaceutical exports from Mexico and for 15 percent of all chemical exports. Within the chemical industry steroids were second only to phosphoric acid in export value; three of the steroid hormone companies were among Mexico's top ten chemical exporting firms. On the overall list of industrially produced export items steroids ranked tenth.[3]

The rapid growth of Mexican steroid exports has, until recently, never been in doubt. What is a major question, however, is the degree to which this growth has resulted in real

[2] Hong Kong is primarily an entrepôt trade center, while Mexico's exports come from its own production facilities.

[3] Unpublished data obtained from the Dirección General de Estadística of the Secretaría de Industria y Comercio, Mexico.

industrial progress for Mexico. Since the late 1950s the industry has been controlled by half a dozen vertically integrated
TNC subsidiaries, whose primary goal has been to supply the
needs of their parent companies. Industry critics contend that
the value of export sales from Mexico has been diminished
because the local subsidiaries undervalue the Mexican products sold to their parents through "transfer pricing," and that
Mexico's tax intake is further reduced by the concentration of
industry profits in tax havens such as Puerto Rico, Panama,
and the Bahamas. It is also claimed that the TNCs pay the
peasants too little for gathering the barbasco and that they
have neglected to pay the Mexican nation any fee at all for
the plant's value as a natural resource. In terms of local drug
manufacture there is another complaint: the TNCs have ex-
tracted and processed over one million tons of barbasco since
they entered the industry, yet Mexico is still not producing
significant quantities of finished (consumer) products to satisfy its internal needs.

Early in 1975 the Mexican state decided to take a more active role in the industry. Through the creation of a state-
owned firm (Proquivemex), a restructuring of the industry
was attempted that would allow Mexico to use its sovereignty
over barbasco as a lever by which the TNCs could be forced
to contribute more to the national goals of local industry
growth and peasant welfare. At the heart of the resulting
conflict was the issue of foreign control and the limits it
placed on Mexican development.

SITUATIONS OF DEPENDENCY AND FOREIGN CONTROL

The relationship between foreign control and national development has been the central concern of historical-structural
dependency studies. As has already been seen, at the most
general level dependency analysis attempts to explain how
the global expansion of capitalism has led to various situations
of dependency in third world countries that restrict or retard
their possibilities for national development. The presumption

55

is that the underdevelopment of the third world is perpetuated by deep conflicts of interests or contradictions embedded in the international capitalistic economy that systematically favor the developed nations more than the underdeveloped ones.

Special emphasis has been placed on the role of the TNC in this process since its transnational organization establishes a direct link between the advanced countries at the center of the worldwide industrial system and the industrializing, dependent nations in the periphery. The dependency approach claims that the interdependence (or interconnectedness) of the center and the periphery in the world system masks the basic underlying feature of asymmetrical control in the relationship, which creates for the center countries and the TNCs consistent net advantages. The instruments for exercising this control are varied, ranging from trade to technology to state power. What is important for this analysis is that TNCs are widely assumed to reflect this conflict of interest in their own strategies for development. In support of this critical view research produced by the dependency school has taken issue with virtually every benefit the conventional economics literature has ascribed to TNCs operating in underdeveloped countries and found instead a national cost.[4] What distinguishes the dependency perspective from other literatures that are critical of TNCs is an emphasis on the internal structures and political options of the dependent nation. Its focus on concrete situations of dependency in the host country allows the social, political, and economic aspects of development to be dealt with as an integrated whole; this leads to the framing of questions that are relevant to national policy.

THE steroid hormone industry has always been an export enclave in Mexico. As such, it has depended on foreign buyers,

---

[4] For a useful synthesis and systematic comparison of the major propositions in the conventional, critical, and neoconventional literatures on TNC impact in third world countries, and with an appraisal of their validity for the case of Nigeria, see Biersteker (1979).

foreign technology, foreign markets, and finally foreign investment. The nature of foreign control in steroid hormones is different, however, from that exercised in other types of industries. As a result, these industries not only present different situations of dependency, they also imply different strategies for lessening or breaking with that dependency. Two types of industries can be compared with steroid hormones in terms of the limitations and possibilities associated with foreign control in each: the extractive export industries (such as copper, petroleum, sulphur, natural gas, iron ore, and bauxite) and the modern manufacturing industries where TNCs set up subsidiaries to produce for the host country's internal market (such as automobiles, electrical and nonelectrical machinery, and chemicals).

In extractive industries the TNCs enjoy a big initial advantage. The foreign companies have near-monopoly control over the techniques and resources needed to locate the raw material deposits, set up the mines or wells, and begin steady production. They will not make the huge investments required unless they are promised substantial returns from the host country. Over time, however, the balance of power begins to shift in favor of the host government: the uncertainty about the existence of natural resource deposits and about the structure of production costs is greatly reduced, and the host country begins to move up a learning curve of bargaining skills and operating experience with respect to the industry. As the value of the foreigners' services declines, the host country's power increases; it can demand—and get— more benefits from the TNCs.[5]

Whereas the foreign-controlled natural resource industries

---

[5] Whether or not the host country in fact makes such demands for greater national benefits from the TNCs depends largely on whether key domestic elites find it in their *private* interests to do so (see Moran, 1974*b*). For a detailed analysis of the changing balance of power between TNCs and the host government in a foreign-controlled extractive export enclave in Mexico see Miguel Wionczek's study of the Mexican sulphur industry (Wionczek, 1967).

57

are almost always export enclaves, TNCs also have found it in their interests to locate in modern manufacturing industries that serve the *internal* markets of host countries.[6] This latter type of relationship between TNCs and the host country has been analyzed in the model of "associated-dependent development" (Cardoso, 1973). The central idea of this model is that the interests of the foreign corporations in the local manufacturing industries are compatible, to at least some extent, with the internal prosperity of the dependent countries. This is in direct contrast to the older view of economic imperialism which holds that the basic relationship between a developed capitalistic country and an underdeveloped country is one of extractive exploitation that perpetuates stagnation. Thus, while host country dependency still exists in the foreign-dominated, internally oriented manufacturing industries because the TNCs control the package of financial, technological, organizational, and marketing resources needed to assure advanced industrial growth, the fairly rapid development of at least some sectors of the internal market (especially the urban middle and upper classes) is now an added condition for TNC success. This path to development entails definite costs to the host country,[7] but they are the costs or contradictions typical of internal capitalism rather than external exploitation per se.

Foreign control of the steroid hormone industry in Mexico presents a different sort of problem to the host country. Unlike the internally oriented manufacturing industries, the

[6] These modern industries utilize large plants and capital-intensive production techniques; they show high growth rates and dominate production of capital, intermediate, and consumer durable goods. The highest concentration of TNCs tends to be in the consumer durable industries.

[7] Data generated during the Brazilian "boom" based on associated-dependent development point to a number of potential costs of this pattern of development: 1) it is based on a regressive profile of income distribution; 2) it emphasizes luxury consumer durables as opposed to basic necessities; 3) it generates increasing foreign indebtedness; and 4) it contributes to social marginality and the underutilization and exploitation of manpower resources (Cardoso, 1973: 149).

steroid hormone industry has never been interested in sales within Mexico; 95 to 98 percent of its production has been consistently destined for export. Thus the TNCs in the industry have no direct interest in promoting the growth of the local economy because the goods they produce are sold outside it. And unlike the case of the extractive export enclaves Mexico cannot increase its bargaining power in steroid hormones by climbing learning curves or through the reduction of uncertainty since the source of TNC control is not at the raw material production stage located in the host country (as is true of the extractive industries) but rather at the finished products stage where it is protected by patents and trademarked brand names. Because steroid hormones is a *nonextractive* export industry (barbasco being a self-renewing natural resource found on the surface of the land), the TNCs have no huge capital investment to protect; rather, the control in steroids is centered in knowledge and demand creation that are beyond Mexico's reach. In short, the steroid hormone industry is neither a "traditional" export industry nor a "modern" manufacturing one but a hybrid combining characteristics of both.

Foreign control in Mexico's steroid hormone industry has two key characteristics: it is structured (i.e., part of a persistent pattern) and it is increasing. It is *structured* because the foreign buyers of Mexican steroids have always controlled the manufacture and sale of the finished products (where industry profits are concentrated) as well as the development of new products and the creation of new demand[8] on which the con-

[8] Demand has been created for steroid hormones by the two classic strategies of capitalistic marketing: 1) widening the market by increasing sales of existing products through the incorporation of new groups of consumers, and 2) deepening the market by introducing new products sold to a reduced number of consumers with a high capacity to purchase or with specialized needs. Widening the market is most obvious with respect to the oral contraceptives, especially the attempts to extend their use to the more populous developing areas of the world. The market has been deepened by the sale of effective, specialized products (such as Syntex's Synalar for the treatment of skin inflammation and Searle's Aldactone, a steroid

tinued existence of the Mexican industry depends. This control has also been *increasing*, since Mexico's position as a raw material supplier in the world industry has become more and more marginalized. The two main causes of this trend are: 1) the development of equally efficient and politically "safer" raw material substitutes for Mexican barbasco, and 2) the added cost of synthesizing complicated steroid drugs, which is now out of proportion to the cost of the starting material.[9] Thus, both the absolute and the relative value of Mexico's contribution to the industry have continued to decline.

This is not to deny that Mexico has received benefits from the TNCs in the steroid hormone industry: these include fiscal revenues and foreign exchange from export sales, seasonal employment for 25,000 peasants and 3,000 workers, and the training of several hundred Mexican technicians and some scientists. The benefits are inherently partial and unstable, however, because they derive from TNC calculations based on criteria of global efficiency that often conflict with national criteria for promoting local growth and welfare. This points to the real nature of the dependency resulting from foreign capital: all attempts to promote national goals that are not in the direct interests of the TNCs will be resisted by the foreign firms because the national benefits are transnational costs.

Notwithstanding the achievements of the dependency school in gaining strong leverage on conflicts of interests as they affect the process of national development and host country policy, most of its studies suffer from two weaknesses in their evaluation of the impact of TNCs in the less developed countries. First of all, dependency analysis either ig-

diuretic) as well as by the discovery of new uses for steroid hormones (such as the treatment of menopause, cardiovascular therapy, insect control, and estrus control in farm animals).

[9] When production costs are a small part of the total sale price, as is typical in pharmaceuticals, one consequence is that technological adaptation is less likely to occur (Vernon, 1971: 183, citing a study by W. A. Yeoman).

nores the question of feasible alternatives to transnational investment in a given country or industry or it assumes a priori that national firms would produce results socially superior to those of a group of transnationals. Second, and in related fashion, dependency analysis tends to sidestep the welfare implications of a national (as distinguished from international) strategy for development for one of two reasons: 1) national autonomy rather than national or consumer welfare is taken as the ethical yardstick, or 2) socialism rather than "autonomous capitalism" or "renegotiated dependency" is taken as the alternative to national dependency.

Main Hypotheses and a Crucial-Case Test

Given that Mexico's steroid hormone industry is characterized by multifaceted relationships of foreign control, one should expect to find two major consequences resulting from this dependency: first, an inequitable distribution of benefits from the industry's growth favoring the central capitalistic economies and the TNCs more than Mexico; and second, at the level of Mexico's domestic policy formulation a stunting or restriction of choice among local development options, since these are likely to conflict with global priorities implied by the dependent situation. The consequences of dependency, in other words, are both economic and political.

These two hypotheses will be evaluated longitudinally with respect to three phases in the development of the Mexican steroid hormone industry. The first phase, 1944 to 1955, begins with the founding of Syntex as a Mexican firm and the establishment of a domestic steroid industry in Mexico and ends with the sale of Syntex to a U.S. industrial holding company. The second phase, 1956 to 1974, covers the "denationalization" of the Mexican steroid hormone industry. During this period, six Mexican manufacturers of bulk hormone products were displaced and replaced by six wholly foreign-owned TNC subsidiaries. The third phase, 1975 to 1982, encompasses the creation and operations of a government firm named Proquivemex in the industry. The goal of the state was to redefine Mexico's dependency and to establish new development priorities that were more national in orientation.

In reality this is not a study of one case but of three because each of the phases of industry development mentioned above will be considered as a distinct situation of dependency. Three sets of related factors work together to form a situation of dependency at the level of national industries: 1) the external (the international structure of the industry in question), 2) the transnational (the global strategies of the TNCs in the industry), and 3) the domestic (the policy—or lack of policy —by the host country state regarding national priorities for development). In the Mexican steroid hormone industry each of these factors reflects the significance of foreign control, although state inaction will be explained by other conditions as well. The relative weight and specific content of these factors change, however, from one situation of dependency to the next. My aim will be to analyze the differences in developmental outcomes produced by the three dependent situations.

Although case studies are by far the most frequent kind of study made in the social sciences, their role in the theory-building process is generally underestimated. In a definitive article on the subject, Harry Eckstein (1975) discusses two kinds of case studies useful for theory that are particularly relevant to my dependency analysis: disciplined-configurative studies and crucial-case studies.[10] "Disciplined-configurative studies" are based on the premise that the interpretation of particular cases can, and indeed must, be derived from established theories or, lacking them, provisional ones; the soundness of any given interpretation depends on the validity of these theories. Disciplined-configurative studies are thus tied to theoretical inquiry in both a passive and an active way. By

---

[10] In total, Eckstein (1975) identifies five distinct types of case studies, the other three being configurative-idiographic and heuristic studies, and case studies as plausibility probes. All but the first type are important for theory.

passively applying general laws or probability statements to particular cases, these studies can impugn established or provisional theories that ought to fit the case but do not. The application of theories to cases can also have an active feedback effect on theorizing by indicating a need for new theory in neglected areas. In short, disciplined-configurative case studies provide special opportunities not only for fact gathering but also for the application and elaboration of middle-level generalizations.

Historical-structural dependency analysis lends itself easily to this form of case interpretation, since, as I indicated in Chapter 1, the holistic dependency argument is primarily contextual in nature and needs to be "filled in" by various theories relevant to the case at hand. In my examination of the Mexican steroid hormone industry I will be basing major portions of my interpretation on widely accepted propositions drawn from the theoretical literatures on Mexico, the nature of the pharmaceutical industry, the behavior of TNCs, the state, etc. I feel that the theories I combine satisfy the criterion of mutual compatibility, and thus they produce conclusions that are consistent overall.

A "crucial-case study" is much more demanding than the disciplined-configurative studies. Whereas the latter are concerned with applying (and sometimes elaborating) theories, the former is interested in subjecting theories to a critical test. Crucial or limiting cases are those that ought to invalidate or confirm theories if any cases can be expected to do so. They may be divided into two types: "most-likely" and "least-likely" cases. The best-known example of a "least-likely" case is probably Michels' (1911) investigation of the ubiquitousness of oligarchy in organizations. His argument was that grass-roots democratic political parties would be least likely, or very unlikely, to be oligarchic if oligarchy were not universal. His intensive analysis of such parties in Germany and elsewhere led Michels to his famous conclusion that there is an "iron law of oligarchy" that makes democracy and large-scale social organization incompatible. A classic example of a "most-likely" case is Whyte's (1943) study of a Boston slum society that, according to prevailing theory, should have displayed a high level of social disorganization but in fact displayed the very opposite. What is a most-likely case for one theory, of course, becomes a least-likely case for its antithesis, and vice versa (e.g., the Boston slum was a least-likely case for the ubiquity of social organization). The distinction is determined by one's research design and objectives and not by the inherent characteristics of a case. In my analysis of the steroid hormone industry in Mexico I hope to show that it is not only amenable to a disciplined-configurative interpretation but also that it constitutes a "least-likely" case for dependency theory (or, conversely, a "most-likely" case for autonomous and integrated national development).

Chapters 3, 4, and 5 will deal with the periods 1944–1955, 1956–1974, and 1975–1982, respectively. In Chapter 3 I will outline the conditions that make the steroid hormone industry in Mexico a "least-likely" case of dependency: Mexico had exclusive access to the best raw material for an expanding segment of the world pharmaceutical industry, a Mexican firm (Syntex) dominated the industry in output and technology for almost a decade, and the local industry originally had active support from the Mexican state; yet ultimately, these circumstances proved insufficient for Mexico to retain national control. The key question is: How and why did Mexico, a world leader in the production of steroid hormones, allow its industry to become denationalized? Chapter 4 describes and offers an explanation for the entry of TNCs into the Mexican steroid hormone industry. Given the resulting situation of total foreign control of the industry the chapter provides an evaluation of the distributional effects of the TNCs in terms of national welfare (defined as local industry growth) and consumer welfare (defined as identical or better products at lower prices), using the expected performance of national firms as a counterfactual basis for comparison. Chapter 4 also analyzes the topic of restricted choice among local development options. Chapter 5 discusses the issues surrounding the creation of Proquivemex in 1975 and assesses the degree to which the Mexican state has utilized its increased autonomy to alter the distribution of industry benefits in the direction of greater and/or more equitable national development.

THE NATION-STATE, EQUITY, AND POWER IN INDUSTRY STUDIES OF DEPENDENCY

The industry approach to dependency research raises a special problem for the investigator that involves overlapping national and industry levels of analysis. The situation is further complicated when state policy is brought into the picture. On the other hand, there are also some unique opportunities for the elaboration of new conceptual and methodological tools that can be used more widely in the field of development studies. My discussion of these points covers three main areas: 1) the role of the nation and the state in industry studies, 2) the "equity" issue and counterfactual analysis, and 3) bargaining power, structural power, and "nondecisions" in dependency research.

The Nation and the State in Industry Studies of Dependency

In the dependency studies that focus on the development of a single industry in a particular country, structures and processes of dependency are actually observed at two different levels: that of the nation-state and that of a specific industry. These two levels of analysis overlap, but the temporal cuts that mark distinct situations of dependency at each level need not coincide. A country as a whole may be judged more or less dependent during time periods when certain industries within that country show a reverse tendency. The more prominent the chosen industry is in a national economy (e.g., copper in Chile or oil in Venezuela), however, the lower are the chances for a major disjunction of this kind to occur.

Although steroid hormones are not a leading-sector type of

industry in Mexico like oil, automobiles, or petrochemicals,[11] fortunately the periodization for the relevant dependency situations at both the national and industry levels coincides very well. In a recent article on the role of foreign investment and TNCs in Brazil and Mexico, Gereffi and Evans (1981) outline four situations of dependency common to both countries: the export enclave economy (1880–1930); "horizontal" import-substituting industrialization (1930–1955); "vertical" import-substituting industrialization (1955–1970); and diversified export promotion (1970–present). These periods parallel, in content as well as timing, the main phases in the development of the steroid hormone industry in Mexico. The 1944–1955 period for the industry, like "horizontal" import substitution for the nation overall, was an era when local private capital led Mexican development efforts and direct foreign investment was at low ebb. The entry and predominance of TNCs, which occurred in the steroid hormone industry from 1956 to 1974, was also the chief characteristic of the "vertical" import-substituting industrialization process in Mexico that began around 1955. By the early 1970s "denationalization" was the key word being used to describe the outcome of TNC entry in steroid hormones as well as in the consumer durable and intermediate goods industries that were the basis of Mexico's "vertical" import substitution. In the diversified export promotion phase of Mexican development (1970–present) one of the primary features has been the expanded role of the state in the economy, particularly notable in the guise of many new government-owned enterprises. The behavior of Proquivemex in the steroid hormone industry in the 1975–1982 period can be fully understood only if it is related to this more general pattern of state involvement in Mexico at the time.

Even when the periodization of situations of dependency

---

[11] While steroid hormones are not a leading sector within the country, Mexico nevertheless has for years been a dominant force in the international steroid industry.

coincides at the national and industry levels, as it does in the Mexican steroid hormone case, there is an additional level of analysis problem that must be addressed in industry studies. State policy (or its absence) is an important component of any dependency situation. For the study of one industry in a single country the nature and strength of state policy has to be disaggregated across industries and viewed over time. Dependency analysis, in other words, must attend to the *priority* that the state gives to different national industries and also to *changes* in these priorities. In the Mexican steroid hormone industry state policy varied markedly from one situation of dependency to the next. State interest in the industry was high during the 1944–1955 period, consisting in various forms of support to Syntex in its quest to become Mexico's national champion in the world steroid industry; state involvement in the industry was very low from 1956 to 1974 due in large part to the fact that the state considered other industries like automobiles, petrochemicals, and mining far more strategic in terms of new industrial policy; and with the creation of Proquivemex in 1975, the state's interest in steroid hormones was once again high but this time in support of a government firm rather than a local private company. These changes in the type and degree of state involvement in the industry must be explained in their own right because they are a crucial part of the internal dynamics of dependency.

The "Equity" Issue and Counterfactual Analysis

In the first of my two main hypotheses I emphasize that if Mexico's steroid hormone industry is truly dependent, its growth will be characterized by an inequitable distribution of benefits favoring the central capitalistic economies and the TNCs more than it should and Mexico less than it should. What do I mean by "inequitable" here? Why not, for example, use the seemingly more objective term "unequal" to describe the economic distortions that allegedly result from foreign control in the context of peripheral capitalism?

I do not believe that the dependency argument should be stated in terms of an unequal distribution of benefits between the central and peripheral countries of the world system because most people acknowledge the possibility (indeed likelihood) of a legitimate gap between what is "equal" and what is "just."[12] With regard to TNCs this means that there is no inherent reason to expect that returns from their investments abroad should be equally divided with the host country in order for these returns to be equitable. The oil industry provides an instructive example on this point. After World War II, expanding oil production in Venezuela led to the adoption of a 50-50 agreement between the companies and the host government whereby the two parties divided evenly the sum of royalties and profits. This arrangement was gradually adopted in the Middle East as well. The 50-50 rule had a ring of self-evident fairness about it that for a while obviated discussion. But more oil continued to be discovered. On the company side new entrants brought more competition; and on the country side the formation of the Organization of Petroleum Exporting Countries (OPEC) by various producers in the Middle East and Venezuela led to simultaneous efforts to alter the basis for contracts with the companies and to maintain the prices of oil and related products. New contracts with new entrants were written at 60-40 in favor of the host country, and then at 75-25, with existing contracts gradually modified in the direction of the terms of the new contracts at the margin (Kindleberger, 1969: 154). Thus, in the case of oil an increasingly *unequal* distribution of benefits was advantageous to the oil-producing nations and was perceived as equitable by them.

What empirical standards can one use to make normative judgments about the fairness or unfairness of an existing or

---

[12] Even the communist slogan "From each according to his ability, to each according to his needs" is a formula based on equity rather than equality since people's abilities and needs are not necessarily equal. For a useful conceptual overview of the equality and equity literature see Bell (1974).

expected distribution of benefits? What separates the notion of a just return from that of "exploitation"? The now classic formulation of this problem was proposed by Charles Kindleberger, who conceptualized the relationship between TNCs and host country governments with regard to direct investment as one of "bilateral monopoly" in which the company has control over its services[13] and the country has control over access before the investment is made and over taxation or expropriation afterwards. "In a typical situation, a company earns more abroad than the minimum it would accept and a country's net social benefits from the company's presence are greater than the minimum *it* would accept . . . with a wide gap between maximum and minimum demands by the two parties to the bargain" (Kindleberger and Herrick, 1977: 320). From the host country's point of view, the *lower limit* of this bargaining range would be the price needed to induce the TNC (and others) to invest and/or to prevent it from withdrawing; the *upper limit* would be the scarcity value of the TNC's services to the country (i.e., the price at which the country would rather do without those services). The price ultimately settled on between the two extremes—which could be quite far apart—would be determined by the relative bargaining strengths of the two sides (see Moran, 1978: 81–82).

The problem of foreign exploitation generally assumes that TNCs are already installed in the host economy or that they are eager to come in. The real debate, therefore, centers on the upper limit of the bargaining range: Are foreign investors thought to be siphoning off too much of an economic surplus that otherwise could be devoted to internal development? The outcome of this calculation depends upon the alternative against which one measures the services of TNCs. These alternatives may be of three sorts: 1) local replacement of the TNC's services where feasible, 2) outside alternatives to the

[13] The TNC's "services" include capital, technology, management, and often access to foreign marketing channels.

TNC (rival TNCs, cheaper knowledge through international bodies, etc.), or 3) doing without the TNC's services altogether. An "inequitable" distribution of benefits would mean that foreign control has led to less benefits than some feasible alternative situation would have.[14] In order to confirm my first hypothesis of an inequitable distribution of benefits between TNCs and Mexico in favor of the former, then, I must be able to show two things: that feasible alternatives to TNCs did exist in the industry in question and that these alternatives could have been expected to perform as well as, or better than, the TNCs did in a benefit/cost sense. The identification of these alternatives, however, frequently requires one to employ a technique known as "counterfactual analysis."

Counterfactual analysis is no stranger to the social sciences.[15] Counterfactual propositions are present any time we try to weigh or assess the relative importance of factors leading up to a particular event. If one asks about the causes of the American Civil War, for instance, one generally expects more than a simple enumeration of relevant factors, such as slavery, John Brown's raid, Lincoln's election in 1860, and the firing upon Fort Sumter. One would at least like to know which of these causal factors were "major" and which "minor" and if possible some notion as to which of these factors were "necessary" or "indispensable" conditions for the outbreak of the war. Presumably slavery was more important than John Brown's raid, for example.

What is involved in this or any weighting procedure is a mental exercise in which the analyst removes the relevant causal factors one at a time in order to speculate what the

[14] In the extreme case of a monopoly seller the country can see what prices have been set or bargains struck between that company and previous buyers (nations) in an effort to arrive at a more equitable arrangement. In this way the country can generate its own alternative.

[15] For a sophisticated discussion of "counterfactual speculation" in history, economics, and the new economic history, see McClelland (1975: Chapter 4). Major works in economic history that have utilized this technique include Fogel (1964), Bruchey (1965), North (1966), and McGreevey (1971).

world would have been like in their absence.[16] The removal of minor factors should produce little expected change and that of major factors a great deal of change with respect to the event or situation under consideration. In *all* counterfactuals, established causal generalizations are used to guide or control such speculation; that is, the social scientist uses knowledge of relevant causal processes to trace the likely results of removal. Other things being equal, one's confidence in counterfactuals as a useful approximation to reality is increased under the following conditions: "[t]he more simple the causal process under study; the fewer causal forces of obvious relevance ignored; the shorter the time period; the smaller the changes considered; [and] the more the analysis turns upon the specification of rough magnitudes rather than exact magnitudes . . ." (McClelland, 1975: 167).

Whereas counterfactual comparisons are usually implicit in social science research, I believe it is very important that they be made explicit in dependency analysis. The reason has already been alluded to in Chapter 1: empirical studies of dependency have tended to confuse the costs or problems of in-

---

[16] This type of procedure is associated with causal analysis of events, where counterfactual statements are used to underscore the importance of factors that actually were operative in the situation under consideration. "If slavery had not existed in America, then the Civil War would not have been fought" is an example of this kind of statement. There is a second type of counterfactual speculation that does not directly concern events. Here the procedure is mentally to *add* (rather than subtract) a particular causal factor and speculate about its impact. "If Hitler had invaded England, then Churchill would have been executed" is one example. What is common to both categories of statement is speculation of the "if . . . then . . ." variety, with the "if" clause, or antecedent, made deliberately false (hence, the full name "contrary-to-fact conditional"). Put more formally, the general proposition in counterfactual analysis takes the form of all causal generalizations:

Probably, if $(C_1, \ldots, C_n)$, then E.

"Probably" indicates that we can never know for certain that the conditions $(C_1, \ldots, C_n)$ do indeed constitute the sum total of conditions, positive and negative, which when realized lead the consequent to invariably follow (McClelland, 1975: Chapters 1 and 4).

dustrial development as it occurs anywhere with the more specific costs associated with foreign-controlled development. These studies have failed, in other words, to adequately distinguish problems of capitalism from problems of dependency. One way to separate these two kinds of social costs is to ask what were the *feasible alternatives*, if any, to foreign direct investment in the country or industry under examination. If there appear to have been no feasible alternatives to investment by TNCs, then at least a prima facie case can be made that the associated social costs of foreign investment are endemic to the type of development strategy chosen by the country's ruling elite.[17] If, on the other hand, local firms represented a real alternative to TNC investment, then it should be possible through counterfactual analysis to compare the actual consequences of TNC involvement with the expected consequences of locally controlled development in order to see whether a substantial difference can be attributed to the situation of foreign control. In this way counterfactual analysis helps us see the past in terms of alternative possibilities that may have been open and not simply as a sequence of events that because they *did* occur *had* to occur.[18] In Chapter

[17] An important caveat must be added here. The notion of "feasibility" requires the researcher to adopt very conservative standards regarding admissable extrapolations from the evidence at hand. Actual history, though, is full of significant events and situations that few predicted or thought likely before they happened. Feasible alternatives, therefore, do not exhaust the range of possible historical outcomes at any given moment.

[18] This latter view is known as the "retrospective fallacy." One tends only to take account of connections between actual occurrences; all unactualized possibilities appear never to have been real. In its extreme form the retrospective fallacy leads to the acceptance of historical determinism: when the past is read "backwards"—step by step, exactly as it occurred—the chain of events as a whole seems to be characterized by an inner necessity, an inherent developmental tendency. A prospectively oriented view, on the other hand, examines each event in terms of the many possibilities that, at the time of its occurrence, remained open for future change. When done well, counterfactual analysis is thus able to provide the social scientist with greater insight into the role of deliberation and choice in human history. (For a fuller discussion of the retrospective fallacy see Mandelbaum, 1971: 134–137.)

4, I explicitly consider national firms as a counterfactual alternative to TNCs in Mexico's steroid hormone industry.

Bargaining Power, Structural Power, and "Nondecisions"

My second main hypothesis mentioned above was that if Mexico's steroid industry is dependent TNCs are likely to have caused a stunting or restriction of choice among Mexico's local development options. How can one determine whether domestic policy has been restricted or distorted by the presence of TNCs? To answer this question, the concept of power has to be introduced into the analysis.

With respect to TNCs, two kinds of power are of interest: bargaining power and structural power.[19] Bargaining power is the power to control the outcomes of specific events. Much of the bargaining power literature is written from a "bilateral monopoly" perspective, as already noted. Transnational corporations and the governments of host countries are seen as the two principal actors, and solutions are arrived at based on the relative bargaining strengths of both sides. Three major sets of factors are thought to account for negotiating strength: 1) the characteristics of the investment project, 2) the characteristics of the host country, and 3) the extent of competition in the international industry (Moran, 1978: 82–83; also see Moran, 1974a; Vernon, 1967, 1971; Wells, 1969; Goodman, 1976). Transnational corporations considering projects with low fixed investments, low fixed costs, changeable technology, complex marketing, and high uncertainty (or some combination thereof) will be less vulnerable to host country demands than will TNCs considering projects with the opposite characteristics. Regarding the host country, a small and stagnant local market, an unskilled governmental bureaucracy, an unmobilized populace, and a limited indigenous industrial capacity would predict weak governmental bargaining power.

---

[19] For a very useful review and conceptualization of the power literature as it relates to TNCs and dependency analysis see Caporaso (1978a and 1978b). My definitions of bargaining power and structural power are from Caporaso (1978a: 4).

Finally, low competition among TNCs in the international industry in which the investment is made predicts a weak bargaining position for the host government; increased competition (either at the beginning of a project or over the course of its life) would strengthen the hand of local authorities.

Although this balance-of-bargaining-power approach has proven useful for studies of the relations between TNCs and the governments of their host countries, it suffers from several recurrent weaknesses (see Bennett and Sharpe, 1979: 58–59). First, it tends to conceptualize potential power as consisting simply in each actor's possession of certain resources, with little attention given to the relationships or circumstances that may allow a particular attribute to serve as a source of potential power. Second, the bargaining approach sometimes fails to distinguish between potential power and actual power; it does not consider the possible gap between the potential capability of host governments to control TNCs and their political "will" to do so. Third, studies employing the balance-of-bargaining-power framework usually take as given the agenda of bargaining, thus failing to ask which actors, issues, and interests have been excluded from the bargaining process. To adequately address these concerns, it is necessary to turn to another, more structural conception of power.

Structural power, in broadest terms, is the power to govern the rules that shape bargaining power. This kind of power is a "higher order power" since "it involves the ability to manipulate the choices, capabilities, alliance opportunities, and payoffs that actors may utilize" (Caporaso, 1978a: 4). Structural power is crucial to the understanding of dependency because dependency analysis tries to assess the ways in which international economic and political arrangements, including the global organization of TNCs, "condition," "shape," and "constrain" domestic production structures and domestic political processes. In order to determine the significance of structural power in situations of dependency, the empirical researcher must go beyond actual cases of conflict and overt decisions between TNCs and the host country governments,

74

however, and look at the ways in which nondecisions affect agenda setting and the outcomes of bargaining encounters.

Nondecisions as an area of research in sociology and political science emerged nearly two decades ago in the debate over the nature of community power and how best to study it. Robert Dahl's classic work on New Haven, *Who Governs?* (1961), which epitomized the "pluralist" approach to power, was criticized for looking only at overt decisions[20] while giving no attention to the "mobilization of political bias" in the system whereby powerful individuals or groups defend and promote their vested interests by preventing certain grievances from ever becoming issues within the political process. In a pair of seminal articles Bachrach and Baratz (1962, 1963) showed how nondecisions could be studied to redress this serious flaw in the pluralists' approach. More recently, Matthew Crenson's book *The Un-Politics of Air Pollution* (1971) has extended and improved upon this same technique.[21]

In his excellent and provocative synopsis of the power literature Steven Lukes (1974) outlines three distinct perspectives: the "one-dimensional view" of the pluralists; the "two-dimensional view" of their critics who, like Bachrach and Baratz, emphasize nondecision making and potential issues; and a "three-dimensional view" of power. Lukes (1974: 44–45) argues that the three-dimensional view of power goes

[20] For an early effort by this author to challenge Dahl's methodology see Gereffi (1970).

[21] Crenson (1971) provides a detailed analysis of two neighboring cities in Indiana, both equally polluted and with similar populations, one of which, East Chicago, took action to clear its air in 1949, while the other, Gary, took no similar measures until 1962. Crenson's explanation of the difference is that Gary is a one-company town dominated by U.S. Steel, whose power reputation and behind-the-scenes influence, coupled with Gary's strong party organization, effectively prevented the issue from being raised for many years and decisively influenced the content of the antipollution ordinance that was finally enacted. East Chicago, on the other hand, had a number of steel companies and no strong party organization when it passed its air pollution control ordinance, thus facilitating the issue's earlier hearing there.

75

beyond the two-dimensional position in several ways. First, it is not methodologically individualistic, as are the first two perspectives on power; it shows that the power of a collectivity—whether it be an industrial corporation, a political party, or a social class or group—has systematic effects that are not reducible to the decisions or behavior of particular individuals. Second, it shows how the political agenda was shaped through the exercise of such power by preventing demands from being raised. Third, it does not link nondecisions solely to the existence of actual (overt or covert) conflict; hence, there is a stress on inaction (in Crenson's case, "What U.S. Steel did not do ...") since the most effective use of power is to prevent conflict from arising in the first place.

In my analysis of the Mexican steroid hormone industry I will incorporate aspects of what Lukes calls the two-dimensional and three-dimensional views of power. I will show in Chapter 4 how the dependent status of this industry resulted in nondecisions that greatly restricted its possibilities for further growth. These nondecisions are attributable not only to corporate power but also to institutional inaction on the part of both TNCs and the Mexican state.[22] Finally, the transformation of the potential power of TNCs and the Mexican state into actual power will be seen not just in terms of each actor's possession of certain resources but as a function of the web of relationships in which each actor is enmeshed.

---

[22] In Crenson's (1971) study the inaction of U.S. Steel was the major factor that prevented the Gary citizens' interest in reducing air pollution from being acted on (though other conditions, institutional and ideological, are needed for a fuller account). In his explanation of the world depression of 1929, Kindleberger (1973: 291–292) also places primary importance on institutional inaction—in this case, attributable to the governments of Britain and the United States:

... the 1929 depression was so wide, so deep and so long because the international economic system was rendered unstable by British inability and United States unwillingness to assume responsibility for stabilizing it in three particulars: (a) maintaining a relatively open market for distress goods; (b) providing counter-cyclical long-term lending; and (c) discounting in crisis.

76

Six sets of relations are of particular relevance to this study: 1) the relationships among TNCs in the international industry; 2) the relationships between TNCs and domestic firms in Mexico; 3) organizational constraints within the TNCs themselves; 4) the relationship between the Mexican state and the U.S. government; 5) the relationship between the Mexican state and certain domestic social classes, especially the peasants; and 6) the relationships among the various ministries and agencies of the Mexican state.[23] In Chapters 3, 4, and 5 these relationships will help explain the most important features of the steroid hormone industry's development in Mexico: the reason why domestic steroid firms were established in Mexico in the first place; why Syntex left Mexico for the United States in the late 1950s; the entry behavior of TNCs; inaction by the Mexican state and the TNCs vis-à-vis key local development options; the creation and performance of two state-owned enterprises (Farquinal and Proquivemex); and the limits of state autonomy.

[23] The impact of these relationships in the Mexican automobile industry is analyzed masterfully by Bennett and Sharpe (1979).

CHAPTER THREE

From European Oligopoly to Mexican
Monopoly in the International
Steroid Hormone Industry
(1944–1955)

THE Mexican steroid hormone industry grew out of the struggle between an established European oligopoly and an ascendant American one. A Mexican firm, Syntex, utilized its access to cheap and efficient raw materials to overthrow the Europeans' initial technological lead in the world industry. Soon after, American TNCs were able to break Syntex's Mexican monopoly with the help of direct pressure from the United States government. In slightly over a decade industry control moved from European TNCs to Mexican national firms to U.S. TNCs; the basis of control changed from technology to raw materials.

These early changes will demonstrate that even under ideal conditions, a third world country may not be successful in its quest for autonomous and integrated development in a TNC-dominated industry. In the dynamic international steroid hormone industry of the 1950s Mexico had sole access to the best raw material (barbasco), a local firm that was the world industry leader in technology and production for almost a decade (Syntex), an emerging mass market and a growing clientele of buyers abroad, and active support from the Mexican state. These favorable circumstances ultimately proved insufficient to retain local control, and a situation of dependency developed as transnational interests came to dominate the Mexican steroid industry. To understand why, a close look will be taken at the political dimension of oligopolies. It will be seen that transnational pharmaceutical companies operate abroad not for the purpose of spreading technology but to consolidate and control their own market share. Control is valued over efficiency because control in an oligopoly is the key to industry profits.

WHAT ARE STEROID HORMONES?

In order to understand the basis both for the European oligopoly's early superiority in the steroid hormone industry and for the weakness that allowed this superiority to be overturned, it is necessary to briefly review the chemistry of steroid hormones.

A natural hormone is a chemical that is manufactured in a gland, enters the blood stream, and exerts a specific effect on the activity of another organ or target tissue elsewhere in the body. Some hormones are steroids, and some are not.[1] The word "steroid" means "like a sterol." Sterols are certain solid alcohols that are abundant in animals and plants, cholesterol being the most common sterol in man and other vertebrates. All sterols have a basic molecular structure of four interconnected rings bonded together by carbon atoms. Many other substances have that same basic skeleton. All substances that have it, whether they are sterols or not, are called steroids.[2]

The steroid hormones are of two main types: those that keep the *species* alive, and those that keep the *individual* alive. Both are essential to human life. Those that maintain the species from generation to generation do so by controlling the reproductive systems of both sexes; they are called sex hormones. The three principal groups of sex hormones are: androgens (the male hormones), estrogens (the female hormones), and progestogens (the hormones that regulate preg-

---

[1] The nonsteroid hormones include insulin, thyroid hormone, and a group of hormones produced in the pituitary gland attached to the brain.

[2] In addition to carbon, steroids contain hydrogen, usually oxygen, and sometimes one or two other elements.

nancy and the female cycle). Those steroid hormones that maintain the individual do so by helping to regulate metabolism; they are called adrenocortical hormones because they originate in the cortex (outer wall) of the adrenal glands located just above the kidneys. These adrenocortical hormones are also called corticosteroids, or corticoids.

THE EUROPEAN HORMONE CARTEL AND THE MEXICAN CHALLENGE

The steroid hormone industry originated in Germany, and most of the early discoveries were made by Europeans. Between 1929 and 1935 the sex hormones were isolated in pure form; the isolation of the corticoids followed during the years 1935 to 1938. Soon after, the pharmaceutical companies in Europe and the United States sought methods of producing these hormones.

The early demand for steroids was created by "replacement therapy," which sought to treat human ills caused by hormone insufficiency via the administration of extra doses of what was lacking. Thus, habitual miscarriages were remedied by injections of progesterone, menstrual disorders by extra amounts of estrogen, weakness due to surgery or illness by androgens, and Addison's disease by the administration of a corticoid. The problem was that the supply of these replacement hormones was limited. The sex hormones progesterone, testosterone, and estrone had at first been isolated from tons of sow ovaries, bull testes, and horse urine, respectively. As can be imagined, the process was very inefficient and costly and the output minute.

Scientific research thus moved in a new direction: it tried to duplicate the natural hormones by synthesizing basic sterols found abundantly in nature. Between 1934 and 1940 European chemists developed ways of producing the major sex hormones synthetically; their starting material was cholesterol obtained from animal sources (Syntex Laboratories, 1966: 13, 21).

Three European drug companies—Schering A.G. of Germany, Ciba of Switzerland, and Organon of Holland—formed the core of a cartel in the 1930s built around an involved set of process patents and cross-licensing agreements that gave them virtual control over the production and sale of the synthetic sex steroids.[3] The process patents of these firms covered all possible methods for synthesizing the sex steroids from cholesterol, their favored starting material. Product-and-use patents were also employed; these restricted the number of firms that could legally sell the major sex hormones in the pharmaceutical market.

The output of sex hormones made from cholesterol was limited, and prices were high—topping one hundred dollars per gram in the early days—largely because the procedures used by the Europeans were both intricate and wasteful.[4] In spite of the prices, however, their technological control allowed the three cartel members to dominate the international market for these products. Their American branches were especially successful.

---

[3] In its totality the European hormone cartel was composed of five member firms: Schering A.G., Ciba, Organon, Boehringer & Sons of Germany, and Les Laboratoires Français de Chimiotherapie of France (Chimio). A five-party agreement was entered into on May 26, 1937, that covered the male and female sex hormones and cortin, the adrenocortical hormone. It involved a division of territories regarding exports, with certain parties being definitely excluded from certain areas. The sales of the European firms' American subsidiaries generally were restricted to the United States, its territories and possessions, and Canada. Another main purpose of the cartel agreement was to fix prices, whereby the European parties agreed upon prices that in turn were adopted by their American affiliates. The entire world hormone cartel system was bound together with patents, which had the effect of slowing down research in the United States. The contracts among the American companies were carefully planned and drafted abroad to avoid any appearance of violating U.S. antitrust laws. For more detail on the European hormone cartel see U.S. Congress (1944).

[4] Cholesterol was being obtained primarily from the spinal cords of cattle. A ton of starting material was melted down to ten to twenty pounds in the first step (Applezweig, 1962: 10).

81

The strong showing of the European firms in the United States spurred the U.S. pharmaceutical companies to greater activity in the sex steroid field. Their basic strategy was to undermine the European cartel by looking for a cheaper and more efficient source material for steroid hormones. This would simultaneously allow the Americans to sell steroids at lower prices and to bypass the "captive" technology built around the processing of cholesterol. In addition, the new technology developed to process the alternative raw material could then be patented and turned against the Europeans as a barrier to entry that would limit their ability to compete.

Parke-Davis, one of the American companies making efforts to break the European cartel, sponsored extensive research in the steroid field by a chemist at Pennsylvania State University named Russell Marker. Knowing that the raw material bottleneck in the industry needed to be broken, Marker had turned to plants in his search for a cheap and abundant source of steroid hormones. Marker concentrated on certain steroid substances of botanical origin called sapogenins. He became particularly interested in a scarce sapogenin called diosgenin, which Japanese chemists had isolated in 1936 from a plant of the genus *Dioscorea*. In 1939 in a series of brilliant experiments Marker worked out the molecular structure of sapogenins and demonstrated that they were extremely useful starting materials for sex hormone synthesis. In 1940 he showed that diosgenin could be converted into the pregnancy hormone progesterone.

Marker proved to be as interested in the industrial possibilities of exploiting the newer plant steroids as he was in their structural chemistry. He was soon organizing searches of the American Southwest and Mexico for plants that would yield diosgenin or other sapogenins. Success came when he discovered that a good yield of diosgenin could be gotten from the black, lumpy root of a species of *Dioscorea* which the Mexicans called *cabeza de negro,* a vine growing wild in the jungles of southeastern Mexico. Unable to convince the American drug companies that Mexico was the place for a steroid industry, Marker resigned from Penn State, rented a small laboratory in Mexico City, and started to work at exploiting his own steroid processes.

In 1943 Marker showed up at a Mexican company named Laboratorios Hormona S.A., which was in business to market pharmaceuticals, including natural hormones derived from animal sources. The company was owned by two naturalized Mexicans of European origin, Emeric Somlo from Hungary and Dr. Federico Lehmann of Germany. Marker supposedly brought with him two kilograms of progesterone that he had made from diosgenin, worth about $160,000 (U.S.) at the going price. Somlo and Lehmann immediately recognized the importance of Marker's discovery and persuaded him to join them in setting up a company to industrialize production of the hormone. The new company was called Syntex S.A. and was incorporated in Mexico City in January of 1944.[5]

Based on Marker's exclusive process, Syntex produced several kilograms of progesterone in its first year. This was a healthy percentage of annual world production at the time, and it had a big impact on the world market. By 1945 progesterone prices had dropped from their eighty dollars a gram level prior to Syntex to eighteen dollars a gram.

Marker soon had a disagreement with his two partners, however, and left Syntex without ever revealing his process. Somlo, the chief executive of the company, was in urgent need of someone who could synthesize hormones as well as organize their production on a large scale. Hence he brought to Mexico in 1945 a young Hungarian-born chemist named George Rosenkranz, who had been working in a laboratory in Cuba. Rosenkranz had an excellent background in steroid hormones and knew Marker's scientific publications well.[6]

---

[5] The agreement was that Somlo and Lehmann would contribute the initial capital, the installations, and the sales organization of Syntex, for which they received 60 percent of the stock. Marker's contribution was the "know-how," for which he received the remaining 40 percent of the company (Lehmann et al., 1973: 198).

[6] Rosenkranz received his doctorate in Switzerland under the Nobel Prize winner in steroid research, Leopold Ruzicka, whose work had given Ciba its strong patent position in the industry.

Developing a chemical process different from Marker's, Rosenkranz was able to produce progesterone in 1945. He then moved on to hormones that Marker had not made. By 1950 Rosenkranz, as director of Syntex's technical and scientific operations, achieved the synthetic production—from diosgenin—of all four major types of steroid hormones: progestogens, androgens, estrogens, and corticoids (Syntex Laboratories, 1966: 27–29).

Even though diosgenin was thus shown to be a versatile source material for steroid hormones, and although prices for the Mexican products continued to drop, the Mexican steroid industry was still a struggling outsider. Conditions for modern production needs in Mexico were referred to as primitive, and the future availability of *cabeza de negro* was uncertain. Nor was the world demand for hormones sufficient to encourage many buyers to weather patent infringement storms and to finance expensive sales campaigns to capture some of the market held by the hormone establishment.

The patent pressures came from both sides. Syntex's sale of hormones was inhibited by the Europeans' product-and-use patents, which put Syntex customers in legal risk. At the same time Syntex was being sued by Parke-Davis, which had tried to protect itself with worldwide rights on Marker's processes but slipped up by not filing Marker's patents in Mexico, apparently believing that lack of secrecy there would make them unenforceable. Eventually the action of the U.S. Alien Property Custodian in seizing Schering A.G.'s American subsidiary following World War II and the inability of Parke-Davis to stop the Mexicans from allegedly violating their patents opened the flood gates for the rest of the industry to the sex hormone market.[7] From 1947 to 1949, however, there was almost no incentive for the hormone cartel to lower its drug prices to the consumer even though much cheaper steroids were available from Mexico. Syntex's total sales for steroids

[7] The feud between the two firms was finally resolved in 1956 when Syntex and Parke-Davis entered into a series of licensing agreements (Syntex Laboratories, 1966: 50–51; Djerassi, 1979: 249–250).

other than progesterone were still relatively small, and at the time the demand for progesterone itself was limited.

Three discoveries, closely related in time, provided the decisive boost that the steroid hormone industry in Mexico needed to reach world dominance. First, in 1949 a new variety of the *Dioscorea* botanical family, called barbasco, was discovered in Mexico.[8] Barbasco had two major advantages when compared with the *cabeza de negro* originally utilized by Marker: it yielded approximately five times as much diosgenin, and barbasco was practically inexhaustible in Mexico whereas *cabeza de negro* was growing scarce.[9] All uncertainty was now gone about the future availability of diosgenin as the raw material base of Mexico's steroid industry.

Second, in 1949 in the Mayo Clinic in the United States Drs. Edward Kendall and Philip Hench made the momentous discovery that cortisone had anti-inflammatory properties that would dramatically relieve the symptoms of rheumatoid arthritis. Overnight cortisone was labeled a "wonder drug"; demand for the product soared along with the hopes of millions of arthritics. Cortisone was a steroid hormone. It was not yet known, however, whether it could be produced from diosgenin. The sole producer of cortisone in the world in 1950 was Merck & Co. of the United States, and Merck's only source of starting material was ox bile. The supply of cortisone manufactured from ox bile was only a trickle, however, in comparison with the demand generated by millions of arthritis sufferers.

It immediately became obvious that bile acid from oxen

[8] Barbasco (*Dioscorea composita*) is the name given throughout Latin America to all fish poisons. It was discovered, however, that whereas the principal toxic agent in the barbasco from other countries was rotenone, the main active ingredient in Mexican barbasco was glycoside of diosgenin (Applezweig, 1962: 25).

[9] Although it produced a much smaller tuber than *cabeza de negro*, barbasco took only three years to complete its biological cycle, while *cabeza de negro* required twenty years. Furthermore, barbasco was an invasive plant found almost everywhere in tropical or subtropical areas from sea level to sixteen hundred meters altitude.

could not remain the only source of cortisone starting material. Cortisone had to be made in great quantity, quickly, and inexpensively, so that sick people could afford to buy it; the supply of beef bile, on the other hand, was limited, the method slow and complex, and production costly.[10] There thus ensued a worldwide search for other starting materials and new methods.

Third, the great breakthrough in the raw material search was finally achieved by The Upjohn Co. of Kalamazoo, Michigan, in 1951. The basic problem in producing cortisone had been how to attach an oxygen atom to what is called the carbon 11 position of the steroid molecule. None of the available starting materials (such as cholesterol, diosgenin, or stigmasterol) had oxygen at 11, and no method was known of getting it there except Merck's long and expensive process from ox bile acid. Upjohn had decided to try microbiological as well as chemical techniques, and their gamble paid off. Their microbiological team developed a process—the fermentative oxidation of progesterone—that permitted a soil microorganism to introduce oxygen at the necessary position.[11] The task that chemists had found so difficult was done with ease by enzymes.

From the point of view of the Mexican steroid hormone industry this discovery was crucial because it allowed steroids made from diosgenin to be used as *intermediate* materials in

[10] In 1950 it was estimated that the production of enough cortisone from ox bile to treat one patient for one year would require the slaughter of 14,600 head of cattle. The process used by Merck to manufacture this cortisone involved thirty-seven complex chemical steps covering a period of several months. This brought the cost of an ounce of cortisone in 1950 to $4,800, one hundred times the price of gold (U.S. Congress, 1957: 6).

[11] The method was to put the soil fungus (a specimen of the genus *Rhizopus*) in a culture medium and let it grow, then pour a progesterone solution in with the fungus, let it ferment for a day or so, and pour it out again—each of its billions of molecules altered in the same crucial way. The result was 11-alpha-hydroxyprogesterone, which could be converted by chemical stages to cortisone, or its derivative cortisol; the latter was shown to be even more effective than the former in alleviating inflammation.

the manufacture of cortisone and its derivatives. Progesterone was the intermediate material preferred by Upjohn. Whereas before it had been sold in small amounts as a finished sex hormone, now it was possible for Syntex to produce progesterone from barbasco in tonnage quantities to meet the new and rapidly growing demand for corticoids.

SYNTEX DISPLACES THE EUROPEAN CARTEL

When Syntex began producing diosgenin in bulk quantities in the late 1940s, Schering, Ciba, and Organon countered by dropping prices on their specialities, testosterone and estrone, and by also making bulk hormones available to their competitors. The three European firms enjoyed a strong position since both testosterone and synthetic estrone could be made more efficiently from cholesterol than from diosgenin, and these hormones had much wider sales than progesterone, which was Syntex's specialty (Applezweig, 1953).

The scales finally started tipping toward the Mexican firm in 1950 when Syntex began to find the one major element for success it had previously lacked: a mass market. In that year the first impact of the arthritis drugs on the Mexican steroid industry was felt; it came in the form of a false start, however. Some physicians had found that a chemical precursor to cortisone, pregnenolone acetate, induced remissions in their arthritic patients. Since pregnenolone was much cheaper than cortisone and could be mass produced almost immediately from diosgenin, this approach was anxiously pursued. In the ensuing flurry of activity more than two million dollars worth of pregnenolone acetate was produced and sold, almost entirely by Syntex. Unfortunately it was soon discovered that the sole basis for remission in the arthritic had been enthusiasm by the patient or his physician rather than pregnenolone. Although public disappointment was great, the pregnenolone experience was a clear demonstration that Mexican barbasco was a first-class raw material and that the industrial potential was there for large-scale production (Applezweig, 1962: 26).

87

Upjohn's spectacular research triumph the following year finally put an end to all speculation regarding the future of the Mexican steroid industry. In the summer of 1951 Upjohn placed a five million dollar order for ten tons of progesterone to be delivered by Syntex in a twelve-month period (Syntex Laboratories, 1966: 39). No previous hormone order had ever approached this size. Before Syntex was formed, the world output of progesterone was only a few pounds a year; even in 1951 it was less than one ton. Progesterone, which had been selling for $1.75 per gram as a sex hormone, was now driven down in price once again by Syntex to $0.48 per gram, but this time for use as a starting material in Upjohn's microbiological synthesis (see Table 3.1).

Syntex's international competitors could not hope to meet the booming demand for basic steroids at anywhere near these prices. Most of the steroid manufacturers in Europe and the United States were thus forced to abandon their own processes and either use Mexican starting materials or buy their finished hormones from Mexican sources (Applezweig, 1953).

New mass markets had been the turning point in Syntex's battle with the established hormone producers. The Mexican firm's major weapon, however, was diosgenin. In comparison with Merck's bile acid route to cortisone production dios-

TABLE 3.1
Syntex's Progesterone Prices

	U.S. Dollars Per Gram
1943[a]	80
1945	18
1947	12
1949	3
1951	1.75
1952	0.48

SOURCES: Applezweig, 1959: 41; 1962: 29; Syntex Laboratories, Inc., 1966: 30.
[a] This was the world market price for progesterone prior to Syntex's formation.

genin's great advantage was that it was abundant and cheap, whereas ox bile was not. Diosgenin's availability, however, does not by itself explain why it was preferred to cholesterol, the early raw material choice of the Europeans; cholesterol from livestock is also abundant and cheap.

The real superiority of diosgenin lies in its extraordinary versatility as a steroid starting material. When cholesterol is broken down chemically, only two of its intermediate compounds can be transformed into commercial products. Diosgenin, however, produces an intermediate compound known as 16-dehydropregnenolone (16-D), from which chemists can move to almost all other pharmaceutically interesting steroids in any desired ratio (see Figure 3.1).

Although Mexican plant materials did not completely overthrow their rivals, their role in the steroid industry was vastly enlarged. By the end of the 1950s, 80 to 90 percent of the

Figure 3.1
Diosgenin: The Base for the Whole Steroid Family

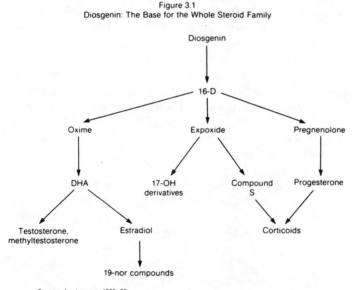

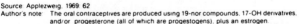

Source: Applezweig, 1969: 62
Author's note: The oral contraceptives are produced using 19-nor compounds, 17-OH derivatives, and/or progesterone (all of which are progestogens), plus an estrogen.

world production of steroid hormones came from Mexico. The locus of industry control thus shifted: the European oligopoly was replaced by a Mexican monopoly. The basis of industry control likewise changed: from technology to raw materials.

U.S. PRESSURES BREAK SYNTEX'S MEXICAN MONOPOLY

Syntex was not the only hormone producer in Mexico in the early 1950s, but it was by far the largest and the most successful. As the major producer of synthetic steroids in the world its vital role in the future of the industry was clear. It thus decided to take steps to consolidate its position and to protect its increasingly heavier investment in research and development.

Syntex was able to limit the activity of its foreign and domestic competitors in Mexico by enlisting the direct support of the Mexican government. This support took two forms: 1) executive decrees placing prohibitive export tariffs on the main products manufactured by the other firms, and 2) a refusal to grant Syntex's competitors the forestry permits needed to gather and transport the barbasco root.

Through protestations to the Mexican government Syntex demanded and got prohibitive taxes placed on the export of *Dioscorea* root and its extracts in 1951 and on diosgenin and 16-D in 1955.[12] Whereas Syntex had the facilities to produce hormones advanced enough to escape the tariff, it thought that its local competitors did not. Syntex thus hoped to maintain its original monopoly through legislation.

With regard to the second tactic, the founders of the three American-owned firms in the industry—Beisa, Labs. Julian, and Pesa—made known to the U.S. buyers of Mexican steroids, and later testified before the U.S. Congress, that their efforts to set up manufacturing operations in Mexico were being blocked because they could not obtain the government permits needed to collect and transport the barbasco

[12] These two executive decrees were published in Mexico's *Diario oficial* on May 7, 1951, and May 13, 1955.

root. Each of the companies claimed that opposition from Syntex was the cause of this problem.[13] According to these competitors, there was no good economic reason in terms of Mexico's national interests that justified the discriminatory protection being given Syntex. Mexico's supply of barbasco appeared practically inexhaustible, and the world demand for steroid hormones was already much greater than all the producing firms combined could handle.

The export decrees and the denial of permits were only partly successful in stopping Syntex's competition. Those firms who could produce intermediates more advanced than 16-D were free of the export tariffs, and small quantities of barbasco kept slipping through to the manufacturers. Thus, Syntex decided to take further steps to protect its position in Mexico.

In a letter written to the Mexican government two months after the 1955 decree was issued, Syntex claimed the legislation was not having the desired effect because some of the other firms had the capacity to go beyond 16-D. Syntex thus asked for prohibitive export taxes to again be extended, this time to the three key intermediate products *after* the 16-D stage—pregnenolone, epoxide, and oxime—each of which could be derived from 16-D by simple chemical processes (U.S. Congress, 1957: 59–60). (See Figure 3.1.)

Syntex also proposed a second and complementary plan to the government that would assure Syntex the lion's share of all future hormone sales from Mexico. According to this plan the purchasers of hormone products would be divided into two categories: "old customers" and "new customers." The former referred to pharmaceutical firms that had previously purchased any of their steroid hormone requirements from Syntex in Mexico or its affiliates in the United States, or from any of the other previously existing local hormone manufacturers (Diosynth and Protex). No firm in the category of an old customer, American or otherwise, would under these ar-

[13] Testimony from the founders of each of these firms is in U.S. Congress (1957): Beisa, pp. 95–97; Labs. Julian, pp. 83–84; and Pesa, p. 127.

rangements be permitted to purchase hormones from a newly organized company in Mexico unless and until they had first purchased substantially the same amount of steroid hormone products from Syntex, Diosynth, or Protex as they may have in the past. Whereas Syntex's previous efforts to consolidate its position in the industry were intended to directly undermine the development of the new companies in Mexico, this most recent proposal was a much bolder move. It meant dictating conditions to the foreign buyers rather than the national suppliers of steroid hormones.

Neither of Syntex's two requests were ever granted. Strong pressure began coming from the U.S. buyers of Mexican steroids and later from the United States government itself protesting the continued Mexican attempts to discourage Syntex's competitors. Between July and November of 1955 at least six American pharmaceutical companies, all of whom were major buyers of steroid hormones, sent sharp letters of protest to the Counselor for American Affairs in the U.S. Embassy in Mexico and/or directly to Mexico's Secretary of the National Economy completely rejecting any policy that would force them to buy from a particular firm.[14] The President of The Upjohn Co., Syntex's biggest client, wrote:

> It is contrary to our concept of good business practice to permit ourselves to become dependent upon a single source of supply for an important raw material. Moreover, to be required to deal with any given supplier violates the principles of free trade and competition which we firmly believe are in the best interests of everyone. (U.S. Congress, 1957: 67)

The two American business groups whose interests were being harmed by the Syntex monopoly—the big buyers in the United States and the small suppliers in Mexico—brought this

[14] The six American companies were: Charles Pfizer & Co., Ciba Pharmaceutical Products Co. (Summit, N.J.), G.D. Searle & Co., Merck & Co., National Drug Co., and The Upjohn Co. Their letters to Mexico are printed in U.S. Congress (1957: 64–71).

matter to the attention of the U.S. government, which found it could claim jurisdiction over the case.

Before World War II, Schering A.G. of Germany had a subsidiary in the United States. This affiliate was always a leader in the hormone field and owned a number of valuable patents. Following the war, these assets became the property of the United States government as reparations. Among the patents taken from Schering's U.S. subsidiary were some of interest to Syntex S.A. of Mexico. In 1952 Syntex signed a licensing agreement with the U.S. government for three of these patents.[15] A standard clause of government licensing agreements is that the licensee will not form monopolies or cartels or engage in the restraint of trade. Since the activities of Syntex were considered to have restricted the number and operations of competitors in Mexico, the firm was hauled before a Senate Committee in the United States in July of 1956 for alleged patent violations. Among the sanctions that could be imposed on Syntex if charges against the company were substantiated was a ban on the sale of Syntex's steroid exports in the United States—by far the company's largest market.

In May of 1956, prior to the Senate Hearings, Syntex was sold to the Ogden Corporation, which was an industrial holding company in the United States.[16] Syntex's founder and principal owner, Emeric Somlo, left the firm, and the new management proclaimed hearty agreement with "the traditional American concept of free enterprise and competition embodied in the Sherman Act and other related antitrust statutes." The Senate Hearings resulted in Syntex signing a consent decree with the U.S. Justice Department in which the company did not admit to restraining trade but promised not to do so in the future.[17] In affirmation of this new image Syn-

[15] The text of these three patent licenses is given in U.S. Congress (1957: 46–52).

[16] The reasons why Syntex was sold to the Ogden Corporation will be discussed in Chapter 4.

[17] Consent agreements are for settlement purposes and do not constitute a legal admission of guilt. They carry the force of law with respect to future actions, however, and civil penalties can be imposed if they are violated.

tex advised Mexico's Secretary of Agriculture by letter in November of 1956 that "... in connection with barbasco root Syntex seeks no favoritism toward itself nor any discrimination against any other company" (U.S. Congress, 1957: 150–151). The doors were now open for new steroid hormone producers to enter Mexico. As a result of the vertical integration that followed, the nature of the nationally based industry soon changed dramatically.

IN summary, oligopolistic rivalry between European and American pharmaceutical TNCs created the opportunity that led to the establishment of a steroid hormone industry in Mexico. The American companies wanted a new, cheap, and efficient source material for steroid hormones to bypass the technological lead and undercut the prices of the European cartel; Mexico's barbasco, it was discovered, fit this need perfectly. Once it got started, however, the Mexican industry's growth was profoundly shaped by the nature of the demand coming from foreign buyers, first in the United States and later in Europe. Syntex sought to counter this oligopsony power of the TNCs by persuading the Mexican state to allow it and a couple of much smaller national producers to organize a virtual Mexican monopoly in the world industry based on their exclusive access to barbasco in Mexico. However, a second major external force intervened in the industry: the U.S. government. The big American buyers of Mexican steroids were supported by their home government in their efforts to secure a cheap and reliable source of raw material supply from Mexico. When Syntex's special relationship with the Mexican government was broken in 1956, direct TNC ownership of supplying companies in Mexico became both feasible and desirable.

CHAPTER FOUR

Denationalization and Dependency in the Mexican Steroid Hormone Industry (1956–1974)

IN 1955 there were seven firms in the Mexican steroid hormone industry (see Table 4.1). Only one of these—Beisa—was the subsidiary of a TNC; the other six companies were set up in Mexico as independent producers of intermediate hormone products to be sold in bulk quantities in the international market. After 1955 nine new private companies entered the Mexican industry; every one of them was a wholly owned subsidiary of a foreign pharmaceutical firm. Mexico's six independents could not survive the onslaught; by 1963 they had all disappeared. In their places were a half dozen TNC subsidiaries whose only reason for being was to supply the needs of their parent companies in the exterior. This change will be referred to as the denationalization of the Mexican steroid hormone industry. In order to understand the nature and consequences of this change with respect to the TNC strategies that promoted it, a clearer notion of these strategies and their relation to dependency analysis is required.

TRANSNATIONAL CORPORATION STRATEGIES AND INDUSTRY DENATIONALIZATION

Transnational corporations consist of a parent firm that is located in one country and a network of affiliates located in one or more other countries. Such a network is bound together by common ties of ownership, it draws on a common pool of human and financial resources, and it responds to some sort of common strategy (Vernon, 1976b: 24). The transnational

95

structure of these companies subjects them to at least two kinds of national influences: those coming from the home country and those of the host economy. At least as important as either of these factors in determining TNC behavior, however, are the imperatives imposed by the basic strategy of the firm itself (Vernon, 1976a: 47–48; 1977: Chapters 3–5).

Like most large bureaucracies, TNCs place heavy emphasis in their search for profits on questions of survival, continuity, and efficiency. The disposition of the transnational firm is thus to minimize any risk that can be minimized, often with strategies leading to greater control over their operations. This is true for both of the levels at which TNC strategies operate: among the affiliates of a single transnational enterprise, where common needs dictate unity and consistency in behavior, and among the leaders of any oligopolistic industry, where common interests generate cooperative policies. For the host country the impact of global imperatives at either level is often mixed—i.e., they may contribute to the achievement of national objectives or they may not.

If Mexico's steroid hormone industry is dependent, however, a much stronger argument than one of mixed results is called for: namely, that 1) TNC strategies benefit the firms themselves and/or their home countries inequitably, at the expense of the host, and that 2) these same strategies impose systematic constraints on Mexico's policy options to increase national industry benefits. The next section of this chapter will examine the first proposition (i.e., biased distributional consequences). It will compare the actual consequences of TNC investment in the Mexican steroid hormone industry against what could have been expected from a national strategy based on a group of Mexican private companies like that led by Syntex before denationalization. The final section of the chapter will examine the second proposition (i.e., domestic policy constraints). An expanded role for the state firm Farquinal will also be discussed as a feasible alternative to the total control exercised by the TNCs. Before moving to distributional consequences and counterfactual alternatives, however, the phenomenon of denationalization itself must be analyzed. I will do this at two levels: the meanings (and nonmeanings) of the concept, and actual TNC entry behavior.

The Meanings (and Nonmeanings) of Denationalization

In its common-sense meaning "denationalization" refers to a situation in which local owners are bought out by foreign firms and the national bourgeoisie is directly displaced by international capital.[1] Before this term can be employed to describe the events in the Mexican steroid hormone industry after 1955, several qualifications are needed.

First of all, denationalization implies that a *national* industry existed prior to the entry of foreign capital. Whether this is true in the case of steroid hormones depends on how "national" is defined. Of the seven original steroid companies in Mexico five were formed by foreign or immigrant entrepreneurs,[2] and one (Beisa) was formed by a foreign corporation. The only original firm founded by native-born Mexicans was the state-owned laboratory Farquinal. Looking at firm founders, there thus appears little evidence of a true national bourgeoisie. One could indeed say that Mexico's steroid hormone industry was always in the hands of foreigners.

From the point of view adopted here, however, the significance of denationalization lies in the shift from national to transnational *norms of control* as a result of direct investment by TNCs rather than the mere fact of foreign ownership per

[1] Two recent empirical studies of TNCs in Mexico that give considerable attention to the phenomenon of denationalization are Newfarmer and Mueller (1975) and Fajnzylber and Martínez Tarragó (1976). For a view of denationalization and dependency in the Brazilian pharmaceutical industry see Evans (1976).

[2] Syntex, Diosynth, and Protex were all founded by Hungarian Jews who left Europe during or shortly before World War II, immigrated to Mexico, and became naturalized Mexican citizens. Labs. Julian and Pesa were established by U.S. citizens.

se.[3] It is precisely a new form of control, and not a new group of owners, that marks the major change in the Mexican steroid hormone industry after 1955. Six of the seven steroid companies that existed in Mexico in 1955 were "independent" producers of bulk intermediate products, with no organizational ties whatsoever to the U.S. and European pharmaceutical manufacturers who bought from them. This meant that the Mexican sellers of steroid intermediates were free to maximize their returns from the foreign buyers. When the Mexican industry became dominated by the subsidiaries of vertically integrated TNCs after 1955, the difference in interests between the Mexican sellers and the foreign buyers disappeared. Both were now joined in the same organization: the transnational corporation. Denationalization meant that the decisions formerly controlled by the independent Mexican producers—such as what products would be manufactured and in what volumes, the prices of these products, and the choice among clients—were now made according to global needs rather than national ones.

This leads to a second qualification of the concept. Denationalization does not imply that the criteria of global efficiency associated with TNCs are inherently inferior to national criteria in terms of national welfare benefits. The distributional consequences of international and national strategies are affected by both country and industry differences; hence, they are not subject to blanket generalizations. For example, the oft-cited phenomenon of transfer pricing by the TNC does not always work to the host country's disadvantage, as is commonly assumed. In industries such as oil, bauxite, and copper the TNC parent tends to benefit most in its intracompany sales when *high* prices are charged by its subsidiary in the host country. Reasons for this relate to barriers to entry at the different stages of the industry, relative

[3] Foreign ownership and foreign control often go together, but not always. A TNC may have management control of a foreign subsidiary even though it owns only a minority share of its stock; likewise, a foreign entrepreneur may totally own an independent company in Mexico yet allow its decision making to retain a national frame of reference.

tax levels, etc. Evidence from the pharmaceutical industry, on the other hand, shows quite the reverse: transfer pricing by transnationals has, in many cases, clearly been detrimental to the host country's interests (see Vaitsos, 1974; Lall, 1973, 1979a). The TNC parent often prefers to buy at low rates and sell at high rates when dealing with its foreign subsidiaries (especially in the less-developed countries), thus minimizing host country income and raising local drug prices to the consumer. Country differences may be just as marked because of divergent corporate tax rates, profit remission policies, and the like. In this chapter all conclusions with respect to TNC strategies and denationalization apply specifically to Mexico's steroid hormone industry.

The third qualification of denationalization that needs to be made relates to the tendency to use it as a static concept, leading to the belief that foreign control of an industry comes with one fell swoop of TNC investments. In reality, the foreign control over an industry that characterizes a situation of dependency is usually multilayered, based on diverse combinations of resources found in the exterior. This was certainly the case for the steroid hormone industry in Mexico. First came the foreign entrepreneurs, then the foreign scientists and the use of foreign technology. Most important of all, perhaps, was the creation of and access to mass markets for steroid hormone products outside of Mexico. By the time the first big wave of TNCs rolled in during the latter half of the 1950s, the Mexican industry was already long dependent on the exterior. Denationalization (defined as TNC displacement of Mexican firms) and dependency were thus not coextensive. Transnational investment was one more element, albeit an especially important one, in a process of dependency that had begun more than a decade earlier.

Explaining TNC Entry Behavior

The entry of TNCs into the Mexican steroid hormone industry can be divided into two distinct periods: the U.S. phase (1956–1961) and the European phase (1963–1970) (see Table 4.1). Six of the seven U.S. TNCs in Mexico's steroid hormone

TABLE 4.1
The Steroid Hormone Industry in Mexico (Major Firms)

"*Independent*" *National Firms (1944–1955)*

	Syntex, SA	Diosynth, SA de CV	Beisa, SA de CV	Productos Químicos Naturales, SA	Searle de México, SA de CV	Steromex, SA	Protex, SA	Laboratorios Farquinal	Proquivemex, SA de CV
	–Founded by independent entrepreneurs (1944)								
1945–		–Founded by independent entrepreneurs as Hormosynth, SA (1947)							
1950–		–Name changed to Diosynth (1951)	–Founded by the Schering Corp. (USA, 1951)				–Founded by independent entrepreneurs (1949)	–Founded by the government (1950)	
1955–					–Founded by independent entrepreneurs as Productos Esteroides, SA (1955)	–Founded by independent entrepreneurs as Labs. Julian de México, SA (1954)			

U.S. TNC Entry (1956–1961)

- Bought by the Ogden Corp. (USA, 1956)
- Bought by the Syntex Corp. (USA, 1958)
- Bought by American Home Products, Inc. (USA, 1959)
- Bought by G.D. Searle & Co. (USA, 1958)
- Bought by Smith Kline & French Labs (USA, 1961)
- Bought by General Mills (USA, 1956)
- Stopped working 1962

1960—

European TNC Entry (1963–1970)

1965—
- Founded by Syntex, SA & brought by Schering AG (Germany, 1963)
- Stopped working (1963)

1970—
- Brought by N.V. Organon (Holland, 1969)
- Name changed to Searle de México (1967)
- Brought by Ciba (Switz.) & name changed to Steromex (1970)

1975—
- Founded by the government (1975)

industry entered between 1956 and 1961: General Mills (1956), the Ogden Corporation (1956), Syntex (1958),[4] G.D. Searle (1958), American Home Products (1959), and Smith Kline & French (1961). The lone exception, the Schering Corporation,[5] ran its Mexican subsidiary as a "pilot plant" from 1951 until 1957 so that the date of its full operations also falls within the concentrated entry period of the other U.S. transnationals. The European TNCs that came into the industry—Schering A.G. of Germany (1963), Organon of Holland (1969),[6] and Ciba of Switzerland (1970)—were the same three firms that dominated world hormone production in the 1930s and 1940s through cartel arrangements. Curiously, they were the *last* new companies to begin Mexican production.

The form and timing of entry of these two groups of TNCs lead to two specific questions about oligopoly behavior. Why did the U.S. TNCs all bunch their entry into such a short time· period (six firms in six years)? Why were the European companies the last to enter Mexico, even though they were the original world leaders in the field?

The concentrated entry of the U.S. TNCs in the Mexican steroid hormone industry can be explained by two different sets of factors, one external to Mexico and the other internal. The external factor is a type of firm conduct known as "oligopolistic reaction": a follow-the-leader pattern of foreign investment in which the rival firms in an oligopoly counter one another's moves by making similar moves themselves. According to Knickerbocker's (1973) path-breaking

---

[4] When Syntex separated from Ogden to become an independent company in 1958, it incorporated in Panama because of that country's favorable tax laws. Syntex's ownership and operations were centralized in the United States, however, and it is thus considered as a U.S. transnational corporation.

[5] The Schering Corporation of Bloomfield, N.J., was the former U.S. subsidiary of Schering A.G. of Germany. The U.S. government held the Schering Corporation in custody from 1942 to 1952, at which time it was sold to the public. It has no connection or affiliation whatsoever with Schering A.G.

[6] Organon merged with the AKZO group of Holland in 1969.

work in the area, oligopolistic reaction is basically a risk-minimizing strategy followed by "product pioneering" firms[7] in rapidly growing industries. Matching a rival's move to set up foreign production facilities is considered a form of insurance. The premium that firms pay to insure a competitive balance in the oligopoly is the cost of making a matching move. The calculation underlying oligopolistic reaction is that if industry rivals mimic an unsuccessful investment by an aggressive competitor, everyone loses together and the competitive balance is maintained. On the other hand, if industry rivals do not match a successful investment, the new investor may break into a lead the others cannot overtake.

The TNCs in the steroid hormone industry were product pioneering firms par excellence. With demand still booming in the late 1950s for corticoids and beginning to grow in the early 1960s for oral contraceptives, the rapid growth of the industry was not in doubt. If anything diminished the extent of oligopolistic reaction in the Mexican industry it was the Mexican government's intervention on Syntex's behalf in the early part of the 1950s, which scared a number of potential investors away from Mexico in search of other sources of steroid raw materials. Nonetheless, six U.S. TNCs were willing to take their chances in Mexico after 1955, and oligopolistic reaction largely explains why they did so in the same period of time.

The internal factor conducive to the concentrated entry of U.S. TNCs in the 1956 to 1961 period was tied to two consequences of the government permits problem faced by Syntex's competitors in the early 1950s. First, the difficulty in getting government permits discouraged TNCs from establishing subsidiaries before Syntex's virtual monopoly was broken in 1956. Second, the quasi-competitors who did exist

[7] "Product pioneering" firms possess one or more of three characteristics: 1) the firms conduct extensive research and development, 2) they employ complex, high technology productive methods, and/or 3) they engage in vigorous and sophisticated marketing activities (Knickerbocker, 1973: 13–14).

were unable to work at full capacity until after 1956 for the same reason. The long delay undoubtedly weakened the financial resources of the independent private companies (Protex, Diosynth, Labs. Julian, and Pesa), thus making their purchase by the TNCs even easier.

The main reason that the European companies lagged behind those of the United States in entering Mexico is what could be called "entrenched technology." When the Europeans dominated the world steroid hormone industry in the 1930s and 1940s, their raw materials were cholesterol and bile acids from animals. Once Mexican barbasco became the new raw material of choice, the established companies were confronted with a dilemma: to try to improve the yields from their own less efficient and more costly raw materials, or to switch over to barbasco at the cost of completely revamping their processes for making steroids (which is the most expensive part of a producer's investment). The big American pharmaceutical companies, which had little or no existing investment in steroid technology to protect, were thus free to rush into Mexico when the conditions seemed best. The Europeans, on the other hand, followed a middle road for a number of years: they worked to improve the yield from their original processes at the same time as they imported large quantities of the cheaper Mexican steroids to use in the manufacture of finished products. By the time the European companies did invest in Mexico, they had a diversified raw material base as well as a wide line of finished steroid products.

The National and International Impact of TNC Strategies on Mexico's Steroid Hormone Industry

The major TNCs in the steroid hormone industry chose one of two strategies with respect to raw materials: they either vertically integrated to the Mexican source of supply or they set out to develop alternatives to Mexico's barbasco. Both strategies aimed at lessening TNC reliance on Mexico.

The group of transnationals that set up producing affiliates in Mexico was of the mind that their raw material dependence could be most effectively reduced by increasing control at their source of supply. This same "drive for unambiguous control,"[8] characteristic of research and advertising intensive industries, led each firm to establish wholly owned subsidiaries. There was a second group of pharmaceutical companies in the industry, however, that felt it could best lessen its dependence on raw materials by spreading its risk among several alternatives to barbasco. Instead of investing in Mexico these firms were content to import large quantities of Mexican intermediate hormones; meanwhile they were busy developing equally efficient and politically "safer" sources of supply at home. Upjohn, the world's largest consumer of steroid intermediates, thus turned in the early 1960s from barbasco to stigmasterol made from soya sterols in the United States as its starting material for the manufacture of corticoids.[9] Some of the European firms, such as Roussel (France) and Organon (Holland), continued to improve their yields from bile acids. And Schering A.G. (Germany) worked to make a success of a new technique—total synthesis—rather than depend entirely on barbasco after 1963. The inevitable result of this diversification strategy was that Mexico's 80 to 90 percent share of world steroid production in the 1950s began to drop.

Regardless of whether a TNC used barbasco or an alternative raw material, an integrated source of supply carried with it a major advantage: the TNC could simultaneously increase its control over industry prices. The consequences of this transnational linkage for Mexico were diverse and far reach-

[8] See Stopford and Wells (1972: Chapter 8) and Vernon (1977: Chapter 4) on this aspect of TNC behavior.

[9] Upjohn has by far the best techniques in the industry for producing corticoids. A number of companies that have developed their own finished products find it cheaper to buy their advanced steroid inputs from Upjohn rather than continue with their own syntheses. Such specialized clients include Squibb, Merck & Company, and the Lederle Laboratories Division of American Cyanamid.

ing. To appreciate its impact, however, it is necessary to look at the transnationals' internal corporate strategy.

Two major goals of a TNC's strategy are to minimize its global tax burden and to protect itself from competition. To help attain these goals, the parent company uses considerable discretion in setting the "transfer price" at which it sells to or purchases from foreign subsidiaries. (Discretion is often required since there may not be an open arms-length market to indicate what the price should be—much to the consternation of tax officials.) Where profits are declared within the corporation's network of affiliates is largely determined by how well they serve the two goals just mentioned. Usually companies show low profits where tax rates are high or at stages in the vertical chain where there are insignificant barriers to entry to new firms (Moran, 1973: 382). This was the case in the steroid hormone industry, and it imposed a double loss on Mexico.

The TNCs with Mexican subsidiaries made extensive use of tax haven affiliates in Puerto Rico, the Bahamas, and Panama. The advantages were twofold. First, their rate of corporate income tax was very low (much less than in the United States, Europe, or Mexico), so the more the TNC could concentrate its profits in tax havens, the more it would benefit. Profits were concentrated by importing into the tax haven at as low a price as possible and exporting at a high price, while keeping local processing costs to a minimum. United States taxes had to be paid only on money repatriated to the U.S. Second, Puerto Rico had the additional advantage that any goods processed there could be re-exported to the United States free of U.S. customs duties.

To protect itself from competition, the TNC found it wise to concentrate its remaining profits where its barriers to entry were highest. The negative effect this had on Mexico becomes apparent in looking at how the pharmaceutical industry is organized. New products are the lifeline of drug companies' profits. Barriers to entry were therefore established to protect this source of revenues. These centered around two corporate resources: research and development, and advertising. The specific devices used to protect company gains derived from these resources were patents and trademarked brand names, respectively. The continuous generation of products was based on new knowledge; patents and brand names gave the TNCs proprietary control over this knowledge.[10] The production and control of knowledge in the pharmaceutical industry are jealously guarded by the TNCs as close to the center of their worldwide operations as possible. This contributes to *a global situation of asymmetrical control* in which industry profits are concentrated by transnationals in their home

[10] More than any other industry, the modern pharmaceutical industry can be attributed with creating the linkages that are so common today between the patent and brand-name systems. The earliest "wonder drugs"—sulfanilamide (the first sulfa drug), penicillin, cortisone, and hydrocortisone—were not patented. Improved versions of these products, such as streptomycin, which was introduced commercially in 1946, were patented, but the patents were licensed widely. As a result, these drugs, which were manufactured by many firms and sold under their generic names, experienced sharp price declines. Penicillin, for example, sold for $60 (10 million units bulk) in 1945, $4.75 in 1950, and $0.21 in 1960; streptomycin's price plummeted from $160 (10 grams bulk) in 1946, to $3.15 in 1950, to $0.36 in 1960 (Ginsberg, 1972: 54). In order to avoid this devastating price competition, innovating pharmaceutical firms began to utilize their patent rights to retain exclusive control over the production of their new drugs instead of licensing these patents to other companies for royalty fees. One consequence of this strategy was that, by not licensing their patents, firms were able to restrict output of their own drugs to levels where monopoly profits could be maximized. In broad-spectrum antibiotics, to take the clearest case, a producers' cartel of five firms—Lederle, Pfizer, Bristol, Upjohn, and Squibb—held the market price for these drugs (most notably, tetracycline) constant in the United States for a decade, from 1951 to 1961. More significant for the pharmaceutical industry in the long run was the fact that the end of patent licensing increased the importance of advertising to drug firms. In oligopolies where price competition is avoided or minimized, advertising becomes the main form of nonprice competition. It is advertising that has allowed company brand names to assume such a prominent place in the pharmaceutical industry. These issues will be discussed in greater detail in Chapters 6 and 7. For a penetrating account of the importance of research and advertising as barriers to entry in the modern pharmaceutical industry see Temin (1979*b*).

TABLE 4.2

Bulk Prices of Steroid Hormones

(U.S. dollars per gram)

	1947	1957	1968
Progesterone	12	0.15	0.08
Testosterone	30	0.35	0.18
Cortisone	200	2.00	0.33
Estrone	100	3.50	0.75

SOURCES: Applezweig, 1959: 41; 1969: 59.

countries or in tax havens. In steroid hormones the ability of Mexico to lessen this asymmetry by bargaining on the strength of "bilateral monopoly" (access to raw materials versus access to technology) was limited by the existence of alternative sources of supply.

The most obvious consequence of this situation on Mexico's steroid industry was a dramatic drop in the prices of its intermediate products (see Table 4.2). In 1957 bulk prices for steroid hormones were nearly one hundred times less than what they had been a decade earlier. By 1968 the prices for these products were lower still, at only one-half to one-sixth of their 1957 value.[11] In line with my previous argument, one reason for this drop is that part of the Mexican producers' profit margins were being shifted to tax havens. More fundamental is the fact that low entry barriers in Mexico allowed fierce competition to continue driving its prices downward. As will be discussed later in this chapter, Mexico lacked the political will to turn this competition to its advantage.

Denationalization had another consequence that was even more harmful with respect to the local industry's future: it converted Mexico from a major producer of original research in steroid chemistry to a consumer of it. As a national firm Syntex S.A. was the major force in the Mexican industry until

[11] In 1968 steroid prices hit bottom. Since then they have been characterized by a slow inflationary rise.

it decided to move its corporate headquarters from Mexico City to Palo Alto, California, in 1959. One of Syntex's directors described the company's research achievements up to that point:

> By 1959, more scientific publications in steroid chemistry had emanated from Syntex in Mexico than from any other academic or industrial organization in the world. . . . In a matter of ten years, Mexico—a country in which no basic chemical research had been performed previously—had become one of the world centers in one specialized branch of chemistry. (Djerassi, 1968: 25)[12]

The case of Syntex shows that original research of the highest quality was not only feasible in Mexico but had actually been carried out successfully for over a decade. Once Syntex became a foreign-based TNC, however, Mexico lost a key opportunity to keep a strong foothold in the international industry.

Why and How Syntex Left Mexico

Why did Syntex move the heart of its operations from Mexico to the United States in the late 1950s? This was perhaps the critical turning point in the history of the Mexican steroid hormone industry. To understand Syntex's action, one has to look at a combination of factors including intrafirm struggles for control, home and host country influences, and key features of the international pharmaceutical industry. Prior to its sale to the Ogden Corporation in 1956 there was a power struggle within Syntex between those who wanted the firm to remain fundamentally a bulk producer of intermediate steroids and those who thought the firm should enter into the finished products market. When the leader of the former faction, Emeric Somlo, left Syntex at the time of the U.S. Senate antitrust hearings involving the firm, victory for the latter re-

---

[12] For a more personalized view by Djerassi of research at Syntex in Mexico see the "Author's Postscript" in Djerassi (1979).

search-oriented group was assured. The big questions now were *where* and *how* to make this transformation from a bulk manufacturer to a producer and marketer of finished, patent-protected drugs.

Both "home" (Mexico) and "host" country (primarily, the U.S. export market) factors led Syntex to decide to move from Mexico. After 1955 the Mexican state was unwilling to give Syntex preferential treatment over its local competitors as a result of the U.S. antitrust pressures. Furthermore, foreign scientists working at Syntex were encountering annoying bureaucratic delays with respect to visas and necessary pharmaceutical imports. Shifting the firm's headquarters to the United States was an attractive option for a number of reasons. There is some evidence to show that both marketing and research are more effective when carried out in a company's largest market—in Syntex's case, the United States. Also, the U.S. Food and Drug Administration's stringent regulations for new pharmaceutical products generally required a U.S. clinical testing site. Finally, the problem of attracting and keeping highly qualified research personnel could be easily solved by locating near a prestigious and modern academic complex. In choosing Palo Alto as the locale for its new headquarters in 1959 Syntex could fully avail itself of the facilities of Stanford University, where its onetime research director, Carl Djerassi, had accepted a chemistry professorship. Syntex thus became a full-fledged transnational corporation: its legal place of incorporation was Panama because that country offered substantial tax benefits; the center of its administrative, research, and marketing operations was in Palo Alto in the United States; the manufacturing of bulk steroid intermediates continued to be done in Mexico; and finished drugs were produced in Syntex plants in Puerto Rico and the Bahamas, again for tax avoidance purposes.

In order to actually join the ranks of finished drug producers, however, Syntex had to overcome the two major barriers to entry in the pharmaceutical industry: generating sufficient resources for high-level research and development

(R&D) activities, and developing a marketing network and brand name reputation to ensure sales of the company's products. Both challenges were met via innovative institutional arrangements. To help expand its R&D program, Syntex entered into a cooperative research agreement with Eli Lilly and Company in 1959 through which Lilly contributed heavily to Syntex's annual research costs, with both companies having the right to market products resulting from Syntex's research efforts. Thus Lilly had access to new products, and Syntex had added funds for research. The patents remained in Syntex hands, as did the direction of the chemical research. The joint agreement was phased out in 1966.

To handle its marketing problem, Syntex decided to license some of its best finished products to companies that already had extensive marketing networks. Norethindrone, for example, which Syntex first produced commercially in 1956, was licensed to erstwhile competitors such as Parke-Davis and E.R. Squibb of the United States and Schering A.G. of Germany.[13] Other Syntex products were licensed to Ciba and Organon. In the oral contraceptives market Syntex licensed the active ingredient to two of the first three U.S. "pill" manufacturers (Ortho Pharmaceutical Corporation and Parke-Davis) until Syntex marketed a birth control pill under its own label (the pill was called Norinyl) in 1964. Syntex avoided an overspecialization in the oral contraceptives market with the introduction of Synalar in 1961 as an extremely successful steroid diuretic. By 1965 steroids for the treatment of inflam-

[13] Syntex has had more than just licensing ties with Schering A.G. When Syntex decided to concentrate on finished pharmaceuticals, the capacity of its huge plant in Orizaba, Mexico, was judged far in excess of the company's bulk needs. Syntex thus entered into a five-year sale agreement with Schering A.G. in 1963, whereby the German TNC bought the Orizaba plant (whose name was changed to Productos Químicos Naturales S.A., or Proquina) and from this was to supply Syntex with all of its requirements of bulk steroids. Once Schering was installed in Mexico, however, it reneged on its supply contract with Syntex. The latter was forced to build a new plant in Cuernavaca, Mexico, in the late 1960s to insure that its bulk chemical needs would be met.

matory diseases (including the Synalar group) accounted for 48 percent of the company's total sales; the oral contraceptives represented less than 40 percent of total sales (for details, see Syntex Laboratories, 1966).

By the mid-1960s Syntex was thus able to free itself of both its research and marketing ties to other TNCs. It had become large enough to finance all of its own research and development. It had built its own worldwide marketing network so that products developed in its laboratories could now be sold under the Syntex label. And Syntex had also become a diversified pharmaceutical company, no longer depending almost exclusively on oral contraceptives for the great bulk of its income. Syntex's transformation as a pharmaceutical manufacturer is strikingly illustrated in Table 4.3, which traces the company's sales by their channel of distribution from 1961 to 1976. In 1961 bulk sales to other manufacturers comprised over one-half of the value of the firm's total revenues and sales by licensees another one-third, with the percentage of finished drugs sold under Syntex's own label standing at just 15 percent. By 1976 the situation was totally reversed. Syntex subsidiaries accounted for over 85 percent of the company's total sales, with distributors handling almost all the rest. Bulk sales of steroids and sales by licensees are an insignificant part of Syntex's operations today.

The general point is not simply that a single decision by a major corporation like Syntex can limit development in Mexico. What is essential is that the structure of the steroid hormone industry—i.e., the way it is organized internationally—forces Mexican intermediate goods producers to become, or to affiliate with, finished products manufacturers. The reason, relatively simple, bears repeating: pharmaceutical industry profits lie in new and successful finished drugs because their value can be protected (as well as created) by patents and trademarked brand names. This argument is supported by the experience of the three U.S. TNCs who entered the Mexican industry but did not last: American Home Products, Smith Kline & French, and General Mills (see Table 4.1). The first

TABLE 4.3
Syntex Sales, by Channel of Distribution
1961–1976

Year[a]	Total Sales (millions of U.S. dollars)	Bulk Sales to Other Manufacturers	Licensees and Distributors[b]	Sales of Syntex Subsidiaries[c]
1961	8.1	53%	32%	15%
1962	11.8	33	31	36
1963	16.3	13	28	59
1964	26.5	14	29	57
1965	35.8	5	43	52
1966	56.3	11	41	48
1967	67.2	15	34	51
1968	73.8	13	27	60
1969	108.7	20	12	68
1970	103.0	15	15	70
1971	117.4	17	12	71
1972	140.3	16	13	71
1973	160.4	8	12	80
1974	217.5	2	13	85
1975	245.9	1	13	86
1976	277.4	1	13	86

SOURCE: Syntex Corporation, *Annual Reports*.
[a] As of 1969, Syntex sales figures incorporate the accounts of three acquisitions: Hoffman-Taff, Diamond Laboratories, and Star Dental.
[b] From 1961 to 1968, sales are for licensees only; from 1969 to 1976, these figures are for distributors only, with most sales to licensees being reflected in the bulk sales category.
[c] From 1961 to 1968, this category included all sales under the Syntex label by subsidiaries and distributors alike; from 1969 to 1976, these sales are those of Syntex subsidiaries only.

two companies were bought by European TNCs (Organon and Ciba, respectively), and General Mills closed its plant. In each case the company had entered Mexico to produce specific patentable products from Mexican raw materials. In each case obstacles prevented these original products from being manufactured as planned.[14] Once their profitable proprietary outlet disappeared, the TNCs did also.

The costs of foreign control in the Mexican steroid hormone industry are now evident: successful national firms were displaced, the prices for Mexican products plummeted, and significant local research and development was pulled away. We will also see in the following pages how denationalization, among other factors, impeded greater local drug production in Mexico. But a crucial question arises. Were there feasible alternatives to the TNCs, and if so, could they have been expected to perform as well, or better? If both parts to this question cannot be answered in the affirmative, then the costs of TNCs may be considered part of the price endemic to the industrialization process itself.

National Private Firms as a
Counterfactual Alternative to TNCs

It is clear that there were feasible alternatives to transnational investment in Mexico's steroid hormone industry since it was dominated by national private firms before the TNCs moved in. The real issue is whether a group of national private enterprises could have done as well in the industry as the transnationals, or perhaps even better. For the purposes of comparison I will look at the performance of TNCs in the Mexican steroid hormone industry and the expected perform-

---

[14] American Home Products was originally thinking of making an oral contraceptive from barbasco, but it later developed a birth control pill (Nordet) that was produced synthetically and did not require barbasco at all. In the case of Smith Kline & French the company had two medicines (anabolic steroids) that were well advanced in clinical testing and it wanted a captive source of raw material supply from Mexico. However, it was suddenly discovered that these two products had extremely dangerous side effects, and in 1964 (three years after it acquired its Mexican subsidiary) Smith Kline & French discontinued all work on steroids. The General Mills subsidiary in the industry, Protex S.A., died in 1963 for lack of a market when its chief customer, Schering A.G. of Germany, bought a manufacturing plant from Syntex and formed Proquina (see footnote 13).

ance of a group of national private firms; both will be measured against two sets of welfare criteria: 1) the national welfare of Mexico in terms of the local capital accumulation
needed for industrial growth, and 2) the welfare of the consumer in terms of product quality and product prices.

National Welfare. The international steroid hormone industry was structured during the latter 1950s and the 1960s via
the creation of high entry barriers around research and advertising so that large profit margins could be obtained only
by manufacturers of finished drug products protected by patents. Once a patent was obtained, a brand name was a cer-
tainty and the product became a "specialty" or "ethical
drug" that could only be purchased with a doctor's prescription. The doctor was thus pivotal in the scheme of things; he
alone determined whether a given company's product would
be sold or not. Not surprisingly, he was deluged with promotional advertising from mighty sales machines set up by each
pharmaceutical firm to convince the physician of its product's
superiority. Much of this work was put in the hands of pro-
fessional advertising agencies who were adept in the art of
the eye-catching photograph, the neat slogan, or the persua-
sive phrase.

Assuming that the TNCs were able to use patents and
brand names in these ways to create high entry barriers to
competition in their home countries, and assuming that low
entry barriers in Mexico gave firms easy access to barbasco as
a raw material, it follows that a handful of local private firms
would probably have been *worse* for local industry growth
than the transnationals were. Under these circumstances the
Mexican steroid hormone industry would have been weaker
with local capital because: 1) a more competitive sellers'
market would exist since the producers of steroid hormone
intermediates would no longer need to double as finished
goods manufacturers, 2) the buyers formed a de facto monop-
sony and would have no obligations to purchase from an affiliate if cheaper source materials were available elsewhere, and

115

3) Mexico would constitute a spill-over market forced to bear the burden of disproportionate fluctuations in demand in comparison to the integrated portion of the industry.

The picture changes, however, if we relax either of the assumptions made above. In this analysis I will discuss only the assumption of low entry barriers in Mexico.

In an asymmetrically controlled international industry such as steroid hormones, a national firm is highly vulnerable without the protection of its government.[15] When raw material access in Mexico was going against the U.S. TNCs in the mid-1950s, they used the power of the United States government quite effectively to quash the Mexican government's efforts to give discriminatory protection to Syntex and a couple of other national producers. What would have happened had Mexico successfully resisted these pressures? That is to say, what could have been expected of a small group of national private firms with the Mexican government's protection?[16]

---

[15] This argument also has been made for TNCs domiciled in relatively small countries like Switzerland (see Niehans, 1977).

[16] There are precedents for a Latin American government to support local private producers and fend off U.S. threats when a key commodity is involved. Brazil, for example, effectively resisted direct American action by the U.S. Justice Department in 1913 and by Secretary of Commerce Herbert Hoover in 1926 who opposed Brazil's attempts to regulate the international coffee market. Brazil has long been the world's leading coffee producer, and coffee was the nation's major source of foreign exchange. In 1906, 1917, and 1921 the Brazilian government financed the withholding of coffee from the international market in order to generate higher and more stable earnings for its coffee exports. Agencies in the United States, the world's leading coffee-consuming nation, protested that such efforts violated both the Sherman Antitrust Act and the Wilson Tariff Act. Ultimately Brazil's activist stance toward its principal commodity export was upheld; the U.S. Department of State even entered into negotiations with the Justice Department on Brazil's behalf (for a full account, see Krasner, 1973). The reason Brazil succeeded in resisting U.S. pressures is that its policy toward the international coffee trade, on which it was highly dependent, was clear and unified: increased efficacy, higher returns, and price stability. The American government was unable to formulate a consistent policy because coffee did not impinge on security issues. The result was that the official U.S. response to Brazil was ineffectual or contradictory. One implication is that as a country's economic activity becomes more diverse, its national economic interest may become less clear.

116

If it is assumed that Syntex would have stayed in Mexico and would have continued with its high-level research, then the chances of local industry growth under the control of national firms look very good. Neither of these assumptions should be problematic since government protection and incentives could probably have made Syntex's stay in Mexico as profitable as if it had located anywhere else. The advantages to Mexico under these conditions would have been numerous. Export sales could have been maintained through price competition at the bulk level, with particular attention given to the nonintegrated TNC buyers. Continued research could have led to the development of Syntex's own "specialty" products. (Again, this is not farfetched since Syntex was producing immediate precursors to the birth control pill while still in Mexico in the mid-1950s. By 1964 Syntex had developed three of the first four oral contraceptives that became available in the United States.) Proprietary control by Syntex over *finished* products, as well as its acknowledged leadership as a bulk producer of *intermediate* steroids, would probably have provided a great incentive for Syntex to "close the gap" between the two by becoming a fully integrated steroid hormone company *within Mexico*. The effects of this as a boon to the growth of Mexico's steroid hormone industry would have been without parallel compared with TNC contributions.

The burden of this counterfactual argument need not fall solely on the achievements of Syntex as an exceptional company. Evidence from a study of the pharmaceutical industry in Argentina shows a general tendency for local firms there to engage in significant amounts of innovative activity. These local firms account for nearly 50 percent of total sales and own nine of the top twenty-five companies. The major national pharmaceutical enterprises were reportedly maintaining a flow of new products by investing as little as 1 percent of their sales in research and development; on the basis of such new products the local firms' market share relative to that of the transnationals increased between 1962 and 1970 (Katz, 1974: 111–114 and 62). If national firms were able to outperform the TNCs in Argentina's pharmaceutical industry,[17] the possibility should certainly be kept open that as a group they could have done the same in Mexico.

In conclusion, I find that the prospective national welfare contribution of national private firms in Mexico's steroid hormone industry turns on a key assumption: whether or not local government protection would have been extended to them. If government protection had been lacking for local firms (as in fact it was after 1955), thus keeping barriers to entry in Mexico low, TNCs would have been the best alternative for local industry growth. If national private firms such as Syntex had been given the protection and incentives needed to stay operating in Mexico, they would probably have generated more growth in the national industry than did TNCs.

Consumer Welfare. With respect to consumer welfare, the case is much clearer: national private companies in Mexico would have—and did—benefit the general consumer as much as, and often more than, the TNCs. Here analysis is conditioned by the fact that the local companies in Mexico were primarily manufacturers of intermediate steroid products sold internationally in bulk quantities; thus the standard of comparison will be the price at which the same products were sold on the world market (and in particular, in the United States) by national and transnational enterprises.

As was shown in Chapter 3, the original European hormone cartel was overthrown almost entirely due to Syntex's efforts in Mexico to produce greater outputs of steroid hormones at lower prices than the Europeans. These efforts were dramatically successful, and consumers were able regularly to use drugs whose previous price had been prohibitive (such as cortisone). Once again, this argument is not limited to Syntex's achievements only. By the early 1950s other national firms in Mexico were able to underbid Syntex for contracts with big hormone buyers in the United States (U.S. Congress,

[17] For a fuller discussion of Argentina's pharmaceutical industry see Chapter 7.

118

1957: 115). Thus, before denationalization a group of national producers existed in Mexico that was offering high quality steroid hormones at the lowest prices in the world.

It has been noted that the prices for Mexican intermediate materials continued a downward slide after TNCs became established in the national industry (see Table 4.2). On the one hand, this could be interpreted to mean that competition (e.g., from alternative raw materials to the barbasco found in Mexico) was continuing to drive Mexican intermediate prices down, to the international consumer's benefit. A second possibility is that while prices for Mexican intermediate products were going down, TNC prices for their final products remained high, thus constituting a transfer of oligopoly profits from Mexico to the TNCs with no real benefits to the consumer. If the first interpretation is correct, it merely shows that the TNCs were continuing benefits to the consumer previously initiated by national firms in Mexico. If the second interpretation is valid, it demonstrates that TNCs were benefiting the consumer much *less* than local firms in Mexico had done; whereas the latter had allowed competition to lower their selling prices, the former would be using competition in Mexico to increase corporate profits rather than to increase consumer welfare. Available evidence supports the second interpretation.

The data I am referring to come from the U.S. Congress's administered price hearings on drugs, which extended from December 1959 to October 1962 and were chaired by Senator Estes Kefauver. What is immediately apparent is the tremendous profitability of the drug companies. The rate of return on investment, after taxes, in the ethical drug industry was higher than that of any other industry in the country. The Schering Corporation is a particularly good example. It is a member of Mexico's steroid hormone industry and was the first company to market an improved cortisone derivative—prednisone, in 1955—that was more potent than cortisone against inflammation and in addition had fewer side effects. With the introduction of prednisone, Schering's profits on net worth after taxes jumped from 12 percent in 1953 and 11

119

percent in 1954 to 47 percent in 1955 (Kefauver, 1965: 42). In the hearings it was learned that prednisone's cost to Schering was around 1.5 cents per pill; its markup to the druggist was from 1.5 cents to 17.9 cents per tablet, with the retail price to the consumer set at 30 cents. One of Schering's competitors, McKesson & Robbins, began selling prednisone on a nationwide basis under its generic name. (Schering used the brand name Meticorten.) McKesson & Robbins' price to the druggist was 2 cents per tablet and the price to the public 3 cents; both transactions turned profits. The other major cortical steroid companies who marketed prednisone under brand names—Merck, Upjohn, and Pfizer—sold at exactly Schering's high price. Although Schering did 89 percent of the business in prednisone, its retail price remained the same from 1955 through the early 1960s. The competitors' prices at the retail level did not change either (Kefauver, 1965: 11–15).

As a side note, it was Syntex of Mexico that prevented Schering from gaining complete monopoly control over prednisone. Syntex contested Schering's patent application in the U.S. Patent Office; as the patent fight dragged on, Syntex began to ship bulk prednisone into the United States. Syntex's market was the small American drug companies who did engage in price competition, particularly on sales to large buyers (like hospitals and state and local governments) who purchased products under their generic rather than their brand names. As a result of the Mexican firm's competition Schering's net profits dropped to 23 percent by 1958, still high by normal standards but roughly half those that prevailed in 1955 (Kefauver, 1965: 43).

The track record of TNCs vis-à-vis the international consumer in steroid hormones is poor. The major firms did not sell their products at lower prices than Mexico's national producers; on the contrary, the TNC price was usually many times higher. Although Mexican prices at the intermediate level continued their downward spiral, finished drug prices of the TNCs remained high. The result: income lost to Mexico was coming to rest in TNC coffers, to the consumer's detriment. If consumer welfare is the issue, national private firms in Mexico were a feasible alternative to the transnationals, and, pricewise, probably a better one.

DEPENDENCY AND RESTRICTED LOCAL DEVELOPMENT

So far I have dealt with the external and transnational factors leading to the foreign control of Mexico's steroid hormone industry. If this foreign control has created a situation of dependency in Mexico, it should be manifested in a stunting or limiting of local options for development. In this section I will show that this has indeed taken place: dependency has restricted the formulation of domestic policy that could have promoted increased growth in the national industry.

Four possibilities will be considered that were open to Mexico and would have resulted in greater local drug production in its steroid hormone industry: 1) using prohibitive export tariffs more extensively to encourage local drug manufacture; 2) carrying out the fermentation of steroids in Mexico; 3) expanding the role of the state-owned firm in the industry, Farquinal; and 4) bargaining by the Mexican state for increased national benefits from the TNCs during their entry period of oligopolistic reaction. These national policy options were complementary, and thus they could have been followed individually or in tandem. None of them was carried out. My question will be: To what extent has this lack of development been a consequence of Mexico's dependency in the steroid hormone industry? This dependency, as mentioned in Chapter 2, is produced by the interplay of three factors: 1) the structure of the international industry, 2) the global strategies of the TNCs, and 3) the lack of autonomous action by the Mexican state to assert national priorities for development.

Industrialization by Decree

In the 1950s two executive decrees were issued in Mexico that had the effect of encouraging more industrial processing

121

of steroid hormones to be done nationally. Through prohibitive export taxes the 1951 decree required Mexican processing of steroid hormones to go at least as far as diosgenin; in 1955 a second decree required national processing to go at least one step beyond 16-D to pregnenolone, epoxide, and oxime. There was a proposal by Syntex for a third decree that would have forced national production to go one step further still in order to break free of the export tariff (see Chapter 3). Neither this latter decree nor any other was ever issued for the industry after 1955.

The first question that arises is: Why didn't Mexico continue to use prohibitive export tariffs to promote the increased industrialization of its steroid hormone industry? The reason lies in the structure of the international industry in terms of demand and production organized according to criteria of global efficiency.

The discovery that cortisone had miraculous anti-inflammatory powers (1949) and that it could be produced microbiologically in giant quantities from diosgenin-based steroid hormone intermediates (1951) created a tremendous demand for the corticoids (i.e., cortisone and its improved derivatives). These products have continued to be the most sought after form of steroids. In 1969, even after the new boom in steroid demand caused by the oral contraceptives, the corticoids still accounted for about 95 percent of the volume of all steroid materials used (Applezweig, 1969: 62). They led in steroid sales as well, but not by as big a margin due to the greater profitability of the oral contraceptives[18] (see Table 4.4).

Unlike the oral contraceptives and the sex hormones, corti-

[18] The dollar volume of the corticoids was hurt because the earliest products, cortisone and hydrocortisone, were not protected by patents, and prednisone and prednisolone, two early modified corticoids, were widely licensed. As a result, heavy competition eroded prices. The oral contraceptives, on the other hand, had much better patent protection. Eventually their prices were cut by almost one-half, but this was more than compensated for by the fact that their dosages were reduced by 90 percent (from 10 mg. of steroids per tablet to 1 mg. or less) (Applezweig, 1969: 58 and 62).

TABLE 4.4
U.S. Steroid Sales
(millions of dollars)

	1960		1964		1968	
Corticoids	$120	78%	$135	64%	$215	58%
Oral						
Contraceptives	4	3	45	21	110	30
Sex Hormones	30	19	32	15	45	12
Total	154	100	212	100	370	100

SOURCE: Applezweig, 1969: 59.

coids could only be produced on a large scale by means of fermentation. Upjohn was the first to use this process; later, steroids were fermented in Europe as well. Fermentation of steroids was not done in Mexico, however. This fact effectively limited Mexico's use of prohibitive export tariffs since the country did not want taxes to hinder its sales of the two products that were required in giant quantities for fermentation abroad, progesterone and Compound S (each derived in one step from pregnenolone and epoxide, respectively).[19]

Fermentation

If fermentation was needed to make corticoids to supply a big and growing world demand, and if Mexico had the capacity to produce the steroids needed for fermentation, why wasn't fermentation done in Mexico? For a Mexican firm, fermentation would have been difficult because TNCs controlled the technology and would only license it at extremely high prices, if at all. For the TNCs with subsidiaries in Mexico local fermentation has not been done because it implies transnational costs rather than national welfare. These costs are both economic and political in nature.

[19] Efforts to push national production in the direction of the noncortical steroid hormones would have been blocked by patents.

123

Some Mexican firms, such as Syntex, decided to have their fermentation done by an international specialist—the Royal Netherlands Yeast and Alcohol Factory located in Delft, Holland,[20] for example—on the grounds that it would cost them less than any other alternative, given their needs. TNCs with Mexican subsidiaries, such as Schering A.G. of Germany and the U.S. Schering Corporation, had their own fermentation plants in their home countries. They obviously had no interest in Mexico taking fermenting business away from their own plants. In addition, they stood to make extra profits on intra-company sales: their Mexican subsidiary could export intermediate steroids at prices well below those prevailing in the "open" market to its affiliate firm in Europe or the United States, which does the fermenting; the steroid is then sent back to Mexico as an import after fermentation, but this time at greatly inflated prices. This form of "double transfer pricing" would of course be impossible if fermentation were carried out within Mexico since there would be no need to export ("cheap") and re-import ("expensive") the same basic product. (Some examples of actual transfer pricing in the industry are given in Chapter 5.)

Fermentation in Mexico would not only mean relative economic losses for the TNCs in the industry; it would imply a much greater political risk as well. With Mexican fermentation facilities the TNCs in steroid hormones would find themselves in a position similar to that of foreign companies in the extractive enclaves. They would have a much bigger capital investment to protect, and as host country technicians mastered the process of fermentation, the TNCs would become more vulnerable to national demands for increasing benefits. In short, fermentation is still not a reality in Mexico. It is clear that the TNCs do not want it to be. And it is equally clear that the Mexican state has made little or no effort to try to encourage or force this issue with the foreign firms.

[20] The Delft company's big business has traditionally been the fermentation of alcohol and yeast. Later, on a much smaller scale, it began to ferment enzyme detergents, antibiotics, and steroid hormones.

This brings up the third possibility that existed for increased industrialization in Mexico's steroid hormone industry: autonomous state action. Two different options will be discussed: 1) expanding the role of the state firm, Farquinal, and 2) using the period of oligopolistic reaction among TNCs in the industry to drive a hard bargain for increased national benefits.

Farquinal: A State Alternative

Labs. Farquinal was part of a much larger state-owned firm, Industria Nacional Químico Farmacéutica S.A. de C.V., that was created in 1950 to administer the chemical and pharmaceutical subsidiaries Mexico had taken over from the Axis countries (particularly Germany and Italy) during World War II.[21] Farquinal's general objective was to promote the development of a national chemical-pharmaceutical industry by manufacturing products made from Mexican raw materials. Almost all of Farquinal's attention was given to producing steroid hormones from barbasco.

Farquinal was one of Syntex's main Mexican competitors in the early 1950s. The government firm's big limitation was that it only produced the most elementary steroid hormones, mainly diosgenin. When Syntex requested the executive decree that placed a prohibitive tax on the export of diosgenin and 16-D (issued in 1955), it was hoped that Farquinal's export business would be hurt, if not discontinued. The government intervened, however, and gave Farquinal a subsidy equivalent to what it had to pay in export taxes. (The Mexican government thus found itself in the curious position of supporting Syntex's monopoly and one of Syntex's main com-

[21] Throughout the 1940s these firms were in the hands of an administrative junta. The junta was unauthorized to make investments to modify or expand the plants, however, and pressure began to grow from national industrialists who had previously depended on these companies for basic chemicals and pharmaceuticals. Industria Nacional Químico Farmacéutica was formed because the government preferred to remain with these firms rather than turn them over to the private sector.

petitors at the same time.) In spite of this apparent concern for the firm the state gave Farquinal no funds to advance its productive capacity, and it was thus forced to relinquish its competitive position in the Mexican industry. By 1962 it had stopped functioning altogether.

The question here is: Why didn't Farquinal make a more lasting contribution to the development of Mexico's steroid hormone industry? Unlike the previous two possibilities examined, Farquinal's failure to expand Mexico's productive capacity in steroids was due neither to the structure of the international industry nor to the global strategies of the TNCs that set up subsidiaries in Mexico (although both factors would obviously condition the actions of the state-owned firm). The real problem plaguing Farquinal was the failure of the Mexican state to formulate a clear and effective national industrialization policy for steroid hormones.

This is reflected at two levels: 1) the management of Industria Nacional Químico Farmacéutica, and 2) uncertainty at the top levels of government concerning what the state really wanted to do about TNCs. According to an agreement reached in 1955 between Mexico and the former Axis powers, the firms being administered by Industria Nacional Químico Farmacéutica could be sold back to their original owners. Thus in 1956 and 1957 all the pharmaceutical houses were returned, leaving Farquinal as the sole remaining division of the larger firm engaged in pharmaceutical production. The directors of Industria Nacional Químico Farmacéutica turned almost all their attention to the chemical side of the firm's operations. They neither allowed Farquinal to become independent, nor did they allow the laboratory to make additional investments. It was under these conditions that Farquinal terminated its activities in 1962. Shortly thereafter, Industria Nacional Químico Farmacéutica was converted into a state petrochemical company.[22]

_____

[22] In 1964 Industria Nacional Químico Farmacéutica became Industria Petroquímica Nacional S.A. by means of a presidential agreement (pub-

At the level of more general policy as well, the state was ambivalent about how TNCs should combine with national forces in the industrialization process. Mexicanization (i.e., majority local participation in foreign-owned firms) was just being tried out on an informal basis at the very end of the 1950s, as were industrial integration programs that increased the percentage of local content in products manufactured in Mexico. Perhaps the strategy that would have most benefited Farquinal was that established for the petrochemical industry in 1958 in which the state reserved for itself the production and sale of all "basic" petrochemical products, restricting private sector participation to the more advanced manufacturing stages.[23]

If Farquinal would have been granted a state monopoly to produce "basic" steroid hormones such as diosgenin and 16-D, Mexico's dependency on the TNCs would have been greatly reduced. It was certainly a feasible move since Farquinal already possessed the required technology. And it would have had the very desirable effect of increasing Mexico's marketing flexibility in the exterior since a number of pharmaceutical companies that were not vertically integrated to a source of raw material supply did have the capacity to produce advanced steroids but needed to buy source material from an intermediate goods manufacturer. The big disadvantage with a state plan of this type was that Mexico would lose its integrated group of foreign buyers who had a

---

lished in the *Diario oficial* on December 15, 1964). This new company represented a certain amount of competition for Petróleos Mexicanos (Pemex), the state-owned firm that had been granted a monopoly in 1958 over the production and sale of all "basic" petrochemicals in Mexico. Thus, in April of 1967 Industria Petroquímica Nacional was dissolved. Its assets were subsequently divided between Pemex and the state fertilizer company, Guanos y Fertilizantes de México, which used the added productive capacity for fertilizer inputs.

[23] "Secondary" petrochemicals could be produced by private companies provided that foreign ownership of their stock did not exceed 40 percent; "tertiary" petrochemicals could be manufactured freely by private companies of any type.

vested interest in purchasing from their Mexican subsidiaries.[24]

The range of reasons that could account for why the state
did not follow the same course of action in steroid hormones
as it did in petrochemicals need not be considered here. What
is more important from the point of view of this analysis are
the factors that explain the general inactivity of the Mexican
state in the steroid hormone industry in the late 1950s and
early 1960s when the intense competition among TNCs
should have made them vulnerable to demands for increased
national benefits.

Oligopolistic Reaction as a Basis for Bargaining

In 1962, the year Farquinal stopped operating, Mexican barbasco was supplying over 75 percent of the world total of
steroid intermediates, the American TNCs had been flocking
into Mexico to set up subsidiaries, and an efficient substitute
for barbasco had not yet appeared. Why did Mexico not use
the period of oligopolistic reaction (its point of greatest
strength) to get a better bargain from the TNCs?

One reason is corruption. From the days of Syntex's original monopoly in the industry as a national firm in the 1940s
and the 1950s until the last TNC entered at the turn of the
1970s, corruption has been part of "business as usual" in the
steroid hormone industry. It was first used to garner state
protection for a national firm, then to encourage the state's
benign neglect of the TNCs. Bribes were also considered to
have played a role in Farquinal's failure to receive the official
support it needed to survive in the industry. Nevertheless, al-

---

[24] Even the potential loss of established TNC buyers would not have
been an insuperable obstacle since the Mexican government conceivably
could have used Farquinal as the basis for a forward integration push in
the local industry. In the late 1950s Syntex may well have been open to a
plan of this type because it wanted to utilize its technological expertise to
enter the market for finished pharmaceuticals and it preferred to rely on
another firm for its bulk steroid hormone supplies (see footnote 13).

though prevalent, corruption appears to be a supporting rather than a determining factor in explaining the lack of nationalistic state policy during or shortly after the TNCs' period of oligopolistic reaction.

A much more important reason for state inactivity is the fact that in the late 1950s and the early 1960s the steroid hormone industry was simply not strategic in terms of national development priorities. As has already been mentioned, several new and major policy initiatives were being undertaken at the time in big industries whose production would go to the internal market: Mexicanization was being used as an informal bargaining lever for the first time in the chemical industry in the late 1950s;[25] "industrial integration" programs were started for automobiles in the early 1960s; and the use of a state firm in this same period to produce "basic" products in petrochemicals was novel and encountering resistance from the private sector. In contrast to the problems presented in these strategic areas, the steroid hormone industry was specialized (to the point of being exotic), export oriented, and

[25] Interestingly enough, one of the original founders of Syntex, Emeric Somlo, was indirectly involved in one of the first Mexicanization schemes carried out in the chemical industry. Du Pont, the giant American chemical firm, had been importing titanium dioxide pigment for paints and other materials into Mexico for a number of years. A group of Mexican investors headed by Somlo approached the government about setting up a plant to manufacture titanium dioxide locally. Somlo, it was rumored, was looking for a good place to invest his share of the proceeds from the 1956 sale of Syntex to the Ogden Corporation. The government agreed to close the border to imports of titanium dioxide if a Mexican group would undertake local production. Du Pont had no experience with joint ventures at the time, and in what in all likelihood appeared to be a mere formality, the government told Du Pont it could no longer sell titanium dioxide in Mexico unless it was willing to participate in a joint venture with majority Mexican capital. To the surprise of the government officials and Somlo, Du Pont accepted the offer. It set up the required new firm, Pigmentos y Productos Químicos S.A. de C.V., in 1959; Du Pont was the minority partner with a 49 percent share, and one of the large Mexican banks, Banco de Comercio, owned the remaining 51 percent of the enterprise. Pigmentos y Productos Químicos was Du Pont's first joint venture in Mexico and its first minority-owned joint venture in the world.

successful. The prevailing mood was to "leave well enough alone" rather than to strike a better bargain. This mood was reinforced by Mexico's desire not to further alienate the transnational pharmaceutical companies, who had still not forgotten the Mexican state's intervention in support of Syntex's national monopoly in the 1950s. Given that these TNCs supplied Mexico's domestic market with finished pharmaceutical products as well, from the Mexican government's point of view it was not wise to start attacking them unless there was a strong political demand to do so.

The multifaceted, dynamic nature of dependency needs to be stressed again here. TNCs were able to constrain policy in Mexico both directly and indirectly in their roles as domestic producers and as foreign purchasers of bulk steroid hormones. If the Mexican state would have had enviable foresight and sufficient political will, it might have been able to use the forces of oligopolistic competition between TNCs to Mexico's advantage. Even here, however, the state found itself restricted to at least some degree by the fact that the TNCs in the steroid hormone sector of the pharmaceutical industry were also major manufacturers of many other kinds of finished drugs used in Mexico, thus increasing their ability to raise the costs to Mexico of any governmental action affecting the steroid producers. The determinants of state inactivity, in other words, were both internal and external to the state itself.

In conclusion, the two main dependency hypotheses put forth in Chapter 2 have been examined and supported in this chapter. Evidence shows that TNC control in Mexico's steroid hormone industry in the 1956 to 1974 period led to 1) biased distributional consequences that favored TNCs and their home countries more, and Mexico less, than a comparable group of national private manufacturers would have, and 2) domestic policy constraints that restricted Mexico's best chances for increased industrialization of steroid hormones at the national level. In Chapter 5 the emphasis will shift from the structural power of the TNCs to their bargaining power, as they confront the Mexican state in a head-on clash over local development priorities. I will attempt to show how Mexico's deteriorating terms of trade in the world industry and growing pressure from the peasants (*campesinos*) interacted to finally force the state to take strong and autonomous action in the steroid hormone industry during the last years of the Echeverría administration. As will be seen, however, the ultimate effectiveness of state autonomy was limited by the various aspects of dependency it had to combat.

CHAPTER FIVE

The Renegotiation of Dependency and the Limits of State Autonomy in Mexico (1975–1982)

IN January 1975 Productos Químicos Vegetales Mexicanos S.A. de C.V. (Proquivemex) was created by the Mexican state to control all transactions related to the gathering, processing, and sale of barbasco.[1] Proquivemex bought "green" barbasco from the peasants, put it through a drying process (in which it loses 80 percent of its volume by weight), and then resold the barbasco to the six TNCs in the industry at a price fixed by Proquivemex. Thus, the TNCs no longer had any direct contact with the peasants; all business was mediated by the state-owned firm. Proquivemex was created largely in response to barbasco's declining share in the world production of steroid hormones and to internal pressure stemming from the exploitation of the peasants in the industry. The TNCs were labeled the cause of both problems and were also chosen as the main mechanism for financing solutions.

The efforts by the state to try to establish new priorities in Mexico's steroid hormone industry via Proquivemex will be analyzed as a case of "reformist nationalism" in which the Echeverría government was not trying to make a total break with the dominant powers in the capitalist system, nor was it abandoning a capitalist path to internal development. Rather,

[1] Eighty percent of Proquivemex's capital stock of 15 million Mexican pesos is owned by the government, with the remaining 20 percent divided equally among the six TNCs in the industry. See *El mercado de valores*, Nov. 17, 1975.

132

it was proposing "a redefinition of dependency that, at the same time it [was] accelerating the development process, [was] also expanding the margin of autonomy and the bargaining power of the internal power centers" (Labastida, 1975: 33).

In carrying out this analysis I will first discuss the problem of Mexico's barbasco in both a world industry and national context. Second, I will outline the state's strategy for using barbasco as a lever to increase its autonomy vis-à-vis the TNCs in order to get them to contribute more to national goals of internal growth and welfare. Finally, I will show how the TNCs defended their interests by broadening their base of private sector support in Mexico, thus converting Proquivemex's forceful program into mild reforms.

BARBASCO

The fundamental problem faced by Mexican barbasco in the world market is that it was losing ground rapidly to alternative source materials for steroid hormones. Whereas in the late 1950s diosgenin from Mexico's barbasco accounted for 80 to 90 percent of the world production of steroids, by the early 1970s this percentage had dropped to 40 to 45 percent. To make matters worse, the rate of Mexico's decline as a supplier of steroid source materials appeared to be accelerating. From 1963 to 1968 the world demand for steroid raw materials nearly doubled, while Mexico only upped its diosgenin output by 33 percent; from 1968 to 1973 world demand rose by another 50 percent, but the production of Mexican diosgenin increased by only 10 percent—from 500 metric tons to 550 (see Table 5.1).

There are both external and internal reasons for the declining share of Mexican barbasco in world steroid production. Clearly there was an effort on the part of the pharmaceutical buyers of steroid intermediate materials to lessen their dependence on Mexico (a near-monopoly supplier in the 1950s) by developing alternate source materials. In particular there

TABLE 5.1
World Steroid Raw Material Sources

Country	Material	Production[a]		
		1963	1968	1973
Mexico	Diosgenin	375	500	550
	Smilagenin	—	10	—
United States	Stigmasterol	60	150	280
	Total Synthesis	—	—	30
Guatemala	Diosgenin	10	30	—
Puerto Rico	Diosgenin	—	20	—
France	Bile Acids	20	50	50
	Total Synthesis	—	50	50
Germany and Netherlands	Cholesterol and Bile Acids	5	10	—
Germany	Total Synthesis	—	—	70
Africa	Hecogenin	20	40	40
India	Diosgenin	10	30	—
China	Diosgenin	—	80	250
Canada	Conjugated Estrogens	—	—	100
Total		500	970	1,420
Mexico's production as a percentage of total world production		75%	53%	39%

SOURCES: Applezweig, 1969: 64; Bremer et al., 1976: 12.
[a] Production figures expressed as tons of diosgenin.

has been a sharp increase in the percentage of politically "safe" raw materials coming from the home countries of the TNCs—the United States, Germany, and France. Nevertheless, in and of itself the external challenge to barbasco is not decisive in explaining Mexico's decline as a raw material supplier in the industry. With the exception of stigmasterol, used by Upjohn in the United States, no other raw material approaches diosgenin's quantitative importance as a steroid source material.[2] One reason is that diosgenin is still more versatile than most of its rivals. Another is that the TNCs with producing subsidiaries in Mexico have a vested interest in using diosgenin rather than its substitutes.

There is an internal reason that helps explain why the Mexican production of steroids has not kept pace with world demand: barbasco appears to be growing scarce. The cause is that more and more of the land where wild barbasco grows is being cleared for agriculture and livestock use. Of the 7.6 million hectares in Mexico that are suitable for barbasco growth, 80 percent has already been converted to other uses, leaving only 1.5 million hectares from which barbasco can still be gathered.[3] Complicating this problem is the fact that the average yield of diosgenin from barbasco has dropped (from 6 percent to 4 percent).[4]

Mexico was not facing an acute shortage of barbasco in the mid-1970s. Yet these two trends—external substitutes for barbasco and its potential internal scarcity—created a fear that Mexico's steroid hormone industry could become internationally marginalized and that as a result the six TNCs almost surely would decide to leave the country for better prospects elsewhere.[5] Mexico would thus suddenly lose a major

[2] The diosgenin produced by China also comes from the barbasco plant. Internationally it is an unstable source of supply, however, since China only exports diosgenin if there is an excess after its own huge internal demand for steroids has been satisfied.

[3] The data come from a study conducted by Mexico's Instituto Nacional de Investigaciones Forestales and were cited in *Excelsior*, Oct. 30, 1974.

[4] Proquivemex claims this is due to an irrational exploitation of barbasco by the TNCs, who have been harvesting immature plants. The foreign companies don't deny they have been gathering immature barbasco, but they claim these plants are taken from land soon to be cleared for other purposes. Thus, they say, their collection policy is rational since the alternative would be to let this source material go to waste.

[5] This fear is certainly not allayed by comments such as the following made by Syntex's General Manager in Mexico:

If [the foreign firms in Mexico's steroid hormone industry] have the possibility of obtaining their raw material at more convenient prices elsewhere, then naturally they will not need to keep their local facilities operating in the country. If they buy in other nations, logically the local plants will disappear. (*El sol de México*, Aug. 21, 1976)

source of foreign exchange, and twenty-five thousand peasants would lose an important source of income.[6] Politically, therefore, the steroid hormone industry suddenly became much more strategic to the Mexican state during the 1970s. In addition, Mexico's dependence on the foreign manufacturers of finished steroid products remained as strong as ever since the country had to continue importing costly quantities of steroid drugs and oral contraceptives. After thirty years of producing for the rest of the world, a national industry that could supply the Mexican population still did not exist.[7]

THE STRATEGY OF THE MEXICAN STATE

Confronted with these circumstances, the state adopted a strategy in which it could use its sovereignty over barbasco to

[6] Mexico had already suffered several major setbacks in rural industries due to the arrival of synthetic substitutes that largely displaced the demand for the natural products. When plastics, for example, greatly decreased the demand for the henequen fibers cultivated in Mexico, government subsidies to the unemployed peasants rose to P $2 million a day (*El universal*, Mar. 13, 1976). Similar problems have shaken Mexico's cotton and natural rubber industries as a result of the rapidly growing demand for synthetic fibers and synthetic rubber. Mexico is thus quite sensitive to the internal disturbances that could result if the world demand for barbasco drops because of external substitutes.

[7] A similar situation exists in Brazil with respect to insulin. The raw material for insulin comes in the form of insulin "crystals" manufactured from the pancreas of cattle and hogs. In Latin America the only place where this raw material is produced is Eli Lilly's plant in Argentina. Between 1945 and 1960 insulin had been manufactured in Brazil by a local firm called Laboterápica. But in 1957 Laboterápica was bought out by Bristol-Myers, which decided that the Brazilian market for insulin was unsatisfactory and therefore ceased production. Brazil, with one of the largest cattle populations in the world, now exports some four hundred tons of pancreas a year. Yet the country pays about eleven thousand dollars per kilogram to import insulin, which it already possesses the know-how and the resources to manufacture (Ledogar, 1975: 65–67). In case of a shortage that might affect the lives of many citizens, such as occurred in Brazil in April and May of 1975, the country is completely at the mercy of a foreign supplier.

force a negotiation with the TNCs regarding new contributions they would be expected to make to promote greater national development of the steroid hormone industry. The key to this strategy lay in the state's ability to impose upon the TNCs *new conditions of access to barbasco.* There were three conditions, two formal and one informal, that were eventually proposed by the state.

The two formal conditions were: 1) that the TNCs pay a much higher price for the processed barbasco (which they would now be receiving from Proquivemex) than they had in the past, and 2) that the TNCs devote a certain percentage of their installed capacity to produce finished steroid hormones for Proquivemex (to be used either as exports or for sale to the internal market). Although the exact amounts with respect to price and the installed capacity requirement later became negotiable, it was made clear that if an agreement satisfactory to the state was not reached on both counts the TNCs would not receive any barbasco. A third condition emerged out of the direct negotiations between the state and the TNCs. Although not made a formal requirement of access, it did appear that the Echeverría government strongly desired the Mexicanization of the six TNC subsidiaries in the industry, all of which were 100 percent foreign owned.[8] The state plan was to be implemented by Proquivemex since the state-owned firm controlled all the buying (from the peasants) and the selling (to the TNCs) of barbasco.

In April 1975 Proquivemex began selling its dry (i.e., processed) barbasco to the TNCs at a price of P $20 (20 Mexican pesos) per kilogram;[9] before Proquivemex, the same material had cost the foreign firms P $10 to $12 per kilogram. Then at its January 1976 board of directors meeting the state com-

[8] The government wanted at least some part of the stock in these companies to be sold to Mexican partners. It did not specifically request that Mexicans be given a majority share, however, nor that this share be sold to the government.

[9] Unless otherwise noted, all figures in pesos refer to an exchange rate of 12.50 Mexican pesos to one U.S. dollar.

pany made two major changes: it raised the price of dry barbasco from P $20 to P $70 a kilogram, and it required that the six TNC subsidiaries turn over 20 percent of their installed capacity to "toll manufacture" the products selected by Proquivemex.[10]

In order to understand the purpose of these demands, it is necessary to take a closer look at the goals and assumptions of the state strategy, which were different in kind, not just degree, from those of the TNCs. Proquivemex saw its goals as social and national in nature; the objectives of the TNCs, on the other hand, were eminently private and global.[11] This is the fundamental reason that the conflict between the two sides became so prolonged and bitter.

Proquivemex had two primary goals: to improve the welfare of the peasants, and to defend Mexico's rural natural resources. The peasant policy makes clear the social nature of the state firm's goals. One of the main factors leading to the creation of Proquivemex was social protest. It came especially from student groups in the barbasco-producing states who felt that the peasants were being exploited by the TNCs because they were paid too little for the barbasco they gathered.[12] Before the panic-buying characteristic of 1974 when

[10] The proposed arrangement was that Proquivemex would choose from among those products that each TNC had been producing in Mexico or elsewhere in its corporate family. Proquivemex would supply free barbasco and then pay the foreign subsidiary its processing costs plus a reasonable profit. The supply of barbasco to be "toll manufactured" would be additional to that which the TNCs contracted to buy for their own use. According to Proquivemex (1976: 46–47), the TNCs in the industry were only operating at 67 percent of their installed capacity in the early 1970s.

[11] According to one major study, the objectives of the TNCs can be characterized as private, simple, well-defined, and permanent: namely, "profitability and growth, evaluated for the integrated whole of their operations at the level of the world market and in a long-range perspective" (Fajnzylber and Martínez Tarragó, 1976: 131).

[12] The first sustained criticism of alleged TNC exploitation in the industry came out in a series of three newspaper articles published in *Excelsior* on October 30 and 31 and November 1 of 1974. The government immediately proclaimed that the TNCs would, in the future, be granted no more

TNC prices rose as high as P $2.00 (due at least in part to the transnationals' anticipation of Proquivemex), the top price paid the peasants was alleged to have been around P $0.60 per kilogram of collected root.

In reality, however, the TNC pricing policy was a reflection of the extremely low standard of living characteristic of rural Mexico in general. For example, in 1970 the price of P $0.60 per kilogram of collected barbasco was equal to, and in some cases even double, the average daily income of the peasants in all five of the barbasco-growing states.[13] In addition, setting a low price for barbasco was made even easier because gathering the plant was a complementary economic activity; the peasants' main source of income came from cultivating their traditional crops (such as corn, beans, rice, coffee, and fruit). In short, the TNCs took advantage of the fact that the peasants in Mexico have consistently paid more of the costs and received less of the benefits from Mexican development than has any other sector of the population (see Hansen, 1971). Proquivemex was much more concerned about this general problem than it was about giving the individual collectors of barbasco more money; in fact, in 1974 the state firm paid the gatherers approximately the same as the TNCs did.[14]

permits to extract barbasco (thus breaking with the policy that had been in force since the 1950s); only peasants organized in *ejidos* would henceforth be eligible to receive permits (*Excelsior*, Nov. 2, 1974).

[13] In 1970 the five states where barbasco is gathered had the following average daily incomes: Oaxaca, P $14; Chiapas, P $17; Puebla, P $21; Tabasco, P $27; and Veracruz, P $28 (*IX Censo General de Población 1970*, Dirección General de Estadística, Secretaría de Industria y Comercio, cited in Proquivemex, 1976: Table 5.8). A peasant can gather, on the average, fifty kilograms of barbasco daily. At a price of P $0.60 per kilo, this means a daily income of P $30, which is above the average of the most prosperous barbasco-producing state (Veracruz) and more than double the normal daily income in the poorest state (Oaxaca).

[14] The peasants received P $1.50 to $2.00 per kilogram of "green" barbasco from the TNCs in 1974. The Proquivemex pricing policy was to pay the peasant gatherer P $1.50 per kilogram of unprocessed barbasco for his labor, with P $0.50 going to the *ejido* from which the plant was uprooted for *derechos de monte* (see footnote 22) and a remaining P $0.10 going to a

The real aim of Proquivemex was to improve the basic structure of the peasant economy in the barbasco-growing regions of Mexico. The general means used to achieve this end were: 1) to increase peasant resources at the level of the *ejido* (an area of land collectively owned by peasants in rural Mexico) in order to undercut the power of rural middlemen and *caciques* (local political bosses), and 2) to develop new rural industries using vegetable or plant resources other than barbasco. With respect to the *ejidos*, Proquivemex designed programs to give them more autonomy in three areas usually controlled by the *caciques*: transportation, the sale of basic foods, and credit. First, the state firm provided the *ejidos* with freight trucks that were used to transport both barbasco and the peasants' traditional crops (since the two harvest periods do not overlap). This allowed for reductions of up to 75 percent in the freight charges previously set by the *caciques*. These same trucks also served a second major function: they helped lower the price for basic foods. A program was established with Conasupo (the state firm controlling basic food supplies) whereby, rather than returning empty, the freight trucks would come back to the countryside filled with basic foods at official prices after delivering their load in Mexico City. The price the peasants were paying for corn, for example, was cut by nearly 60 percent by this program—from P $4.50 per kilogram (in rural stores, often owned by the *caciques*) to the official price of P $1.95 per kilogram. A similar program was set up with the state fertilizer company, Guanos y Fertilizantes de México (now known as Fertimex). Finally, the stable price set by Proquivemex for collected barbasco relieved the onerous dilemma that confronted the peasants when prices were much lower: since they were often short of cash, they either had to harvest their crops early or go to the *caciques* for short-term credit. With respect to new rural industries, Proquivemex's projects included the production of

common *ejidal* fund managed by the Fondo Nacional de Fomento Ejidal. Thus, Proquivemex's total payment to the peasants was P $2.10 for each kilo of "green" barbasco they collected.

quinine from cichona tree bark and the production of citric concentrates used in the manufacture of Vitamin C products. The national emphasis of Proquivemex's program can be seen in its ideas for defending natural resources. Whereas a foreign subsidiary in Latin America usually thinks of a natural resource as a raw material to be exported, Proquivemex adopted the increasingly common posture of resource-rich developing countries: natural resources are best protected by industrializing them in their country of origin. This point of view was repeatedly expounded by Proquivemex's general director: "For us to remain at the level of exploiting raw materials would be to accept technological and economic dependency" (*Excelsior*, Oct. 11, 1975).

> What we want is to compete on equal terms with [the TNCs], within the regime of the mixed economy. We are the owners of barbasco; they, of the technology, and each must defend himself as he can. . . . We are looking for the vindication of a natural resource, and in that respect we will not take one step backward. We are unable to accept being mere providers of raw material. We want to participate in research and industrialization. (*Excelsior*, Aug. 19, 1976)

In an effort to develop a Mexican owned and operated productive capacity for basic steroid hormones, Proquivemex announced early in 1976 its plans to build three diosgenin manufacturing plants. It also decided to formulate basic pharmaceutical products and its own birth control pill (Mestril). And in order to assure the future supply of barbasco, it began to rationalize the collection of the natural resource.[15]

The big catch in Proquivemex's whole plan was that the TNCs had to finance it. The state hoped that the TNCs were

[15] Both the TNCs and the Mexican government have made attempts to cultivate barbasco in Mexico. So far the method has proven too costly and the returns too limited for cultivated barbasco to be internationally competitive.

141

still dependent enough on Mexico as a source of supply to make them vulnerable, at least in the short run, to increased demands. It also hoped that because the subsidiaries in Mexico were vertically integrated to parent companies that produced final steroid hormone products, the raw material price in Mexico could be raised above what the international market would bear for an "independent" intermediate goods manufacturer since the raw material costs could be paid out of accumulated profits further along the integrated production line. What the state plan did not anticipate was the possibility that the TNCs would find local political allies to help them build a strong defense.

THE TRANSNATIONAL CORPORATIONS' DEFENSE

In January 1976 Proquivemex raised its price for dry barbasco from P \$20 to P \$70 per kilogram. The state firm insisted that the price was not arbitrary. Rather, it tried to capture the greatest quantity of resources possible from the raw material with the condition that the price of dry barbasco to the TNCs, plus the costs of transforming it, plus reasonable profit margins (which were left undefined) would not surpass the price of the products obtained from barbasco.[16] The TNCs vehemently claimed that at a price of P \$70 per kilogram of raw material Mexican steroid hormone exports could not remain internationally competitive and that in fact Mexico's share of the world market had been declining at the pre-Proquivemex costs of P \$12 per kilogram or less due to the strong competition from alternative source materials.[17]

[16] Proquivemex calculated its price for barbasco by working backwards from the price of the finished steroid hormone products to the raw material cost, subtracting the costs of transformation and overhead. The sample of final products on which this calculation was based ranged from the most advanced to the most elementary.

[17] An economic study commissioned by the six TNCs concluded that at a price of P \$12 per kilogram of dry barbasco the TNCs could export P \$612 million of steroid hormones, at a price of P \$20 exports would drop to P \$548 million, and at the P \$70 price the value of Mexico's steroid exports would plummet to P \$30 million (Bremer et al., 1976: 28).

142

Faced with the new P $70 price, the front-line defense of the TNCs was not to buy any barbasco from Proquivemex. This strategy was made viable because most of the TNCs had built up an inventory of barbasco sufficient to carry them through 1976. The possibility that the TNCs could refuse to buy from Proquivemex for one year represented a series of dangers to the state firm's plan. First of all, the end of 1976 corresponded with the end of a sexennial administration in Mexico; if the TNCs could hold out until Echeverría left office there was a chance the incoming president would not allow Proquivemex to play such an active role in the industry. Second, Mexico's steroid exports would drop drastically, thus creating economic pressures to arrive at a settlement. Third, with Proquivemex's warehouses already full, it would not be able to continue buying from the peasants at a normal rate, thus aggravating rather than improving their situation in the countryside.

Proquivemex therefore decided to rely on strong mass support from the peasants to try to break the stalemate with the TNCs. This time, however, the demands were not for payment of the higher barbasco price; they were for nationalization. Spurred on by reports that the TNCs were threatening Proquivemex with a boycott as a result of the new price increase,[18] the state firm helped organize a mass assembly of peasants in the state of Veracruz calling for President Echeverría to nationalize the steroid hormone industry.[19] In August another mass meeting of one thousand *ejidal* leaders representing more than one hundred thousand peasants was held, this time in Mexico City.[20] Nationalization was again called

---

[18] Ironically, this report was first published by the *Wall Street Journal* (Mar. 8, 1976); it was quickly picked up by a major Mexico City newspaper (*El sol de México*, Mar. 9, 1976). The TNCs tried to recoup their prestige by placing full-page ads in all of Mexico City's main dailies denying the veracity of the story and making countercharges of their own. (This ad, dated Mar. 11, 1976, appeared in most papers the following day.)

[19] Newspaper accounts of this meeting were printed on March 13, 1976. The peasant unions formally published their demands for nationalization a few days later. See *Excelsior*, Mar. 15, 1976.

[20] The meeting was held on August 15 and 16.

for since the TNCs (with one exception[21]) had still not bought a gram of barbasco from Proquivemex in 1976.

Echeverría did not respond to either request for nationalization. It is quite likely that the outbursts by both sides in the press as well as the ability of Proquivemex to mobilize the peasants took top government officials by surprise (especially the Veracruz meeting in March). On both occasions, however, the results were the same: the idea of nationalization was discarded, the conflict was quickly pushed out of the press, and direct negotiations were opened up between the six TNCs and the government. Significantly, Proquivemex was not invited to participate in these negotiations. The probable reason is that the state firm had overstepped its boundaries for autonomous action as determined by top officials in the state bureaucracy. After the March protest the vehicle for these negotiations was a joint government/private sector study commission; three government members (one each from the ministries of National Patrimony, Industry and Commerce, and the Presidency) and three industry members represented each side. Between March and August this commission only met twice, however, perhaps hoping that the interest shown by the government and the at least implicit reprimand given Proquivemex would improve relations between the two sides. Such was not the case.

Whereas the March meeting of peasants against the TNCs presented a generalized demand for nationalization, in August Proquivemex's directors supported this demand with two specific offenses charged against the foreign firms. The first was that they owed the peasants P $470 million for neglecting to pay *"derechos de monte"* to the *ejidos* over the past twenty-five years.[22] The second charge was that the TNCs

[21] The one exception was Diosynth, which ran out of its barbasco reserves in May and agreed to "toll manufacture" 160 tons of dry barbasco into intermediate products for Proquivemex in June. Diosynth later discontinued its operations for the state firm, however.

[22] *Derechos de monte* refer to the Mexican law stating that in order to exploit natural resources lying on the surface of the land—such as trees for lumber or surface mining to get at ore deposits—one must pay the owner

had defrauded the federal treasury in Mexico at a rate of P $1 billion per year. The charge of tax fraud refers to the TNC practice of transfer pricing and will be commented on in some detail.

When transfer pricing is used to try to reduce a TNC's global tax burden, exports to an affiliated company are often undervalued, whereas imports from an affiliate have a higher than normal price. The objective is to transfer funds out of a given country without paying taxes on them. According to Proquivemex's director, the real value of the TNCs' steroid hormone exports from Mexico should have been P $1.4 billion annually (based on world market prices for their products) instead of the P $400 million they were charging. This represented an annual loss to Mexico of P $1 billion of taxable income. At current tax rates this meant the Mexican government was losing P $420 million (42 percent corporate earnings tax) and the workers in the industry were losing P $80 million that should have been distributed to them as shared profits (*El sol de México*, Aug. 17, 1976).

The mechanism that accounts for such a big difference can be seen in the following examples in which the export price for a given product is compared with the price at which the same product was imported into Mexico. (It makes no difference from the point of view of national taxable income whether the exporting and importing are done by the same firm or by two different ones.) In 1972 one of the TNCs in Mexico imported the hormone progesterone at a price of P $30,000 a kilogram, while the value given to progesterone as an export by a second TNC in the same year was P $1,365 a kilogram. The case of estradiol is particularly dramatic. Whereas it was exported by Syntex for slightly over P $11,000 a kilogram, estradiol was imported into Mexico by another

---

of the land for the resource used. This law thus separates payment for the natural resource (e.g., to the *ejidos*) from payment to those who gather the material. The TNCs claim this charge is without any legal basis since no government authority had ever previously requested that such a payment be made for the *Dioscorea* plants. See *Excelsior*, Aug. 17 and 19, 1976.

company for P $1 million a kilogram, 88 times the export value given by Syntex.[23]

Actually, the overpricing of steroid hormone imports into Mexico was neither new nor was the information needed to demonstrate it hidden. Detailed product and country-specific data on steroid hormone imports have been published by Mexico's Ministry of Industry and Commerce since 1965. In each year significant overpricing of imports is evident. Table 5.2 summarizes this published information for five well-known steroid hormone products imported into Mexico in 1974. The rate of overpricing was not estimated on the basis of international reference prices for imported drugs, as Vaitsos (1974) and others have done, but instead takes the minimum price at which a specified product was imported into Mexico and deems any excess over this minimum price to be an overprice. Since low prices may sometimes result from large bulk purchases of drugs, the minimum or reference prices are based on small annual orders (five kilograms or less) whose volume is always below, and usually far below, the other import sources used in the comparison. If anything, then, this method understates the overpricing in the industry.

The findings from Table 5.2 indicate that the overpricing of imports in the Mexican steroid hormone industry was widespread and economically very significant. The rate of overpricing is more than 1,000 percent in several cases, reaching a high of 5,650 percent for progesterone imported from the Netherlands. In relatively few instances is the rate of overpricing less than 300 percent. For all five of the products considered, the highest rate of overpricing is linked to one of the European home countries of Mexico's steroid hormone TNCs (the Netherlands, the Federal Republic of Germany, or Switzerland). Overpricing of imports, in other words, in all likelihood was one of the main mechanisms used to transfer unde-

---

[23] See Proquivemex (1976: 43–44). The estradiol example is also mentioned in *Excelsior*, Mar. 20, 1976. For more information on transfer pricing in the pharmaceutical industry in Latin America see Vaitsos (1974) on Colombia and Katz (1974: 33–34) on Argentina.

clared profits from Mexican subsidiaries to TNC parent companies in Europe. Potentially large amounts of taxable income were lost to Mexico in this way. The total amount of overpricing for the five products listed in Table 5.2 is almost P $5 million. When you consider that there are sixty-five different import codes for steroid hormone products entering Mexico and that there is evidence of overpricing in almost every one the concerns about fraud expressed by Proquivemex certainly appear justified.

The *derechos de monte* and tax fraud charges led the TNCs to realize that their original defense of not buying barbasco was insufficient since they were exposing themselves to political attacks that could allow the mass pressure for nationalization to become overwhelming. Thus, the transnationals decided to try to obtain a broader base of support among the main private sector business groupings in Mexico. In order to do this the foreign firms had to successfully redefine the nature of their battle with Proquivemex from a foreign/national conflict between six TNCs and the Mexican nation over peasant welfare and natural resources to a generalized struggle between the private sector in Mexico (national and foreign) and an increasingly interventionist Mexican state. This is exactly what happened.

After the mass meetings and charges made by Proquivemex in August 1976, the president of Concamin (the mandatory confederation of all industrialists in Mexico) denounced the state firm on two grounds. First, he claimed its charges were without legal basis. Concamin's president affirmed that he was not trying to defend the TNCs per se but rather a principle of law. In a very able move he pointed out that either the accusations made by Proquivemex were false or Proquivemex was implicating the corresponding federal authorities for corruption since the TNCs had never before been informed by either the Secretary of Agrarian Reform (with respect to *derechos de monte*) or the Secretary of the Treasury (with respect to the alleged tax fraud) that they were committing any offenses. Concamin's second, and principal, complaint with

147

TABLE 5.2
Overpricing of Imports in the Mexican Steroid Hormone Industry, 1974

Product	Country of Origin	Kilograms	Pesos	Unit Price	Rate of Overpricing[a] (percentage)	Amount of Overpricing[b] (pesos)
Progesterone	Federal Republic of Germany	2	1,032	516	—[c]	0
	France	35	67,745	1,936	375	49,685
	Spain	5	32,060	6,412	1,243	29,480
	Netherlands	37	1,078,620	29,152	5,650	1,059,528
Total		79	1,179,457	14,930	2,893	1,138,693
Prednisone	Italy	3	6,026	2,009	—[c]	0
	France	137	1,037,565	7,573	377	762,332
	Brazil	10	102,660	10,266	511	82,570
	Netherlands	20	350,365	17,518	872	310,185
Total		170	1,496,616	8,804	438	1,155,087
Prednisolone	United Kingdom	5	31,250	6,250	—[c]	0
	Panama	29	292,750	10,095	162	111,500
	France	21	246,150	11,721	188	114,900
	Federal Republic of Germany	11	171,725	15,611	250	102,975
	Italy	6	118,063	19,677	315	80,563
	Netherlands	23	620,223	26,966	431	476,473
Total		95	1,480,161	15,581	249	886,411

Estradiol	France	5	56,999	11,400	—[c]	0
	Federal Republic of Germany	10	309,466	30,947	271	195,466
Total		15	366,465	24,431	214	195,466
Hydrocortisone	Netherlands	5	35,919	7,184	—[c]	0
	Federal Republic of Germany	7	68,330	9,761	136	18,042
	Bermuda	9	601,020	66,780	930	536,364
	Switzerland	13	1,006,355	77,412	1,078	912,963
Total		34	1,711,624	50,342	701	1,467,369

SOURCE: México, Secretaría de Industria y Comercio, 1975, pp. 166–168.

[a] The rate of overpricing is based on a minimum price at which a selected steroid hormone product was imported into Mexico in 1974. Any excess over this minimum price is considered to be an overprice. To reduce the possibility of bias from low discount prices for bulk purchases, the selected minimum (or reference) price for each product is derived from import totals whose volume is always lower than that of any of the other import sources used in the comparison.

[b] The amount of overpricing is calculated by multiplying the minimum unit price by the number of kilograms received from each importing country and then subtracting this result from each country's actual import total in pesos.

[c] The unit price from this import source is the minimum, or reference, price.

Proquivemex was that its directors were trying to agitate the peasants and create conflict in the countryside, which would be to the detriment of the private sector as a whole (*El sol de México*, Aug. 18, 1976). The president of Concamin claimed that the problem was particularly grave because "it puts social tranquility in danger since the peasant problem is the most serious that exists in the country; the businessmen do not want these irregular situations to be started and fomented, only to be blamed later for what is happening" (*Novedades*, Aug. 18, 1976).

The president of the National Chamber of Chemical-Pharmaceutical Laboratories in Mexico also spoke out sharply against Proquivemex. Again the main concern was not with the charges made against the TNCs per se. Rather, it was a more general problem: the danger that Proquivemex, with its production of finished pharmaceuticals,[24] would displace privately owned Mexican laboratories from the big government market for pharmaceutical purchases in Mexico.[25] The criticism leveled against Proquivemex was that it was guilty of "disloyal competition" vis-à-vis the private Mexican labs since the state firm had access to credit at lower rates of interest than the private firms did and it was exempt from taxes that the private companies had to pay (*El heraldo*, Aug. 19, 1976).

The government quickly took heed of this new situation. The direct negotiations that followed were placed in the hands of the Secretary of National Patrimony rather than the three ministries that were represented on the study commission. The government claimed the price of barbasco could be lowered considerably if the TNCs "toll manufactured" for

---

[24] The Proquivemex product that seemed to worry the national laboratories most was the antibiotic ampicillin (the second-generation penicillin). Many firms knew how to make it and it was bought in large quantities by the government.

[25] The government market accounts for about 25 percent of all pharmaceutical sales in Mexico. It was estimated to be worth $240 million (U.S.) in 1976 (*Business Latin America*, Mar. 24, 1976, p. 90).

Proquivemex. The government also made known its desire to have the TNC subsidiaries "Mexicanize" by selling part of their stock to local partners. Somewhat ironically, it is clear that not having acquired local partners before Proquivemex was created was a big tactical error by the TNCs. Mexicanization may serve very conservative ends. By becoming "partly Mexican" a TNC becomes much less vulnerable politically without being required to improve its performance in Mexico, either with respect to the internal or the external (i.e., export) market.

Negotiations continued through the sexennial change of government at the end of 1976 in which José López Portillo replaced Echeverría. The devaluation of the Mexican peso (beginning August 31, 1976) helped the TNCs considerably in their bargaining with the government, however. By November 1976, for instance, the government price for barbasco had dropped from P $70 to P $55 a kilogram, with the TNCs offering to pay P $25 (*El sol de México*, Nov. 4, 1976). The value of the Mexican peso at the time, however, was only *one-half* what it had been before the devaluation in comparison with the U.S. dollar (P $25 to $1.00 U.S. after the devaluation, as compared with P $12.50 to $1.00 U.S. before). Thus, the dollar value of the TNCs' offer for dry barbasco at the end of 1976 was the same as what they were originally paying for the raw material in 1974, before Proquivemex had been created.

A workable agreement between the two sides was not reached until April 1977, at which time the TNCs consented to pay P $60 per kilogram for dry barbasco (approximately P $30 at predevaluation exchange rates). Proquivemex's total payment to the peasants was also raised, from P $2.10 during 1975 and 1976 (see footnote 14) to P $4.50 (*El día*, April 14, 1977). In the agreement no mention was made of the government's previously stipulated conditions that 1) the TNC subsidiaries "Mexicanize," and that 2) they "toll manufacture" finished products for Proquivemex. Thus, the government finally got the TNCs to pay a higher price for processed barbasco, but in so doing it dropped its demands for related industry change.

From 1977 to 1980 Mexico's position in the world industry continued to deteriorate. Whereas Mexican diosgenin accounted for 75 percent of the world supply of steroid raw materials in 1963 and nearly 40 percent in 1973 (see Table 5.1), by 1980 this percentage had dropped to 10 percent. Several of the TNCs with subsidiaries in Mexico began switching to alternative raw materials and to processes that did not require barbasco; thus, the total amount of barbasco purchased from Proquivemex by the six TNCs dropped from 6,800 tons in 1977 to 2,800 tons in 1978. Proquivemex's primary response was to try to increase at all costs the vertical integration of the industry within Mexico (*El universal*, Oct. 18, 1978). This vertical integration was to proceed in three main directions: 1) the production from barbasco of all the diosgenin used in Mexico, 2) the production of intermediate steroids, in particular 16-D, hydrocortisone, and eventually the diuretic spironolactone, and 3) the production of fermented steroids in Mexico. Mexico also planned to use hecogenin from the sisal plant grown locally to manufacture without fermentation some steroid products that would require fermentation if barbasco were used as the starting material. Transnationals thus became increasingly marginal to the development of the steroid industry in Mexico.

Overall there are three principal reasons why Proquivemex was unable to impose its program of reforms on the TNCs in the Mexican steroid hormone industry. The first is economic. Mexico's overall plan for development continued giving an extremely high priority to exports, which began to fall off sharply as of 1975 (see Table 5.3). It was apparently felt that the TNCs could stave off Mexico's deteriorating position in the world industry better than a newly created state firm could. The second reason is political. Proquivemex did not have the support it needed at the top levels of government to carry through its reforms. One clear demonstration of this in 1975 is the fact that the Mexican government allowed the

TABLE 5.3

The Mexican Steroid Hormone Industry: Exports and Imports
1965–1976

Year	Exports*		Imports*		Percentage of Total Production Exported**
	Pesos[a]	Kilos[b]	Pesos[a]	Kilos[b]	
1965	173	156	39	12	97
1966	205	179	51	7	97
1967	214	186	51	11	88
1968	208	199	89	3	80
1969	234	247	46	5	92
1970	224	208	58	11	93
1971	262	235	83	6	94
1972	217	227	111	117	94
1973	372	250	117	6	95
1974	448	236	140	8	98
1975	380	161	147	11	NA
1976	291	119	100	5	NA

SOURCES: * México, Secretaría de Industria y Comercio, 1966–1977.
** Olizar, 1975–1976: 155.
NOTE: NA= not available.
[a] Expressed in millions of pesos.
[b] Expressed in thousands of kilograms.

TNCs to import diosgenin from the People's Republic of China, thereby directly undermining Proquivemex's pricing policy with respect to barbasco. In addition, by mid-1976 the state firm had been replaced as the chief negotiator with the TNCs in the industry by members of the state bureaucracy. The third reason is technological. Mexico's "technological dependence" in the steroid hormone industry is still very real. Mexico imports the vast majority of the active ingredients used in steroids and in the other pharmaceutical products consumed nationally. Had nationalization occurred, it would have seriously jeopardized the stream of technologically sophisticated pharmaceutical products controlled by foreign manufacturers.

STATE AUTONOMY AND ITS LIMITS VIS-À-VIS TNCs

A brief recapitulation of my conclusions about the Mexican steroid hormone industry as a crucial-case test of dependency theory is in order. Whereas most dependent countries are prevented from attaining integrated and relatively autonomous national industries by the absence of one or more critical factors of production, Mexico by the early 1950s could boast of possessing all that it needed to be the world leader in a dynamic and technologically sophisticated segment of the pharmaceutical industry: it had exclusive access to the most efficient and versatile raw material, barbasco; a local firm, Syntex, led the world industry in both output and steroid technology; and the Mexican state had taken an active role in supporting established local producers. Given these advantages, why was Mexico unable to develop a fully integrated steroid hormone industry that could make finished as well as intermediate steroid products? From Mexico's point of view, this forward integration would have been highly desirable. It would have 1) increased the value and diversity of the country's steroid exports, 2) had a positive impact on manufacturing value-added and local employment opportunities, and 3) reduced the prices of finished drugs to Mexican consumers.

The reason why Mexico was unable to obtain the benefits of full industrial development in steroid hormones, I have argued, stems from the multifaceted dependency relations in which the country was enmeshed. "Dependency," as the concept has been used in this study, is not implied by capitalism per se, as some Marxists would have it, but rather refers to the pattern of foreign-controlled capitalist development that is so common in many third world nations. This foreign control was manifested not only by the wholly owned TNC subsidiaries that took over the Mexican industry in the late 1950s and early 1960s and whose global strategies often conflicted with the country's national and social priorities; foreign control was also an inherent part of the structure of the international industry. Mexico's steroid hormone output had to be sold in mass markets abroad and the most important market of all was the United States. This fact allowed the U.S. government to play a key role in forcing the Mexican state to stop protecting domestic producers of steroid intermediates prior to the entry by U.S. and European TNCs. The dependency represented by this foreign control led to an inequitable distribution of industry benefits favoring the central capitalistic economies and the TNCs more than Mexico and to a restriction of Mexico's choices in pursuing its development options, as shown in Chapter 4.

The structural power of the TNCs clearly limited the bargaining power of the Mexican state in the steroid hormone industry, although state inaction at certain junctures could also be explained at least in part by conflicting priorities within the state bureaucracy, inadequate administrative capabilities for monitoring and regulating the activities of TNCs, and corruption. When the state in Mexico did begin to act against the foreign firms in 1975, this new-found political will appeared to be sparked by alleged abuses involving the peasants; later the state's initiatives, embodied in Proquivemex, were tempered when the local private sector sided with the TNCs to protest the growing peasant mobilization that accompanied the state's involvement. Thus an understanding of the dynamics of dependency and Mexico's attempts to reverse it involves not just the issue of foreign control but also an analysis of the social class relations that made this control possible. This raises the general questions of how third world states use their autonomy to try to control TNCs and what factors increase the state's probability of success.

The relationship between the state and foreign capital in third world countries is complex and has changed rapidly in recent years. In his book *The State and Society*, Alfred Stepan (1978: Chapter 7) reviews some of these changes and, more generally, attempts to assess the capability of the state to

155

control foreign capital. One of the most interesting features of his analysis is Stepan's identification of a bargaining cycle relating the potential power of the state to its ability to control foreign capital, with particular emphasis given to the case of Peru since 1968. This bargaining power model is considered applicable to manufacturing as well as extractive industries (Stepan, 1978: 242) and thus might provide a useful framework for drawing some conclusions from the Mexican steroid hormone case.

There are two main dimensions to Stepan's bargaining cycle model: the importance to the state of attracting foreign investment in a particular economic sector (low priority or high priority), and the status of foreign investment prior to bargaining with the state (uncommitted or "sunken"). In Table 5.4 this model is adapted to the case of Mexico's steroid hormone industry. According to Stepan's formulation, the state is in the *strongest* position to control or exclude foreign capital at a minimal economic and political cost if the proposed investment involves an area of the economy given a low priority by the state and there is no existing foreign investment in the sector (cell 1). The state is in the *weakest* position to control foreign capital, on the other hand, in those sectors where foreign investment has a high priority in the state's development plan and foreign investment is still uncommitted to the sector (cell 4); in these circumstances the state may have to forego exacting conditions for entry and may even have to extend special subsidies to attract foreign capital. Between these extremes fall two intermediate positions of potential state power. When foreign investment is "sunken," Stepan argues, it is vulnerable to the broad range of control measures the state can apply. The state is in a stronger position in cell 2 (low priority) than in cell 3 (high priority), however, because in the former situation local factors of production are available that can adequately meet planned investment targets in the sector.

When these phases of the state-foreign capital bargaining cycle are related to the case of Mexico's steroid hormone in-

TABLE 5.4

The State-Foreign Capital Bargaining Cycle,
Adapted to the Case of Mexico's Steroid Hormone Industry
1944–1982

[handwritten marginalia: "← Gereffi's study show diff'nt pattern"; "Also, differ frm Moran's cycle"]

Previous Status of Foreign Investment	Importance to the State of Attracting Foreign Investment	
	Low Priority	High Priority
	1	4
Uncommitted	State can bar entry of foreign capital at almost no economic or political cost	State has to offer incentives to attract foreign capital
	1944–1955: Local private capital phase	Not applicable
	2	3
"Sunken"	State can control or even eliminate foreign capital but at some economic and political cost	State cannot eliminate foreign capital but has some capacity to impose greater controls and exact greater rents
	1956–1974: Transnational corporation phase	1975–1982: State enterprise phase

[handwritten marginalia: "↓"; "← strongest"]

SOURCE: Stepan, 1978: 244. The dates refer to the three phases of dependency in Mexico's steroid hormone industry.
NOTE: Scale of state potential to control foreign capital:
1 = highest
4 = lowest

dustry, it can be seen that the Mexican state's power should have been greatest at the beginning of the industry's growth (cell 1) and weakest at the end (cell 3). In fact, my analysis of the industry does not fully support the predictions of Stepan's bargaining cycle model. The power of the Mexican state was probably weakest, or least in evidence, during the middle period when the TNCs' domination of Mexico's steroid hormone industry was greatest (cell 2). The state's role in the industry is most prominent, on the other hand, in the era of Proquivemex, when the bargaining cycle model predicts the state to be weakest (cell 3). And when the state should have been strongest (cell 1), local private capital enjoyed its only real moment of glory in the industry, with the state playing a supporting but definitely subordinate role. To explain these apparent inconsistencies, a closer look at the assumptions underlying Stepan's model is called for.

First of all, the notion of high or low priority of foreign investment to the state is more complicated than the bargaining schema implies. "Priority" has both an economic and a political dimension, and these need not coincide. Steroid hormone exports gave the industry a high *economic* priority in Mexico in phases 2 (1956–1974) and 3 (1975–1982). What changed over this period, however, was the industry's *political* priority to the state, which went from low in phase 2 to high in phase 3. The issue of alleged exploitation of the peasants by the steroid hormone TNCs first surfaced in Mexican newspapers at the end of 1974. It was this politically volatile peasant issue, more than economic issues, that prompted an expanded role for the state through the creation of Proquivemex in early 1975.

The ties of foreign capital to the prospective host country point to another aspect of Stepan's model in need of further refinement if it is to help explain what happened in Mexico's steroid hormone industry. "Uncommitted" foreign investment, as used in Stepan's bargaining framework, implicitly refers to TNCs only in their capacity as potential local producers. It is clear from the steroid hormone case, however, that TNCs may be linked to a host country in at least two separate ways: as producers and as foreign buyers.[26] In phase 1 (1944–1955), TNCs as producers were essentially uncommitted to Mexico (with the sole exception of the Schering Cor-

[26] A third role, applicable to transnational banks, is that of financier.

poration's subsidiary, Beisa, which operated as a pilot plant). United States TNC buyers of Mexican steroid hormone exports in this period, on the other hand, were heavily committed to Mexico for their raw material supplies. Because their reliance on Mexico was so great, these TNC buyers helped pressure the U.S. government to break Syntex's virtual monopoly in Mexico. This opened the floodgates to the direct foreign investment that led in phase 2 to the denationalization of the Mexican steroid hormone industry. Transnational commitment, like state priority, is thus not a unidimensional concept. The high degree of commitment by TNC buyers limited the options of the Mexican state prior to the influx of TNC producers.

Finally, Stepan's model assumes that in manufacturing industries, as in extractive ones, the moment of new investment is the company's moment of greatest bargaining strength (Stepan, 1978: 242). As time passes, "sunken" foreign investment is likely to become increasingly vulnerable to host country demands. The experience of TNCs in steroid hormones and other manufacturing industries does not seem to support this generalization, however.[27] Unlike industries in the extractive sector, manufacturing industries are not characterized by the reductions in uncertainty and the host country "learning curves" that cause shifts in bargaining power from companies to the host government after the initial investment is made and that frequently lead to the nationalization of extractive industries (see Moran, 1974a). In the manufacturing sector nationalizations are rare because, for one thing, rapidly changing technology is a continuing source of corporate strength and this technology is beyond the reach of most host governments. Even more important is the fact that over time manufacturing TNCs tend to forge domestic alliances with local suppliers, distributors, and creditors, among others. What this means for the manufacturing TNC is that the mo-

[27] See Bennett and Sharpe's (1979) analysis of Mexico's automobile industry, which shows how and why TNCs increased their bargaining power with the state over time.

ment of initial entry may be its *weakest* bargaining point because the government controls the terms of access to the local market. Once established, however, manufacturing TNCs begin to acquire domestic allies and their bargaining position vis-à-vis the government improves. This ability to count on help from the local private sector explains why the steroid hormone TNCs in Mexico remained largely unscathed in phase 3 (1975–1982) even though the government directed an intense assault against them.

This study, then, tells not just of the exercise of state autonomy in Mexico but also of its limits. One should not infer from this account that the Mexican state fully and straightforwardly represented the interests of all the Mexican people. Although acting in the name of the nation, the state's development plan favored certain groups in the population over others. What greater state autonomy vis-à-vis TNCs in Mexico really represents is a shift in the locus of responsibility for development decisions: along with other national actors, the state now plays a larger role in setting development goals and also in establishing the means to reach these goals.

Transnational corporations, on the other hand, claim that they more than anyone else have promoted development in Mexico's steroid hormone industry. If so, it is development as defined by an international strategy rather than a national one. This international strategy has had some clear costs. Exports have been generated, but they are of intermediate products rather than finished drugs. The finishing continues to be done in the home countries of the TNCs where the big industry profits are made. Taxes have been paid in Mexico by the transnationals, but their amount has been reduced to a minimum through the use of tax havens and transfer pricing. And knowledge creation, the most valued resource of private drug companies, has remained tightly controlled near the center of each transnational organization.

Nor is there much solace for Mexico in the belief that these costs are inextricably bound into the industrialization process itself. The counterfactual analyses carried out in Chapter 4 indicated that national alternatives—i.e., both private and state-owned firms—are likely to have been at least as beneficial as the TNCs, and perhaps more so, with respect to national welfare (as defined by local industry growth) and consumer welfare (as defined by lower drug prices).

Mexico's options in the steroid hormone industry have been narrowing. Mexico has access to raw material supply, and the TNCs have patents, technology, and marketing networks. Unfortunately for Mexico, its basis of strength has been weakened due to the development of substitute sources of supply and to the decline of raw material costs as part of the final sales price of steroid drugs. On the other hand, the TNCs still have a vested interest in maintaining their local subsidiaries' direct access to the Mexican source of supply since this has long been part of their strategy to gain a competitive edge internationally. Bargaining, therefore, continues to be viable.

What is good public policy for Mexico under these conditions? In a vertically integrated industry such as steroid hormones, one national strategy is for Mexico to get as much of the oligopoly profits and the value added as possible at the stage it controls. More specifically, it can follow any combination of policy measures, such as: 1) formulating an optimal excise tax on exports; 2) demanding a percentage of the final product price; 3) policing transfer pricing closely; and 4) demanding more local processing (fermentation, toll manufacturing, etc.). Again, however, Mexico's bargaining power in each area is constrained because technology is controlled and there are alternative sources of supply. The TNCs threat that "they can go elsewhere" is credible.

At present Mexico has opted for a second national strategy: the use of a state-owned enterprise as a flexible policy instrument for dealing with both national development goals and TNCs.[28] Such a strategy has a number of advantages. First, it

[28] Under Echeverría this strategy was particularly prominent in major rural industries such as tobacco, coffee, sugar, and barbasco. Each of these four industries employs large numbers of peasants: sugar, about 300,000; coffee, 95,000; tobacco, 45,000; and barbasco, 25,000. In each of these in-

still allows bargaining with TNCs to be carried on for limited gains in which neither side feels it is in an all or nothing situation. Second, state resources can be used more directly to promote welfare goals that private firms, national or transnational, would ignore. In steroid hormones the state firm tried to eliminate exploitative middlemen, to lower the price of basic goods to the peasants, and to develop new rural industries to stabilize the peasant economy should demand for barbasco decline. A third advantage in using state firms as a policy instrument is that the state need not represent a direct threat to the private firms in the industry, thus lessening the chance of mutually destructive opposition. A good example of this is Central de Medicamentos (CEME), a state pharmaceutical company in Brazil created in 1971. The objective of CEME is to produce and distribute basic, generic name drugs without charge to that part of the population which receives the official minimum wage or less. This is exactly that sector of the population which is normally excluded from the commercial market for medicines. Thus, CEME is not likely to take any customers away from private firms. Furthermore, a large part of the medications distributed by CEME are purchased from the private sector, which probably hopes that its own market will be expanded someday as members of this poorer group acquire additional income (Evans, 1976: 133–136).

---

dustries a major state-owned firm was either created or revitalized during the Echeverría administration as part of its rural development program. In the sugar industry a decentralized agency called the National Commission on the Sugar Industry was created in 1970. The tobacco state-owned enterprise, Tabacos Mexicanos (Tabamex), was created in 1972. In the coffee industry an existing firm called the Mexican National Coffee Institute (Inmecafe) was revitalized. Finally, in the case of barbasco there was the creation of Proquivemex in 1975. Although these industries are quite diverse in their overall structure, it appears that the function of state-owned firms in each was similar: 1) to increase the economic strength and stability of these industries and of the rural areas depending on them, 2) to reduce the exploitation of the peasants, particularly by rural middlemen, and 3) stemming from the above, to increase the regime's legitimacy and political support in the countryside.

A national strategy based on state enterprises as a policy instrument has disadvantages also. First of all, state firms may grow to a size where they are beyond the control of normal bureaucratic measures. Implementing a flexible state policy may be further complicated by the fact that an in-grown cadre of technical experts develops in these larger enterprises (a form of "state bourgeoisie") that gives them a life of their own. Second, formulation of the policy that these firms should follow may become tangled in a maze of bureaucratic politics at the middle levels of government as groups representing different interests all try to bring their weight to bear. A third problem is that publicly owned enterprises may greatly increase the state's political risk in an industry. Especially in cases where a particular *stage* of the industry is monopolized, like Proquivemex is attempting to do in steroid hormones, the state may often be called to bear the brunt of the responsibility for employment or price fluctuations caused by external or internal supply and demand changes completely beyond the state's control.

Evidence regarding the role and performance of state-owned enterprises in Mexico and other third world countries is sparse. It appears, however, that many of the larger nations are beginning to increase their use of state firms as a key element in national strategies for development. The results of some of these efforts will be looked at more closely in Chapters 6 and 7.

For their part, TNCs will continue to challenge the state in defining development priorities. Their global spread means their control in industries is not easily broken, especially where it rests with technology and marketing expertise. Until the developing countries gain their own control over knowledge creation, they will be forced to try to shape the contribution of foreign firms to national needs. This will require that national sovereignty and state autonomy be flexed, not buried. The challenge for nations will be to combine the elements of a strong state with those of a just society.

PART THREE

CROSS-NATIONAL DEPENDENCY ANALYSIS: THE PHARMACEUTICAL INDUSTRY IN A THIRD WORLD CONTEXT

CHAPTER SIX

The Internationalization and Structure of the Global Pharmaceutical Industry

HEALTH is a basic human need. Because pharmaceutical products directly affect the health of a nation they have greater social relevance than the products of almost any other industry. As a result, the pharmaceutical industry has tended to operate in a highly politicized environment in all countries, subject to an exceptional degree of government scrutiny and control. At a minimum most countries have enacted and enforced legislation setting high standards for drug purity, drug safety, and drug efficacy. Many governments also seek to foster the development of pharmaceutical production within their national frontiers. In addition to helping meet the health needs of the people, the local manufacture of drugs often involves other national considerations: a country may wish to increase exports, to economize on foreign exchange by minimizing imports, to improve employment prospects, or merely to secure a foothold in a dynamic industry.

The global pharmaceutical industry is dominated by a relatively small number of TNCs. In general these companies have vigorously resisted the expanding range of national demands being placed upon them by developed and less developed countries alike. The conflict arises over the fact that national priorities and the corporate goals of transnational drug firms are frequently at odds. This chapter and the next focus on both pharmaceutical TNCs and third world states in an effort to identify the sources and extent of these conflicts and the likelihood of their solution through policies that ensure an

167

adequate supply of reasonably priced drugs for developing nations. Although both advanced and developing countries share some areas of common concern toward drug manufacturers (for example, in guaranteeing product safety), I argue that the health needs and economic capabilities of industrialized and third world nations are clearly different. Diverse national policies toward pharmaceutical TNCs are thus called for. In the third world this generally includes some sort of state participation in the production and/or distribution of drugs.

The analysis of Mexico carried out in Chapters 3 through 5 detailed the structure and mechanisms of dependency for a single national case. In order to broaden our understanding of the pharmaceutical industry in the third world, Chapters 6 and 7 will look at foreign and local drug firms and the state in various Latin American, African, and Asian nations. Since dependency analysis requires that the situation of specific countries be related to larger world system dynamics, Chapter 6 will outline how and why the pharmaceutical industry expanded internationally. In addition it will attempt to specify the role that third world countries play in the global pharmaceutical industry. The core, semiperipheral, and peripheral status of countries will be linked to the level of development they have attained in the industry.

Chapter 7 then turns to the concrete impact of the pharmaceutical industry in third world societies. First, I will assess the "appropriateness" of pharmaceutical TNCs in terms of third world priorities and developmental goals. The categories used to judge TNC performance include: appropriate prices, appropriate products and technology, and appropriate marketing. Second, I will highlight the role of pharmaceutical TNCs and the state in fourteen selected third world countries. Generalizations about alternative development strategies in the industry are drawn from these cases. The book concludes by reviewing several kinds of public policies concerning drug supply in third world nations that, I am hopeful, can help bring the benefits of the pharmaceutical industry within reach of the majority of their populations.

THE INTERNATIONAL EXPANSION OF THE PHARMACEUTICAL INDUSTRY

The modern pharmaceutical industry is young by industry standards, emerging with the wave of new "wonder drugs" that were discovered after World War II. In the 1930s the pharmaceutical industry was a commodity business. The major companies were full-line drug houses that manufactured and sold a complete array of all the ingredients the pharmacist needed to compound the doctor's prescriptions. Advertising was done in newspapers and popular magazines, therapeutic advance was slow, and drug companies engaged in very little research (Clymer, 1975: 138). By the end of the 1950s the pharmaceutical industry had transformed itself into a research- and advertising-intensive business. Drug firms had grown rapidly and concentrated on specialty (as opposed to commodity) products whose value could be protected by patents and heavily promoted brand names. The vertically integrated company that combined drug discovery, production, and marketing functions in a single corporate network came to dominate the industry. As government regulations created a class of drugs that could not legally be sold without a prescription, advertising increasingly was directed at the medical profession (Temin, 1979a, 1979b).

There are more than ten thousand companies around the world that could be called pharmaceutical manufacturers. Of these, however, no more than about one hundred companies are significant in terms of international market participation. These one hundred firms supply about 90 percent of total world shipments of pharmaceutical products for human use, whose estimated worth in 1976 was $50 billion. The top fifty drug companies headquartered in market economies account for nearly two-thirds of this total, while the leading twenty-five enterprises account for about one-half (Schaumann, 1976: 16–17; Agarwal, 1978: 6).

Table 6.1 provides a listing of the top fifty pharmaceutical companies in 1977. The table merits several comments. First, all of the firms on the list are transnational corporations.

In each case they sell their products in foreign markets and usually also are engaged in production and research and development operations abroad. The trend toward transnationalization came first and in its most pronounced form in European companies, who even prior to the 1930s had responded to small domestic markets by moving extensively abroad, often in concerted fashion under cartel arrangements. United States-based drug companies are also highly transnational, however, with overseas sales representing 40 percent of their global sales of ethical pharmaceuticals in 1977 (PMA, 1978: 3). Profits on foreign sales have been estimated at over 50 percent of the total profits of U.S. drug manufacturers (*Business Week*, 1974: 73). Furthermore, as the process of drug development and regulatory approval in the United States has become lengthier and more costly, American firms have shifted a large part of their clinical testing function overseas as well. Even Japanese pharmaceutical companies, which traditionally have been closely

TABLE 6.1
The Top Fifty Transnational Pharmaceutical Companies, 1977[a]

Rank / Company	Domicile	Millions of U.S. Dollars in Pharmaceutical Sales[b]	Pharmaceutical Sales	
			Proportion of Total Sales	Product Lines Included in Pharmaceutical Sales[c]
1 / Hoechst-Roussel[d]	FRG	1,573	16	1
2 / Merck and Co.	USA	1,446	84	1, 3, 4
3 / Bayer	FRG	1,273	13	1, 3, 5, 7
4 / Ciba-Geigy	SWI	1,150	28	1, 3, 7
5 / Hoffmann-La Roche	SWI	1,145	51	1, 4
6 / American Home Products	USA	1,116	39	1, 3, 5
7 / Warner-Lambert	USA	1,025	40	1, 2, 7
8 / Pfizer	USA	1,016	50	1, 7
9 / Sandoz	SWI	935	48	1
10 / Eli Lilly	USA	911	53	1

TABLE 6.1 Cont.

The Top Fifty Transnational Pharmaceutical Companies, 1977[a]

Rank / Company	Domicile	Millions of U.S. Dollars in Pharmaceutical Sales[b]	Pharmaceutical Sales	
			Proportion of Total Sales	Product Lines Included in Pharmaceutical Sales[c]
11 / Upjohn	USA	744	66	1, 2
12 / Boehringer Ingelheim	FRG	735	77	1
13 / Squibb	USA	668	50	1, 3, 7
14 / Bristol-Myers	USA	666	30	1, 7
15 / Takeda	JPN	646	65	1
16 / Rhone Poulenc	FRA	614	13	1, 3
17 / Schering-Plough	USA	606	63	1
18 / Glaxo	UK	594	72	1, 2, 3, 4, 6, 7
19 / Abbott Laboratories	USA	581	47	1, 4, 5
20 / Beecham	UK	524	36	1, 3, 5
21 / Johnson and Johnson	USA	518	18	1, 3
22 / Montedison	ITA	487	8	1, 3
23 / Cyanamid	USA	484	20	1, 4
24 / Schering	FRG	456	51	1, 4
25 / AKZO	NLD	442	10	1
26 / ICI	UK	414	5	1
27 / SmithKline	USA	411	53	1
28 / Wellcome[e]	UK	385	65	1
29 / G.D. Searle	USA	382	51	1
30 / Baxter Travenol	USA	355	42	1, 7
31 / Boehringer Mannheim[f]	FRG	353	78	1
32 / Revlon	USA	334	29	1, 2, 7
33 / Dow	USA	333	5	1, 2, 6
34 / Astra	SWE	307	73	1, 2
35 / Shionogi	JPN	286	78	1
36 / Fujisawa	JPN	285	80	1
37 / E. Merck	FRG	275	44	1
38 / 3M	USA	266	7	1
39 / Sankyo	JPN	245	79	1
40 / Richardson-Merrell	USA	235	28	1

TABLE 6.1 Cont.

The Top Fifty Transnational Pharmaceutical Companies, 1977[a]

Rank / Company	Domicile	Millions of U.S. Dollars in Pharmaceutical Sales[b]	Pharmaceutical Sales	
			Proportion of Total Sales	Product Lines Included in Pharmaceutical Sales[c]
41 / Sterling Drug[g]	USA	232	14	1, 3
42 / Pennwalt	USA	217	26	1, 2, 7
43 / Syntex	PAN	216	69	1, 4, 5
44 / A.H. Robins	USA	212	69	1, 2, 4, 5
45 / BASF	FRG	210	2	1
46 / Meiji Seika	JPN	175	32	1
47 / CM Industries[h]	FRA	165	62	1, 2, 3
48 / Altana (formerly Varta)	FRG	158	47	1
49 / Miles Laboratories	USA	158	33	1, 7
50 / Tanabe Seiyaku	JPN	154	51	1, 5

SOURCE: United Nations Centre on Transnational Corporations, 1979: 110–111; revised and emended by author.

[a] Corresponds to corporate fiscal year 1977.

[b] All exchange rates to U.S. dollars as of 1 January 1977.

[c] 1. Ethical drugs; 2. Proprietary drugs; 3. Veterinary products; 4. Vitamins and fine chemicals; 5. Nutritional products; 6. Agrochemicals; 7. Hospital and laboratory supplies and equipment.

[d] Hoechst acquired a majority interest in Roussel Uclaf (France) in 1976.

[e] Because of a lack of appropriate data in the Wellcome annual report, the percentage of ethical pharmaceutical sales to total sales was estimated using the 1973 ratio in James (1977: 249).

[f] *Chemical Insight* estimated Boehringer Mannheim's pharmaceutical sales at $353 million for 1977 in its December 1978 issue, no. 1/164. Because of lack of appropriate data, the percentage of ethical pharmaceutical sales to total sales is the 1973 ratio in James (1977: 249).

[g] Because Sterling only provides a product line breakdown of its U.S. sales, 14 percent for pharmaceuticals, the same percentage was taken of its total foreign sales of $496 million and added to the U.S. sales figure of $163 million. By this method, a conservative estimate of Sterling's worldwide pharmaceutical sales is $232 million.

[h] Estimated on the basis of figures for the first eight months as in Société de Documentation et d'Analyse Financière, S.A. (DAFSA), Analyse de Groupes, November 1977. CM refers to Clin Midy.

THE GLOBAL PHARMACEUTICAL INDUSTRY

tied to their large national market, have turned more and
more to transnational activities during the past fifteen
years. In general the degree of transnational commitment
of pharmaceutical TNCs decreases as one moves from
sales, to the formulation and packaging of drugs, to the
manufacture of active ingredients, to basic research and development.

Second, all of the TNCs on this list are diversified, with
varying interests in other industries. Strictly speaking, "pharmaceutical" refers to ethical drugs that are promoted primarily to the medical, pharmacy, or allied professions and
usually require a doctor's prescription. Available corporate
data, however, often include several other product lines in
the category of pharmaceuticals. When this is the case, Table
6.1 identifies which of the six lines most frequently merged
with ethical drugs are included in the pharmaceutical sales
figure.

The diversification of these TNCs is also evidenced by the
fact that in all cases pharmaceutical sales represent only a
portion of total company sales.[1] The proportions given in
Table 6.1 vary widely. By and large this variation is explained
by the origins of today's major drug companies. Most of the
TNCs in the industry started out either as pharmaceutical
supply houses or entered the pharmaceutical field from technologically related industries, the most important being dyestuffs and chemicals (James, 1977: 255). Almost all of the large
United States-based TNCs are pharmaceutical houses by origin, and pharmaceuticals remain their main products (e.g.,
Merck & Co., American Home Products, Warner-Lambert,
Eli Lilly, Upjohn, Squibb, Bristol-Myers, Schering-Plough,
SmithKline, G.D. Searle). The situation in Europe has been
quite different. The principal companies in Switzerland and
the Federal Republic of Germany began as manufacturers of
dyestuffs (Hoechst, Ciba-Geigy, Sandoz) and organic chemi-

---

[1] The fifty companies in Table 6.1 are ranked according to the volume
of their pharmaceutical sales only.

cals (Bayer, Hoffmann-La Roche).[2] For these enterprises and the other major chemical firms in the drug industry (Montedison, AKZO, ICI, Dow) pharmaceutical sales represent a far smaller share of total sales than tends to be the case for those companies whose initial activity was in pharmaceutical supplies.[3]

Table 6.2 shows that among the major pharmaceutical TNCs, United States-based enterprises are clearly dominant both in the number of companies and in pharmaceutical sales volume. The U.S. TNCs consistently account for just under one-half of the sales of the top 10, 25, and 50 firms in the world industry. The second and third place countries, ranked by the aggregate sales volume of their pharmaceutical TNCs, are the Federal Republic of Germany and Switzerland. Taken together these three nations account for 34 of the top 50 TNCs in the industry—23 from the United States, 8 from the

---

[2] A number of the current major German pharmaceutical TNCs— Hoechst, Bayer, Schering, E. Merck, and BASF—were affiliated with or owned by the giant conglomerate I.G. Farben prior to World War II. I.G. Farben of Germany was the largest industrial corporation in Europe and the largest chemical company in the world (see Stocking and Watkins, 1947: 411–414; Borkin, 1978). It was Gerhard Domagk's research on the bacteria-killing properties of dyestuffs for the Bayer division of I.G. Farben that produced Prontosil (sulfanilamide), the first of the remarkable new sulfa drugs (Cooper, 1970: 42–43). This success in the 1930s attracted other big chemical companies into the pharmaceutical industry since it became clear that the active ingredients of drugs would be increasingly manufactured from synthetic substances and less from materials of vegetable or animal origin. Later, after the discovery and ensuing great demand for penicillin and the other antibiotics in the 1940s and 1950s, chemical firms with experience in fermentation were led into involvement with pharmaceuticals because this microbiological technique was found the most efficient for large-scale production. The entry into the U.S. drug industry of both Pfizer and Cyanamid (Lederle) followed this latter pattern.

[3] A percentage breakdown of the nonpharmaceutical sales activities of the twenty-five top pharmaceutical TNCs is given in UNCTC (1979: 118). By way of exception it should be noted that several of the large European drug TNCs also began in the pharmaceutical supply field, most notably Glaxo and Wellcome of the United Kingdom and Boehringer Ingelheim, Boehringer Mannheim, and E. Merck of the Federal Republic of Germany.

TABLE 6.2

Pharmaceutical Sales of the Major Transnational Pharmaceutical Companies,
by Size and Nationality, 1977
(millions of U.S. dollars)

Domicile	Top 10 Companies			Top 25 Companies			Top 50 Companies		
	Number of TNCs	Value of Sales	Percentage of Sales	Number of TNCs	Value of Sales	Percentage of Sales	Number of TNCs	Value of Sales	Percentage of Sales
United States	5	5,515	48	12	9,783	48	23	12,912	48
Germany, Federal Republic of	2	2,846	24	4	4,037	20	8	5,034	18
Switzerland	3	3,230	28	3	3,230	16	3	3,230	12
Japan				1	646	3	6	1,789	7
United Kingdom				2	1,118	5	4	1,917	7
France				1	614	3	2	779	3
Other				2[a]	928	5	4[b]	1,452	5
Total	10	11,591	100	25	20,356	100	50	27,113	100

SOURCE: Derived from Table 6.1.
[a] Italy and the Netherlands.
[b] Sweden and Panama.

Federal Republic of Germany, and 3 from Switzerland—and for nearly 80 percent of total pharmaceutical sales. Transnationals from Japan and the United Kingdom are prominent among the second 25 largest drug companies, with France the only other country with more than one TNC on the list.

The degree to which the top 50 pharmaceutical TNCs are committed to sales in foreign markets is presented in Table 6.3. Because corporate data are often not sufficiently disaggregated to allow a focus on the overseas activity of pharmaceutical products only, the foreign sales proportion given for

TABLE 6.3

Foreign Sales of the Top Fifty Transnational
Pharmaceutical Companies, 1977
(foreign sales volume as a percentage of total sales volume)

Rank / Company	%	Rank / Company	%
1 / Hoechst-Roussel	67	16 / Rone Poulenc	59
2 / Merck and Co.	45	17 / Schering-Plough	43
3 / Bayer	69	18 / Glaxo	61
4 / Ciba-Geigy	98	19 / Abbott Labora-	
5 / Hoffmann-		tories	32
La Roche	90+[a]	20 / Beecham	70
6 / American Home		21 / Johnson and	
Products	31	Johnson	41
7 / Warner Lambert	43	22 / Montedison	42
8 / Pfizer	51	23 / Cyanamid	34
9 / Sandoz	95+[a]		
10 / Eli Lilly	37	24 / Schering	64
		25 / AKZO	88
11 / Upjohn	37	26 / ICI	60
12 / Boehringer		27 / SmithKline	36
Ingelheim	69	28 / Wellcome	86
13 / Squibb	33	29 / G.D. Searle	37
14 / Bristol-Myers	31		
15 / Takeda	6	30 / Baxter Travenol	31

TABLE 6.3 Cont.

Foreign Sales of the Top Fifty Transnational
Pharmaceutical Companies, 1977
(foreign sales volume as a percentage of total sales volume)

Rank / Company	%	Rank / Company	%
31 / Boehringer		41 / Sterling Drug	42
Mannheim	NA	42 / Pennwalt	20
32 / Revlon	28	43 / Syntex	45[b]
33 / Dow	45		
34 / Astra	61	44 / A.H. Robins	30
35 / Shionogi	2	45 / BASF	51
36 / Fujisawa	7	46 / Meiji Seika	3
37 / E. Merck	64	47 / CM Industries	35
38 / 3M	38	48 / Altana (formerly	
39 / Sankyo	2	Varta)	36
40 / Richardson-		49 / Miles Laboratories	29
Merrell	48	50 / Tanabe Seiyaku	6

SOURCE: United Nations Centre on Transnational Corporations, 1979: 113; revised and emended by author.
NOTE: NA = not available.
[a] Estimate.
[b] Foreign sales figure represents non-U.S. sales. Company headquarters are in Panama, but major production facilities for finished drugs are in the United States.

each firm refers to its total sales volume. Although one cannot evaluate the effect of a company's different product lines on its foreign sales performance, a couple of general observations can be made about the relationship of firm size and firm nationality to foreign sales.

First, foreign sales concentration is *not* strongly related to the size of drug TNCs, regardless of whether size is measured by pharmaceutical or by total corporate sales. The 50 firms in Table 6.3 are ranked by their pharmaceutical sales volume, and it can be seen that high and low percentages of foreign sales are distributed almost randomly throughout. Nor does a size ranking based on total corporate sales (which can be derived from Table 6.1) correspond closely to overseas sales activity. There is, however, a definite correlation between foreign sales and the home "nationality" of pharmaceutical TNCs. The Swiss and Japanese TNCs mark the extremes: the 3 Swiss enterprises all realize more than 90 percent of their sales abroad, whereas none of the 6 Japanese drug companies sell more than 7 percent of their output overseas. There is a parallel, although lesser, divergence in the foreign sales activity of the European pharmaceutical TNCs in general versus the United States-based firms. While the great majority of European companies (16 of the 20 listed in Table 6.3) obtain over 50 percent of their sales volume from outside their respective home markets, only 1 of 23 United States-based drug TNCs, Pfizer, obtains over half of its sale volume (51 percent) from outside the United States.

The key factor in explaining these results appears to be the size of the home market of the pharmaceutical TNCs and in particular the great disparity that exists between the United States and Japan (large markets), on the one hand, and individual countries in Europe (small markets), on the other. The biggest national drug markets in Europe are no more than one-third to one-half the size of those of the United States and Japan.[4] Given that any firm acquires important advantages (including government support) from operating in familiar surroundings, the TNCs quite naturally give priority to servicing their home markets before moving abroad. Because the demand for pharmaceuticals in the United States and Japan is especially great, the drug TNCs headquartered in these countries have been able to carry out a majority of their sales domestically. For the European countries with drug TNCs of

[4] The size of the world's largest drug markets in 1980 was as follows (in U.S. dollars): the United States—$14.3 billion; Japan—$9.6 billion; the Federal Republic of Germany—$6.6 billion; France—$5.0 billion; Italy—$3.1 billion; and the United Kingdom—$2.6 billion (IMSworld statistics cited in ALIFAR, 1982: 1).

comparable or greater size than those from the United States or Japan, relatively small national markets imply a much higher degree of foreign sales activity.[5]

A fuller understanding of the internationalization of the pharmaceutical industry can be gained by looking at when and where TNCs have gone abroad, in addition to where they have come from. In Table 6.4 the overseas expansion of the 25 largest U.S. pharmaceutical TNCs is presented by time period and geographical region. Before 1950 the top 25 U.S. drug companies had initially established just 28 foreign subsidiaries. The vast majority of these were located in a few geographically or culturally proximate countries: Canada, Great Britain (including the Commonwealth countries), and Mexico. During the 1950s and 1960s the pace of U.S. expansion picked up sharply, with 152 and 181 pharmaceutical subsidiaries formed in these decades respectively. In the 1950s the outward thrust was primarily directed at Western Europe, the Commonwealth countries, and the relatively advanced nations in Latin America (Mexico, Brazil, and Argentina). Finally, in the 1960s there was a surge of interest in Africa, Asia[6] and the Middle East, and the lesser developed countries of Latin America and Europe. Thus, we can infer from Table 6.4 that over time a significant shift was taking place in the international pharmaceutical industry: local production—generally based on active ingredients imported from the TNC parent—was beginning to substitute for at

[5] Nonetheless the attraction of familiar surroundings is also strong for the European companies, judging from the concentration of their exports within the Western European community. Thus, the Netherlands sells nearly 70 percent of its pharmaceutical exports to other countries in Western Europe, Switzerland and the Federal Republic of Germany about 60 percent, and Italy around 55 percent. The only European nations drawing less than half of their export revenues from Western Europe are the United Kingdom (45 percent) and France (40 percent) (UNECE, 1975).

[6] Although exact data are not available, it is known that very few foreign drug firms had located in Japan by 1970. Therefore the figures for Asia refer almost exclusively to third world countries.

TABLE 6.4
Manufacturing Subsidiaries Established by
the Twenty-Five Largest U.S. Pharmaceutical TNCs,
by Time Period and Geographical Region

Country	Establishment of First Manufacturing Plant			
	Before 1950	1950–59	1960–70	Total
Canada	10	6	4	20
Europe	7	41	64	112
European Common Market[a]	0	25	35	60
United Kingdom	7	8	3	18
Other	0	8	26	34
Australia and New Zealand	3	12	7	22
Latin America	6	65	55	126
Argentina	1	11	4	16
Brazil	0	11	3	14
Mexico	4	12	5	21
Other	1	31	43	75
Asia and the Middle East	0	21	38	59
Philippines	0	8	3	11
Other	0	13	35	48
Africa	2	7	13	22
South Africa	2	7	7	16
Other	0	0	6	6
Total	28	152	181	361

SOURCE: Katz, 1981: 62.
[a] The Federal Republic of Germany, Belgium, France, Holland, Italy, and Luxembourg.

least some of the direct importation of finished pharmaceutical products. As shall be seen below, however, the geographical distribution of drug production still remains overwhelmingly concentrated in a handful of center countries in the world system.

THE ROLE OF THIRD WORLD COUNTRIES

At the end of the 1970s the developed market-economy countries accounted for close to 70 percent of the value of world pharmaceutical production. The developed centrally planned economy countries (the Soviet Union, Eastern Europe, and China) followed with 19 percent, while the share of developing countries in the value of world pharmaceutical output was just over 11 percent[7] (UNCTC, 1981: 3–4). The geographical distribution of production shows that relatively few nations control the bulk of world output. The three largest producing countries—the United States, Japan, and the Federal Republic of Germany—together account for one-half of the world's output of pharmaceutical products. The United States alone supplies more than one-quarter of the global total. In the developing world the geographical distribution in 1977 puts Asia first with 5.6 percent of world pharmaceutical output, followed by Latin America with 5.2 percent, and Africa with only 0.5 percent. A closer look reveals that over two-thirds of third world production came from a half-dozen countries: India, Brazil, Mexico, Argentina, Egypt, and the Republic of Korea (UNIDO, 1978a; UNCTC, 1981: 4).

Most third world countries continue to depend on imports for a majority of their drug needs. The international trade of pharmaceuticals in 1977 was estimated at $8.3 billion. Developing nations imported 33 percent of the total and exported only 6 percent. Developed countries as a whole exported 94 percent and imported 67 percent. Asia and the Pacific accounted for 15 percent of world imports in 1977, Africa 10

[7] The world's pharmaceutical output in 1980 was approximately $84 billion (U.S.) (UNIDO, 1980).

percent, and Latin America 8 percent (UNCTC, 1981: 4–5). These imports come mainly from pharmaceutical TNCs in the developed market-economy countries. They consist of finished drugs, bulk drugs in final dosage form for repackaging, chemicals for dosage formulation, and chemical intermediates that require further processing.

Despite the difficulties involved, many third world nations are trying to establish local manufacturing facilities for pharmaceutical products in the hope of decreasing drug costs and increasing their self-sufficiency in the supply of drugs. Table 6.5 presents the level of development of the pharmaceutical industry in third world countries in terms of five different stages of vertical integration.[8] The countries in the first stage have no pharmaceutical manufacturing activity and therefore must rely entirely on imports of finished drugs to satisfy their health care needs. Countries classified in the second and third stages of development have the facilities to package and formulate imported bulk medicines but lack the capability to produce the latter domestically. The countries grouped in the fourth and fifth stages of pharmaceutical development are characterized by the highest degrees of vertical integration. In addition to formulating and packaging drugs, these countries manufacture a fairly broad range of active ingredients from intermediate and raw materials. The nations that have reached the fifth stage—India, Mexico, Brazil, Argentina, and Egypt—also carry out local research and development on new and adapted pharmaceutical products and processes. Overall Table 6.5 shows that the pharmaceutical industry is most developed in Latin America, less advanced in Asia and the Middle East, and least developed in Africa.

Like the extent of vertical integration, the degree of domestic ownership in third world pharmaceutical industries is

---

[8] Vertical integration may proceed either forwards (e.g., from production to distribution) or backwards (e.g., from production to raw material supply). Developing country drug industries usually vertically integrate in a backward direction, starting with packaging, moving to various kinds of dosage formulation, and ending with the manufacture of bulk drugs or intermediate chemicals.

relatively low. Table 6.6 indicates the share of national pharmaceutical sales held by domestically owned firms for
twenty-five selected countries in 1975. None of the developing nations in this table (excepting South Africa) have
levels of local control that exceed 35 percent. The strongest
domestic pharmaceutical industries (a local share of 65 percent or above), on the other hand, are found in the principal
home countries of drug TNCs: the United States, Japan, the
Federal Republic of Germany, and Switzerland. Other TNC
home countries—the United Kingdom, France, Italy, the
Netherlands, and Sweden—have moderately high local ownership levels (ranging from 55 to 40 percent) in their domestic
drug industries. For the developed market-economy countries, in other words, there is a direct relationship between
being a home base for drug TNCs and national control of the
pharmaceutical industry. Conversely, third world nations
that only host TNCs have very low levels of local control.
Pharmaceutical TNCs are seen, then, as helping the growth
of indigenous production in their home countries while frequently hindering or resisting such efforts in the third world.

A WORLD SYSTEM OVERVIEW OF THE
PHARMACEUTICAL INDUSTRY

While the dependency approach has tended to focus on the
negative effects for the third world of strong ties to center
countries, a more encompassing "world system" perspective
has been created by Immanuel Wallerstein and others that
sees all areas of the world as comprising a single ongoing division of labor. The possibilities open to a given country for
capital accumulation or development are constrained by its
structural position within this division of labor and shaped by
cyclical and secular trends in the evolution of the world system as a whole. Changes in dependency, in other words, are
thus linked to changes in a country's role within the world
economy. In describing the main structural positions of nations in the capitalist world system, both the dependency and
world system approaches use the categories of core, semi-

TABLE 6.5
Levels of Development of the Pharmaceutical Industry
in Third World Countries, 1979

Stage of Pharmaceutical Production	Africa	Latin America	Asia	Middle East
Group 1 Countries that have no manufacturing facilities and are therefore dependent upon imported pharmaceuticals in their finished form. In many of these countries there is insufficient trained personnel, limited public health services, and poor distribution channels.	Burundi Central African Republic Chad Lesotho Rwanda Sierra Leone Somalia Swaziland Togo Uganda Zambia	Honduras	Bhutan Mongolia	Yemen
Group 2 Countries that have started to repack formulated drugs and process bulk drugs into dosage forms.	Ivory Coast Kenya Madagascar Senegal Sudan Tanzania	Bolivia Costa Rica El Salvador Guatemala Haiti Trinidad & Tobago	Afghanistan Burma Malaysia Nepal Sri Lanka Vietnam	Jordan

Group 3 Countries that process a broad range of bulk drugs into dosage forms and manufacture some simple bulk drugs from intermediates.	Algeria Ghana Morocco Nigeria Tunisia	Colombia Ecuador Peru	Bangladesh Indonesia Philippines Singapore Thailand	Iran Iraq Syria
Group 4 Countries that produce a broad range of bulk drugs from intermediates and manufacture some intermediates using locally produced chemicals.		Chile Venezuela	Pakistan Republic of Korea Turkey	
Group 5 Countries that manufacture most of the intermediates required for the pharmaceutical industry and undertake local research on the development of products and manufacturing processes.	Egypt	Argentina Brazil Mexico	India	

SOURCE: United Nations Industrial Development Organization, 1978*b*: 3; revised and emended in IMSworld Publications Ltd., 1979: 40.

TABLE 6.6
Pharmaceutical Market Shares Held by Domestic and
Foreign Firms in Twenty-Five Selected Countries, 1975
(by percentage)

Country	Domestic Share	Foreign Share
Saudi Arabia	0	100
Nigeria	3	97
Belgium	10	90
Venezuela	12	88
Canada	15	85
Australia	15	85
Brazil	15	85
Indonesia	15	85
Mexico	18	82
India	25	75
Iran	25	75
Argentina	30	70
Philippines	35	65
Italy[a]	40	60
Netherlands[a]	40	60
South Africa	40	60
United Kingdom[a]	40	60
Sweden[a]	50	50
France[a]	55	45
Spain	55	45
Germany, Federal Republic of[a]	65	35
Switzerland[a]	72	28
United States[a]	85	15
Japan[a]	87	13
USSR	100	0

SOURCE: Schaumann, 1976: 13.
[a] The home country of at least one of the major pharmaceutical transnational corporations. (See Table 6.2.)

periphery, and periphery (see Wallerstein, 1974a, 1974b, 1976; Evans, 1979a, 1979b; and Gereffi and Evans, 1981).

The external and internal features that lead countries to be characterized as core, semiperiphery, and periphery are also reflected in individual industries. In many respects the global pharmaceutical industry reproduces on a smaller scale the relationships between TNCs, home and host country states, and local social classes that are an integral part of the structure and functioning of the capitalist world system today. Chapter 7 will demonstrate this by examining in some detail the dynamics of the pharmaceutical industry in the third world. What follows here is a preliminary overview of how the drug industry differs in core, semiperipheral, and peripheral nations.[9]

The core nations in the world economy are the vanguard of innovation in the pharmaceutical industry. In order for such innovation to take place these countries have relied on a strong basic chemical industry, very costly experimental and clinical research programs to develop new drugs, an extensive university network to provide a continuing supply of well-trained researchers and technicians, an advanced metal-working sector to supply necessary equipment and machines, an active and competent state regulatory apparatus to assure the quality and safety of the pharmaceuticals produced, and large high-income consumer markets to generate the demand to buy new drugs (see OECD, 1977). This situation characterizes countries such as the United States, Great Britain, Switzerland, France, the Federal Republic of Germany, and Japan. These nations (with the exception of Japan) are the primary exporters of active ingredients for pharmaceutical products, which are produced in bulk quantities and distributed internationally by TNCs or through licensing contracts.[10]

[9] This section draws from Katz (1981).

[10] There were only ten countries in the world in 1978 that exported more pharmaceutical products by value than they imported: the United States, the United Kingdom, Switzerland, the Federal Republic of Ger-

Semiperipheral countries have local drug industries that are capable of synthesizing and formulating many of the active ingredients normally used in manufacturing finished pharmaceutical products. The fermentation process for making antibiotics, for example, as well as the production of vaccines, serums, hormones, etc. are all carried out locally in the semiperiphery. Nonetheless a substantial proportion (ranging from 40 to 60 percent) of the active ingredients employed in making drugs for domestic consumption are imported. Countries that belong to the semiperiphery include India, Brazil, Mexico, Argentina, and Egypt. These nations are the most advanced in the third world in terms of pharmaceutical production (see Table 6.5). They export finished drugs and even active ingredients to less developed countries in their respective geographical spheres of influence. Some research and development is conducted locally, although it tends not to be the kind that would allow these nations to generate significant pharmaceutical innovations. The domestic industry is oligopolistic and controlled in large part by TNCs. There is a variety of local firms, many of them quite small; their technology is often licensed from international companies.

The periphery of the world economy is a very broad term that lacks the precision needed for any type of detailed inquiry. As can be seen in Table 6.5, third world nations that are not in the semiperiphery can be divided into at least four different categories in terms of the level of development of their pharmaceutical industries. For my purposes two broad groupings are sufficient. In the first bloc (corresponding roughly to groups 3 and 4 in Table 6.5) are those countries that do some synthesis and processing of basic drugs but of a rudimentary sort. The fermentation and local production of antibiotics has not yet begun. Chemical synthesis gives way to the packaging of dosage form drugs and the formulation of

many, France, the Netherlands, Denmark, Italy, Ireland, and Singapore (see UNIDO, 1978a). Two-thirds of the nonsocialist world's exports of pharmaceuticals originate from five nations: the United States, the United Kingdom, the Federal Republic of Germany, Switzerland, and France.

bulk products. Practically all of the active ingredients and many of the finished drugs consumed domestically are imported by TNCs. Locally owned pharmaceutical firms are not as prominent as in the semiperiphery, and many of those that do exist are in the state sector.

The least developed peripheral countries constitute a separate bloc (see groups 1 and 2 in Table 6.5). There is no domestic production of pharmaceuticals. All drugs consumed locally are imported. Pharmaceutical research and development is nonexistent, the university system for training technical personnel is very limited, the governmental regulatory apparatus for drugs is weak and fragmentary, and the metalworking sector is unable to produce even elementary equipment. Transnationals participate in the market only as importers. The local companies are often state-owned firms that operate primarily as purchasing agents or distribution networks, especially for the poor majority in these societies.

This overview of the global pharmaceutical industry gives an idea of how it is structured—internationally and within core, semiperipheral, and peripheral blocs of countries. These structural aspects of the industry are powerful forces in conditioning, shaping, and constraining the actions of firms, governments, and social groups, but ultimately they do not fully determine or explain behavior. To understand the kind of impact that the drug industry has had in third world nations and the response it has generated, we need to look at the interaction of TNC strategies with the political and economic strategies of local social classes and host country states.

CHAPTER SEVEN

Transnational Drug Firms and the State in Third World Countries

TRANSNATIONAL corporations and third world states have different, and possibly conflicting, objectives with regard to the pharmaceutical industry. Transnationals are concerned primarily with high profits and maintaining or expanding their market shares at the global level. Developing country states, on the other hand, want to ensure an adequate supply of safe, efficacious, and reasonably priced drugs for their people. At times the goals of TNCs and the needs of third world nations overlap; often they do not, however. Most frequently at issue are divergent and deeply held concerns about drug prices, product selection, and local control.

This chapter will address these conflicts, emergent or actual, by seeking answers to the following questions. How "appropriate" are pharmaceutical TNCs to third world needs? In what ways have third world countries moved to counteract their obvious dependency on transnational drug firms? How successful or unsuccessful have these attempts been? Is there any evidence that TNCs have altered their standard business practices to try to accommodate the specific needs of developing nations? What public policies seem most likely and advisable for the third world in the future?

THE "APPROPRIATENESS" OF TNC PERFORMANCE IN THE THIRD WORLD

The pharmaceutical industry is one of the most lucrative in the world, usually ranking first or second among all industries in profitability since the mid-1950s. In the United States and

190

the United Kingdom in the latter part of the 1960s the industry as a whole earned 21 percent and 26 percent respectively
on capital employed, as compared with 13 percent for all
manufacturing in both countries. The larger firms are considerably more profitable than these average figures would indicate. The two leading British companies in 1972, for example,
earned 45 percent (Boots) and 41 percent (Beecham) on capital employed. Only one nonpharmaceutical company, Rank
Xerox, was more profitable than Boots and Beecham among
the top one hundred British firms in that year. In the 1960s
and 1970s the United States drug enterprises frequently
earned over 40 and even 50 percent profits as a percentage of
net worth.

The profit rates of pharmaceutical TNCs in the third world
are often higher than in the developed countries. Declared
profits on capital employed for three TNC subsidiaries
operating in Egypt in 1967 came to 115 percent for Hoechst,
53 percent for Pfizer, and 52 percent for a Swiss consortium.
In India thirty-three foreign-controlled drug companies
earned 30 percent on capital employed in 1969–1970 as compared to 8 percent for almost two thousand Indian manufacturing public limited firms.[1] Hoffmann-La Roche was one of
the most profitable of the TNCs in India, with its declared
pretax profits in 1968 amounting to over 65 percent of net
worth and over 60 percent of capital employed (Lall, 1975a:
28; Silverman and Lee, 1974: 331).

The persistence over an extended period of time of high
profit rates for the pharmaceutical industry generally is considered a direct consequence of its favorable institutional
context. High barriers to the entry of new competitors
created by patents and trademarked brand names, substantial
seller concentration in therapeutic markets,[2] the captive na-

[1] Deolalikar (1980: 76) found that within the foreign sector of the Indian
pharmaceutical industry TNC subsidiaries made substantially higher profits than did joint ventures with minority foreign participation.
[2] Schwartzman (1976: 131) reports four-firm concentration ratios for

ture of the consumer,[3] and the traditional price insensitivity of doctors are all grounds to expect that the rate of return in pharmaceuticals, even after accounting adjustments,[4] will be considerably above the all-manufacturing average. Profitability measures per se do not provide good grounds for judging TNC appropriateness, however. Locally owned companies as well as TNCs may share in the pharmaceutical industry's high profitability. In addition, if the risks and potential contribution of the industry are great, high profits may be justified as a fitting reward for superior performance. The real appropri-

---

nine major therapeutic categories in the United States in 1973 that range from a low of 61 percent (sedatives) to highs of 96 percent (antiarthritic drugs) and 98 percent (antidiabetic drugs).

[3] In the words of the aphorism made famous by the late U.S. Senator Estes Kefauver, "He who orders [the doctor] does not pay; he who pays does not order."

[4] There are some who claim that the high profitability of the pharmaceutical companies is really little more than an accounting illusion created in large part by the standard accounting practice of treating research and development outlays as expenses against current income rather than capitalizing this item as an investment asset ("Foreword" by Yale Brozen, in Clarkson, 1977: 1–17; Schwartzman, 1976: 155–161). The accounting explanation of high profitability in the drug industry is inadequate for several reasons. First, the accounting bias referred to is characteristically large in all "discovery-intensive" industries (such as pharmaceuticals, oil, and gas), with the overstatement of profitability tending to increase with the intensity of the research and development effort. Under certain circumstances the so-called accounting rate of return can *understate* the "real" or economic rate of return (Stauffer, 1975: 110–113). Second, declared profit figures for pharmaceutical TNCs in many third world countries are likely to be artificially depressed by the transfer-pricing mechanism. Third, by allowing pharmaceutical companies to treat research and development as a current accounting expense, the government in effect is granting them an indirect fiscal subsidy to encourage their risk-taking efforts. This accounting method thus serves to raise the drug firm's profitability in fact as well as on paper. Finally, the accounting explanation of high pharmaceutical profits is misleading because it totally ignores the institutional context that grants substantial market power to the leading drug firms. Whatever the risks in the pharmaceutical industry, its high and steady growth rate strongly suggests that the net returns have more than offset them.

ateness issues for third world countries, then, center on more detailed manifestations of TNC performance. Are their drug prices fair? Are their products and technologies the ones most in need? Are their marketing practices informative and consistent? I will examine each of these questions in turn.

Appropriate Prices

Finished drug prices vary considerably from country to country. In 1967, for example, one hundred 5-mg. tablets of Schering's Meticorten were listed at $22.70 in Canada, $17.90 in the United States, $12.26 in Mexico City, $12.20 in Italy, $7.70 in Australia, $5.30 in Brazil, and $4.37 in Switzerland (Silverman and Lee, 1974: 178, 336–337). Although wide-ranging international differences in finished drug prices are common, a simple explanation of these differences is hard to come by. Since American and Canadian prices for prescription products tend to be the highest in the world, while prices in many third world countries are relatively low, it is sometimes argued that drug prices are likely to be less in the lower income countries. This does not tell us why Bristol's Polycillin was priced at $41.95 in Brazil and $21.84 in the United States, however, or why Ciba's Serpasil was priced at $3.00 in Mexico and at $1.24 or less in well-to-do Switzerland and the Federal Republic of Germany (Silverman and Lee, 1974: 179). Relatively low drug prices prevail in the United Kingdom, Ireland, and New Zealand, but in these cases institutional factors (e.g., national health systems) appear to have increased the willingness of the drug industry to bargain with the countries. Among the other factors that might affect the price of pharmaceuticals in different nations one can mention the size of markets, currency problems, different wage scales, taxes, costs of raw materials, living costs, allocation of research costs, and government regulations. In terms of a generalization, though, the most elemental one still seems the best:

TABLE 7.1
Relative Wholesale Prices of Librium and Valium, 1975
(in U.S. dollars)

Country	Librium[a]	Valium[b]	Price of Librium[c]	Price of Valium[c]
United Kingdom	$0.83	$0.63	100	100
Germany, Federal Republic of	4.38	5.35	528	849
Switzerland	4.75	5.44	572	908
United States	5.80	6.89	699	1,093
Mexico[d]	4.42	6.03	532	957
Costa Rica[d]	7.03	9.13	847	1,449

SOURCES: de María y Campos, 1977: 899; Alfaro Lara et al., 1977: 946.
[a] For 100 10-mg. capsules.
[b] For 100 5-mg. tablets.
[c] As percentages of the U.K. price.
[d] Data are for 1976.

drug prices in different countries tend to be set at the highest level the traffic will bear.[5]

Evidence indicating how the cost of two specific drugs varies internationally is presented in Table 7.1. Librium and Valium are produced by the Swiss TNC Hoffmann-La Roche. It can be seen that the prices of these two products range widely from one country to another, being lowest in the United Kingdom because the national health system in that country negotiates the prices for drugs in a centralized man-

[5] Data compiled by Brooke (1975) on the U.S. antibiotics market show that drug prices within the United States also are set at the highest level the traffic will bear. For eight major multisource antibiotic drugs, Brooke found that high-priced branded products dominated the U.S. market despite the fact that good quality generic drugs were available from a variety of sellers at prices far below those of the dominant firms. Usually the most expensive of the brand-named drugs held the biggest share of the market!

ner and buys in bulk quantities. What is surprising and deleterious from a third world viewpoint is that Mexico and Costa Rica pay more for Librium and Valium than do rich nations like the Federal Republic of Germany, Switzerland, or the United States.

Whereas international differences in *finished* drug prices are a feature of the pharmaceutical industry as a whole, the differential pricing of drug *intermediates* is a problem specifically related to the behavior of TNCs. This practice is known as transfer pricing. Transfer prices are those prices set for intrafirm sales between TNC affiliates located in different countries. When these intrafirm prices are higher than the arm's-length price used in selling to unrelated concerns, the goods in question are "overpriced" and extra funds are transferred via the pricing channel from the buying to the selling units. Conversely, "underpricing" transfers additional funds from the seller to the buyer within a single company's transnational network. Whereas this procedure does not directly affect the level of profits made in each country by the TNC, it does affect where and how these profits are to be declared.

Transfer pricing is more common and the gap between transfer and arm's-length prices is more egregious in the pharmaceutical industry than in any other. This is principally due to both the large volume and the highly specialized nature of the intermediates that account for most of the intrafirm trade in the industry (Lall, 1979a: 63). The main measures to keep transfer-pricing problems in check have been initiated by the developed countries.[6] The considerable

[6] The United States and Canada are beginning joint audits of a number of TNCs (including many drug companies), and the fiscal authorities of various European countries are also coordinating their activities. One tactic used by developed countries with fully or partially government-funded health-care systems is to focus attention on individual products with big sales volumes that are of major fiscal importance to these systems. This principle motivated the cartel offices of the United Kingdom and the Federal Republic of Germany to file suits against Hoffmann-La Roche for its alleged overpricing of Librium and Valium in the early 1970s. It was charged that the high prices paid by the Swiss TNC's U.K. and West Ger-

CROSS-NATIONAL DEPENDENCY ANALYSIS

amount of information now available on the transfer pricing of pharmaceuticals in the third world, however, shows that this practice may be stronger, more persistent, and more detrimental to host country interests there than for developed countries.[7]

Examples of transfer pricing in third world nations are numerous. Colombia is one of the best documented cases. The Colombian government estimated that the weighted average of overpricing for a wide range of pharmaceutical imports in the late 1960s was between 87 and 155 percent depending on the items and time period covered (Lall, 1973: 186). For individual products the degree of overpricing is often astonishingly high. Diazepam, the active ingredient for Valium, was imported into Colombia at a price that exceeded its lowest available price elsewhere by 6,400 percent (Vaitsos, 1974); in Argentina imported diazepam was overpriced by 1,500 percent (Katz, 1974: 33). Another study of Argentina found the prices of drugs in eight submarkets to be 143 to 3,800 percent higher than the minimum import prices for these same products in the same country. The rate of overpricing was particularly high for antibiotics (650 percent), vitamins (730 percent), and sera (3,800 percent) (Krieger and Prieto, 1977: 193). A parliamentary inquiry in Brazil found several in-

---

man subsidiaries to their parent company in Basel were designed to transfer untaxed profits out of the United Kingdom and the Federal Republic of Germany into Switzerland. The West German cartel office ordered price cuts of 35 and 40 percent on Librium and Valium, respectively; the U.K. Monopolies Commission similarly ordered Hoffmann-La Roche to reduce its United Kingdom selling prices by 60 percent for Librium and 75 percent for Valium and in addition to reimburse the health services system for past excessive profits made on these products. Compromise settlements were reached in both cases (James, 1977: 139–144).

[7] Among the characteristics of third world nations that generally induce TNCs to overprice imports and declare their profits elsewhere are the following: exchange controls; profit ceilings (as in India); profit remittance ceilings (as in Colombia); unstable currencies; political instability; tax rates that, although frequently lower than those prevailing in developed countries, are high relative to those in tax havens; and strong local pressures for industry nationalization.

TRANSNATIONAL DRUG FIRMS AND THE STATE

stances of overpricing ranging from 500 to 1,000 percent of arm's-length prices (Ledogar, 1975: 54). And in Mexico, as we saw in Table 5.2, the average rate of overpricing for five steroid hormone imports varied from 214 percent to just under 2,900 percent.[8]

Although host country governments have usually assumed primary responsibility for keeping transfer pricing problems in check, Deolalikar (1980: 86–87) has argued that the best monitors of transfer pricing may be indigenous entrepreneurs interested in local production, and not host government agencies. In his detailed study of India he found evidence that foreign drug companies frequently misrepresented the costs of raw material imports and also the capital cost of putting up the plant for manufacturing the product in question.[9] It was only when an indigenous enterprise prepared a feasibility plan for the production of the same drug, especially if it was being manufactured for the first time in India, that the TNCs' overinvoicing came to light.[10]

Overall, the evidence indicates that TNCs have engaged in

[8] For additional instances of transfer pricing in third world countries see Lall, 1975a: 29–30; Agarwal, 1978: 41–42; and Deolalikar, 1980: 83–84.

[9] Deolalikar's work is part of a larger project entitled "The Political Economy of Science and Technology in North-South Relations: A Study of U.S.-Indian Science and Technology Relations," directed by Ward Morehouse and Brijen Gupta of the Council on International and Public Affairs.

[10] In the case of a particular bulk drug used in the treatment of heart disease a local firm submitted a stage-by-stage cost analysis of its proposed manufacturing process to the government so that the latter could fix a fair selling price for the final product. The local firm indicated a capital cost of putting up the plant of about 25,000 U.S. dollars. Government inspectors then realized that they had already allowed a selling price to the single TNC producing the drug in India that was based on a capital cost of plant and equipment of $1,187,000. The TNC had been importing the basic raw material for this drug from its parent company at approximately $490 per kilogram, whereas the international price of the *finished* product was about $30 per kilogram. Realizing its mistake, the Indian government reduced the previous maximum price allowed the TNC and brought it down to the level of the price allowed the local firm once it began manufacturing the product (Deolalikar, 1980: 84). This demonstrates one of the key advantages of a technologically capable and informed indigenous sector.

197

highly questionable pricing practices. The wide international price differences that have been mentioned are not necessarily related to countries' income levels, as one might expect, and transfer pricing by TNCs has systematically diverted pharmaceutical revenues from many third world markets. The behavior of transnationals, then, has definitely raised drug prices in third world societies well above what would be expected from arm's-length transactions between truly competitive firms in the world industry.

Appropriate Products and Technologies

The "appropriateness" of pharmaceutical products will be assessed according to two criteria: 1) their effectiveness in reducing the mortality and morbidity rates in a nation, and 2) the degree to which the distribution of pharmaceutical sales by therapeutic groups matches the disease pattern in a country. Whereas the first criterion relates to the industry's efficacy, the second refers to social equity since it determines whether the industry supplies goods demanded by the majority of the population. "Appropriate" technology will be defined as technology that uses inputs (labor, capital, or raw materials) in the same proportion as they are found in the local economy (e.g., it uses more labor relative to capital in a labor-abundant, capital-scarce economy).

Unquestionably, new drugs have greatly increased the social and economic well-being of almost all countries. Drug therapy has contributed substantially to economic productivity through lives saved and increased work time on the job. The avoidance or reduction of costly hospital stays, surgery, and physician attention has meant major savings in medical care expenses for individuals as well as governments (see PMA, 1976: 9–18). The cost of prescription medicines, however, is usually the smallest component in the total health-care expenditures of a nation. Analysis of disease trends shows that the environment—food, water, and air—is the primary determinant of the state of overall health of any population (see Illich, 1976: 7–12; Silverman and Lee, 1974: 6–15). With nearly three-quarters of the world's population lacking any form of permanent access to health care, and with 90 percent of the rural population in developing countries (excluding China) not even within walking distance (10 kilometers) of national health facilities of any kind (Agarwal, 1978: 65), the most efficient policy for many third world nations is to focus on primary or preventive health care, with particular emphasis on better nutrition, adequate and safe water supplies, and improved sanitation. The developed countries, although by no means totally free of sickness-producing environmental problems,[11] rely far more heavily on a curative approach to health care premised on continuous drug innovation and regular access to medical practitioners.

Third world nations differ from the developed countries not only in their reduced capability to utilize new drugs in national health care but also in the specific kinds of medicine most needed by their respective populations (see McDermott, 1980). In Pakistan, for instance, systemic antibiotics account for 25 percent of all drugs sold through retail pharmacies; the next most popular therapeutic class is vitamins, with 13 percent of drugstore sales. Systemic antibiotics are also the most widely used class of drugs in the Philippines (19 percent of retail pharmacy sales), Brazil (14 percent), and Venezuela (14 percent). The next largest therapeutic categories in each of these countries are vitamins and cough and cold preparations. In the United States, on the other hand, the leading therapeutic classes of drugs are psycholeptics (tranquilizers/sedatives) and analgesics (pain relievers); in the Federal Republic of Germany the two top drug categories are cardiac therapy and psycholeptics, followed by peripheral vasodilators. Systemic antibiotics account for only 7 percent of drugstore sales in the United States and 4 percent in the Federal Republic of

[11] The environmental problems of most concern to health officials in developed countries today include the safe elimination of toxic wastes, the long-range effects on humans of chemical additives in food, and the threat of radioactive fallout from nuclear power plants.

Germany. The disparities between developing and developed countries in types of drug consumption are even more striking when absolute figures are the basis of the comparison. All of Latin America together, for example, consumes a smaller quantity of antidiabetic drugs than Holland. India consumes only 0.1 percent as many antihypertensive drugs as are used in Belgium, although both drug markets are of roughly equal size. The differences are sharper still when the industrialized countries are compared with Africa (Tiefenbacher, 1979: 213–214).

When these consumption figures are joined with data on disease patterns and the local production of drugs, it becomes clear that third world countries are being supplied with a very inappropriate assortment of products by the pharmaceutical industry. The case of India, which has what is probably the third world's most sophisticated drug industry, affords a good illustration of the problem. The most prevalent diseases in India are primarily parasitic (filariasis, malaria, and dysentery), with leprosy and tuberculosis also being very common. The distribution of pharmaceutical sales by therapeutic group reveals a totally different set of priorities, however. Vitamins, cough and cold preparations, and tonics and health restorers account for nearly one-fourth of the total sales of pharmaceuticals in India.[12] Of the fifteen leading pharmaceutical products by sales in the Indian market during 1978, two facts are noteworthy: 1) there was not a single product on the list used in the treatment of filariasis, dysentery, or leprosy, and 2) ten of the fifteen products were manufactured by subsidiaries of TNCs[13] (Deolalikar, 1980: 64–65).

[12] In Sri Lanka over half the production of the seven private companies that controlled the local industry in 1972 consisted of vitamin preparations, cough remedies, and soluble aspirin. Five of these companies were TNC subsidiaries, and the other two were manufacturing under license from them (Agarwal, 1978: 38).

[13] The situation in Tanzania is similar. Whereas the five patented drugs used most frequently for the treatment of tropical diseases amounted to only 2.6 percent of the national drug budget, sales of Valium and Serenace (a tranquilizer) alone represented more than 3 percent of the drug budget (Yudkin, 1980: 467).

Installed capacities for many important drugs in India are far below licensed capacities. The actual utilization of the installed capacity is still less: only 12 percent for antileprosy drugs, 14 percent for thiacetazone (an antituberculosis drug), and 50 percent for insulin. For nonessential items such as tonics and vitamins, on the other hand, production in several Indian firms greatly exceeds (sometimes by a factor of ten) the licensed capacities (Agarwal, 1978: 39).

Why do pharmaceutical firms fail to provide adequate production capacity for essential drugs needed by a majority of the population in third world nations like India? The principal explanation for this phenomenon relates to the highly unequal distribution of income in these countries. Since middle-income and rich consumers represent the main market for modern drugs, pharmaceutical companies concentrate on furnishing remedies for middle-class ailments like general fatigue, headaches, and constipation rather than for low-income diseases like leprosy, filariasis, and tuberculosis (Deolalikar, 1980: 67). This disparity of attention is reflected in the allocation of TNC research funds as well. Less than 5 percent of the overall research and development effort of the U.S. pharmaceutical industry is directed toward the health problems of the third world, and the amount is growing smaller (Sarett, 1979: 134–135; Wescoe, 1979). Research priorities of the TNCs, like those of developed country governments and foundations, are clearly oriented toward the major maladies of the industrialized societies: cancer, heart disease, mental illness, and neurological disorders.[14] Another reason why drug companies do not cater to the needs of the poor may lie in the fact that there are strict price controls on "essential drugs" in many nations, which greatly reduces the profitability of these items.

A final factor, which is cultural in nature, is required to un-

[14] The World Health Organization has estimated that total world expenditures on tropical disease research are approximately thirty million U.S. dollars per year. This is about 2 percent of the sum spent annually on cancer research alone (see Yudkin, 1980: 473).

derstand why the variety of pharmaceutical products made and sold in the third world is often inappropriate. In an important sense modern medicine not only treats disease, it also "creates" it. This is not a reference to doctor-caused injuries through malpractice, or the overuse of certain prescription drugs or their potentially dangerous side effects, although these all are important problems in the developed and developing countries alike. Disease-creation as a cultural phenomenon refers to the ways in which medical institutions create more illness by redefining normal human experiences such as pain and anxiety as sickness. This "medicalization of life" has weakened individual autonomy and the capacity of people to "suffer their reality"[15] (see Illich, 1976; Mendelsohn, 1979; Renaud, 1975). Third world nations have been encouraged to adopt these western *dis*-eases in large part through the promotional machinery of pharmaceutical TNCs who make and market the remedies. The overwhelming attention that the pharmaceutical industry has given to middle-class ailments and specialized diseases of the rich supports the big-city orientation common in third world health services in which 80 percent of the national health expenditure goes for the needs of just 20 percent of the population (Agarwal, 1978: 65).

With respect to technology the preference of pharmaceutical TNCs for wholly owned operations in the third world with only a minimal amount of technology transfer and centralized research and development is well known. Deolalikar (1980) found that foreign firms in the Indian pharmaceutical industry were more capital-intensive and less labor-intensive than local firms. Since labor is more abundantly available than capital in the Indian economy, this pattern is in direct contrast to the country's relative factor endowments and TNCs can thus be regarded as socially inefficient in this context. This study also found that when foreign technology is transferred to India, indigenous companies are more likely to

[15] For an interesting discussion of why the new politics of "therapeutic nihilism" may be counterproductive for the poor see Starr (1976).

adapt and modify the technology for local use than TNCs are. These conclusions are supported by evidence from other third world countries as well (see Lall, 1975a; Agarwal, 1978; UNCTC, 1983).

The local production of pharmaceuticals, including active ingredients, is by no means beyond the reach of many of the third world nations, however. It is relatively easy to decentralize drug production. Since the manufacture of the active ingredients usually takes place in a number of discrete steps, it is possible to carry out certain stages at one location and the remainder at another. The active ingredient may then be dispatched to a third point for conversion into dosage-form medicines. The volumes involved are small and transport costs are low, which further aids the dispersing of production (OECD, 1977: 49). This is perhaps the main reason why the problem of TNC transfer pricing is more widespread in the pharmaceutical industry than in almost any other. Additional evidence for the decentralizability of drug manufacture comes from the fact that most TNCs maintain one bulk plant in the United States and one abroad, mainly to overcome regulatory barriers against drug exports from the United States.

Within third world countries the growing use of small-scale multipurpose drug plants may diminish the importance of scale economies in basic drug manufacture.[16] UNIDO, for example, is establishing a multipurpose unit in Cuba for the production of fifteen drugs at a cost of about $500,000 (U.S.). Two of India's largest drug companies (Sarabhai Chemicals and the state firm Indian Drugs and Pharmaceuticals Limited) have multipurpose plants; other third world nations including Mexico, Brazil, Egypt, Sri Lanka, and Libya either

[16] Not all drugs can be produced in a single plant. Multipurpose production is only possible when a group of pharmaceuticals is made through similar processes involving common intermediates and using common equipment with minor variations. All sulfa drugs, for instance, can be produced by the same plant, as can a wide range of synthetic drugs such as aspirin, phenacetin, paracetamol, and lodocain.

have multipurpose drug units already or are planning to set them up (Agarwal, 1978: 47–48). The higher costs likely to result from many of these multipurpose plants could be offset by foreign exchange savings as well as by increased local employment opportunities.

Finally, appropriate technologies also should take advantage of a nation's raw materials that can be used in drug manufacture. Third world countries possess many such raw materials, including a wide variety of herbs and plants and animal by-products. The problem has been that these products typically are underutilized from a national point of view because TNCs with the relevant technology usually have chosen to limit manufacture at third world raw material sites to intermediate chemicals at best, with the finished pharmaceutical products to be made at a central plant in the developed countries. This puts some developing countries in the awkward position of importing high-priced medicines that they had previously exported in an intermediate stage because they lack the appropriate technology, and TNCs lack the will, to manufacture the end product locally. A good example of this seen in Chapter 4 was Mexico's inability to acquire fermentation technology to manufacture finished steroid hormone products although its raw material base of barbasco had already made the country a world leader at the level of bulk intermediates.

Overall, one would have to conclude that the products and technologies of the pharmaceutical industry have been far more "appropriate" to the capabilities and needs of the developed countries than they have been to the third world. The imposition of consumption patterns and even specific maladies derived from the middle and upper classes of the industrial societies has served to retard the development of an effective strategy of preventive health care that would meet the needs of the low-income majority in third world nations. In several areas TNC performance was shown to be less efficacious than that of comparable domestic firms.

Appropriate Marketing

The pharmaceutical industry is composed of two distinct sectors: the proprietary drug sector and the ethical drug sector.[17] Proprietary drugs (e.g., aspirin, oral antiseptics) are considered safe for self-medication if package instructions are followed, while ethical drugs generally cannot be purchased without a physician's signature. Since the proprietary drugs are advertised directly to the consuming public and do not require a prescription, the consumer himself makes the buying decision for this class of medicines. In the ethical drug sector where a doctor's prescription is required, the buying decision in the developed countries is made for the consumer by a doctor. The pharmacist typically has been obliged to fill the prescription exactly as it is written. From the consumer's point of view the main criticism made of this situation is that doctors tend to be insensitive to price differences between substitutable drugs.

The situation is different in most of the third world where, although a doctor's prescription may be legally required, many patients commonly and openly obtain these products directly from a pharmacist or an untrained pharmacist's assistant without a prescription of any kind. This system of "self-medication" flourishes not only in the large urban drug supermarkets but also in rural areas and small villages where there may be few or even no health professionals available. Frequently the poorest segments of the population who have little money to buy medicines, much less pay for a doctor's consultation, rely most heavily on the pharmacist's advice, or that of relatives and friends, or the directions given in the package leaflets on how to take the drug and what danger signs to watch for. Under these circumstances the information

[17] In the United States ethical drugs represent about 75 percent of all drugs sold for human consumption, while proprietary medicines account for the remaining 25 percent (Measday, 1977: 256). Pharmaceuticals sold for veterinary use are a growing market, reaching nearly 6 percent of total ethical sales of U.S. drug TNCs in 1977 (PMA, 1978: 2).

that pharmaceutical companies release in standard medical reference manuals and in package inserts or labeling material becomes especially important in determining the situations in which a prescription drug will be used since this information often reaches people with little or no medical knowledge against which to evaluate promotional claims.

Competition of various sorts exists in the pharmaceutical industry, and it is often intense. The exact nature of the competition differs from one country or therapeutic market to another—ranging from new product rivalry to promotional rivalry to price rivalry (or combinations thereof)—depending upon such characteristics as the state of technology, the existence of patents, the power of brand names, and the role of government policy. In general, though, competition in pharmaceuticals is based on the development of new products and on promotion. The degree of price rivalry to be found is still quite limited.[18]

Product rivalry and promotional rivalry in the pharmaceutical industry are closely linked by the workings of patent and brand-name systems. When a new product is developed by a drug manufacturer, it is normally patented and given a trademarked brand name. The assigned function of a patent is to stimulate inventive activity by impeding the imitation of a new product by granting it a period of legally sanctioned monopoly (e.g., seventeen years in the United States, sixteen in the United Kingdom, and seven in India), thereby allowing the innovating firm the opportunity to recoup, or more than recoup, its investment. Often the patent system is only partially successful in forestalling competitors, however. Patents do not preclude the development of duplicative ("me-too") drugs that achieve similar therapeutic ends by means of minor chemical modifications. Furthermore, a patented prod-

[18] The significance of price competition in the drug industry may increase, however, with 1) the continuing expiration of patents for large-selling drugs, 2) the expanded role of the government in both developed and less-developed countries as a principal buyer in the industry, and 3) the declining rate of drug innovation, should it persist.

uct can be licensed to other manufacturers, which can minimize the competitive barrier of the patent itself.

In these situations and others the product brand-name system serves as a critical complement to the patent system. In their positive effects for the drug industry the two systems are similar: they both insulate the major drug companies from price competition. The advantage of the brand-name system is that a brand name may be effective where a patent is not—e.g., for products that cannot be patented, or that are freely licensed, or for which the patent has expired. The brand-name system thus is the foundation of the drug industry's extensive promotional activity, just as the patent system is the cornerstone of its intense research activity. At one level drug promotion is meant to provide doctors with essential scientific information about a wide variety of new products. In addition to this educational purpose, however, the goal of each top pharmaceutical enterprise's promotional program is to gain and maintain market dominance for its products through the creation of strong and lasting brand-name preferences among prescribing physicians and the consuming public alike.

The brand-name system produces a bewildering array of different names for the same drug. For the 700 separate drugs available in the United States, there exist an estimated 20,000 names (Brooke, 1975: 19)—an average of 30 names for each prescription product.[19] The situation is similar in other nations. The number of pharmaceutical brand names registered in various countries in 1974 is as follows: Argentina, 17,000; Belgium, 9,000; Brazil, 14,000; Canada, 17,000; Colombia, 15,000; the Federal Republic of Germany, 24,000; France, 8,500; India, 15,000; Iran, 4,200; Italy, 21,000; Japan, 17,400; and the United Kingdom, 9,000 (UNCTAD, 1977b: 50–51). This proliferation of product presentations has greatly in-

[19] For example, there are forty different brands of tetracycline hydrochloride: Achromycin, Panmycin, Cyclopar, Tetracyn, Sumycin, Robitet, Bristacycline, Kesso-Tetra, Rexamycin, Ro-Cycline, SK-Tetracycline, Tetramax, Tetra-Co, Tet-Cy, Zemycin, etc.

creased the utility of familiar brand names to the physician. Since there are too many drugs to permit a systematic evaluation of quality and price alternatives, doctors probably find it rational to learn about and work with only a few well-promoted brands.

The amount of money spent on product differentiation[20] in the pharmaceutical industry is extraordinary. The drug industry in the United States, the Federal Republic of Germany, Italy, South Africa, Belgium, and Canada annually spends in excess of 20 percent of its total sales on product promotion. The United Kingdom, France, and Sweden are in the 15 to 18 percent range, as are developing nations like India, Turkey, and Indonesia (Slatter, 1977: 102). The absolute level of promotional expenditure in the United States' drug industry in 1978, for example, was $2.05 billion, based on total U.S. human-dosage ethical pharmaceutical sales in that year of $9.34 billion (PMA, 1978: iii). About 55 percent of the U.S. promotional effort was allocated to supporting 26,500 "detail men" who called on 200,000 private practice doctors (about 40,000 of whom are general practitioners) and 7,000 hospitals (Slatter, 1977: 101). It is clear that for a firm to be successful in the pharmaceutical industry as it is currently structured, it must be prepared to build up a large force of sales representatives to visit physicians, pharmacists, and hospital purchasing agents and in addition to expend nearly again as much money on journal advertising, exhibits at conventions, and varied public relations campaigns.

The role of detail men in the pharmaceutical industry in

[20] The term product differentiation refers to the collection of efforts undertaken by companies to make products distinguishable from one another in the marketplace. Product differentiation expenditures include: 1) research and development of the "molecular modification" type usually intended to create duplicative or "me-too" drugs that offer the physician and patient no real clinical advantages over existing products yet are different enough to win a patent, 2) the heavy promotional expenditures of the major drug enterprises aimed at prescribing physicians, and 3) the development of a trademark or brand-name system, which helps generate demand at the level of medical or retail advertising.

Latin America is even more prominent than it is in the United States. Whereas in the United States there is one detail man for every eight to ten doctors, in Ecuador the ratio is about one to eight, in Colombia one to five, and in Mexico, Brazil, and Guatemala there is one detail man for every three physicians (Silverman, 1976: 122). Furthermore, the average detail man in these countries makes a bigger income in salary and commission than does the average doctor.

The drug promotion of TNCs in Latin America has been the subject of detailed investigations (Silverman, 1976; Ledogar, 1975: 25–51). The most systematic and influential research is Silverman's (1976) survey conducted on the promotion of forty different prescription drug products marketed in the United States and Latin America by twenty-three TNCs from the United States, Switzerland, the Federal Republic of Germany, and France. Striking differences were found in the manner in which the identical drug, marketed by a single global company, was described to physicians in the United States and to physicians in Latin America. In the United States the listed indications (or diseases for which a drug is recommended) were usually few in number, while the contraindications, warnings, and potential adverse reactions were given in extensive detail. In Latin America the listed indications were far more numerous, while the hazards were usually minimized, glossed over, or totally ignored.[21] In at

[21] The extent of these differences is evident in the case of the antibiotic chloramphenicol. In the United States chloramphenicol is promoted only for a few life-threatening infections like typhoid fever, Rocky Mountain spotted fever, and certain types of meningitis. Physicians are warned that use of chloramphenicol may result in serious or fatal aplastic anemia and other blood disorders. Latin American doctors, however, are told that the indications for chloramphenicol include not only such diseases as typhoid fever but also tonsillitis, pharyngitis, whooping cough, abscesses, gonorrhea, pneumonia, and ulcerative colitis. In general few or no warnings or adverse reactions are disclosed (Silverman, 1976: 10–11, 13–15). In Brazil a combination of chloramphenicol and tetracycline marketed by a Dow Chemical subsidiary named Lepetit is indicated in the package insert for the treatment of more than eighty different conditions (Ledogar, 1975: 19).

least four of the Latin American countries—Colombia, Honduras, Panama, and El Salvador—such promotion was in clear violation of national law requiring full disclosure of contraindications.

These promotional differences were not simply between the United States, on the one hand, and all the Latin American nations, on the other, however. There were substantial differences in how global enterprises described the same drug product to physicians *within* Latin America. A TNC marketing a prescription drug frequently told one story about it in Mexico, a different one in Guatemala, and gave still other versions in Ecuador, Colombia, or Brazil. If there were corporate or national patterns or policies to account for these variations, they were not readily discernible. This would appear to invalidate, therefore, one of the most widely used industry defenses for differences in promotion: namely, that these reflect "honest differences in opinion" between regulators in the exceptionally stringent U.S. Food and Drug Administration and regulators elsewhere. A second point that should be emphasized with respect to the findings of this study is that Latin America has not been singled out for such treatment by TNCs.[22] At least in the case of chloramphenicol similar differences also are found in non-third world nations such as France, Italy, Spain, Australia, and New Zealand (Silverman, 1976: 107). A third fact worth noting is that most Latin American countries have laws requiring that any drug

---

[22] In Tanzania two temperature-lowering analgesics (or pain killers)—aminopyrine and dipyrone—are contained in thirty-four different ethical drugs listed in the 1978 edition of the *African Monthly Index of Medical Specialties*, a reference book financed by the pharmaceutical industry and sent free of charge to all doctors. The stated indications included toothache and menstrual cramps (dysmenorrhea), even though in the United States these drugs are recommended for use only in patients with terminal malignant disease when safer antipyretics have proven unsuccessful. It is calculated that one out of every 175 people who take these drugs will die as a result, yet enough of the two compounds was prescribed in Tanzania in 1976 to give a five-day course of treatment to 117,000 patients (Yudkin, 1980: 461).

product which is imported must be approved for marketing in the "country of origin." Yet certain prescription pharmaceuticals originally introduced in the United States but later taken off the market by FDA orders—e.g., fixed-ratio antibiotic products—continue to be imported and sold in Latin America. The solution for transnational firms has been simple: the U.S.-based TNC needs only to set up a plant to produce the drug or put it in finished dosage form in Nation X (which is not the United States), get approval for marketing from obliging Nation X officials, and then ship the drug throughout Latin America with Nation X listed as the "country of origin." A similar device has been used by European TNCs with drugs that had to be withdrawn from the European market as ineffective or excessively dangerous (Silverman, 1976: 117).

It appears that the problem of excessive claims and suppressed adverse reactions for prescription drugs might be overcome in Latin America through action by the pharmaceutical TNCs themselves, spurred on no doubt by the publicity this topic has received. Several months after Silverman's *The Drugging of the Americas* (1976) was published, the council of the International Federation of Pharmaceutical Manufacturers Associations adopted a resolution submitted by the United States delegation calling for prescription product labeling to be consistent with "the body of scientific and medical evidence pertaining to that product." Special care was to be taken in appropriately communicating "essential information as to medical products' safety, contraindications and side effects." By 1977 it was evident that some TNCs had already altered their promotion by limiting claims and disclosing hazards in the labeling of some products (Silverman, 1977: 166).

In summary, the marketing techniques of pharmaceutical TNCs are often wasteful and excessive, as many of their product differentiation expenditures show, and unfortunately they can also be dangerous to the health of malinformed drug users. These "inappropriate" marketing practices are a direct

211

result of the TNCs' global profit maximizing orientation whereby demand creation takes precedence over efficiency and continuing sales of existing products abroad makes sense even if there is good reason to believe this is unsafe for the consumer.

PHARMACEUTICAL TNCs AND STATE DEVELOPMENT STRATEGIES IN SELECTED THIRD WORLD COUNTRIES

The pharmaceutical industry's record of inappropriate performance with regard to prices, products, technology, and marketing has made it a target for reform in many third world nations. This section will highlight the nature of the industry, the role of TNCs, and some of the efforts by the state to bring about change in fourteen countries: five from the semiperiphery, three from the more-developed periphery, and six from the less-developed periphery[23] (see Table 7.2).

It is evident in Table 7.2 that the pharmaceutical industry in these three blocs of third world nations differs in quite significant ways. All of the countries in the less-developed periphery have relatively small populations and low absolute levels of drug consumption, low levels of local production, and very high market shares for foreign firms. In effect, the pharmaceutical market in these countries is too small to be of interest to TNCs in terms of local manufacture, yet foreign firms are still dominant because they are able to supply these nations with imports of finished drugs. In the semiperiphery, on the other hand, drug consumption and drug production are at high levels and there are many local manufacturing firms (except in the case of Egypt). The local production of finished pharmaceuticals is generally over 85 percent of total consumption, but the market share of foreign firms is still moderately high (again excepting Egypt, which nationalized all local pharmaceutical plants in 1963). Foreign dominance in the semiperiphery is two-pronged: control over imports

---

[23] These categories correspond to those outlined and discussed with regard to Table 6.5.

The Pharmaceutical Industry in Fourteen Selected Third World Countries

Country	Population (in millions)	Pharmaceutical Expenditure per Capita (U.S. dollars)	Total Drug Production (millions of U.S. dollars)	Total Drug Consumption (millions of U.S. dollars)	Local Production as Percentage of Consumption[a]	Number of Pharmaceutical Firms	Market Share of Foreign Firms (by percentage)[b]	Importance of State Sector
Semiperiphery								
India (1977)	653.0	1.5	822	980	84	116[c]	70	Moderate
Argentina (1978)	44.6	25.0	1,059	1,115	95	220	59	Weak
Mexico (1980)	65.6	15.3	974	1,004	97	443[d]	85	Moderate
Brazil (1979)	119.4	12.7	1,302	1,517	86	428[e]	88	Moderate
Egypt (1980)	39.5	8.1	274	320	86	13	14	Strong
More-Developed Periphery								
Colombia (1978)	25.6	11.7	285	300	95	325	90	Moderate
Indonesia (1975)	130.0	1.2	128	160	80	200	50	Moderate
Thailand (1979)	42.4	7.9	250	335	75	NA	NA	Moderate
Less-Developed Periphery								
Sierra Leone (1980)	3.4	3.2	0.2	11.0	2	1	100	Weak
Kenya (1978)	14.8	2.2	8.0	32.0	25	16	90	Weak
Tanzania (1977)	16.9	0.9	1.2	16.7	7	3	85	Strong
Costa Rica (1977)	2.0	17.5	21.0[f]	35.0	30	24	82	Moderate
Malaysia (1978)	13.3	9.3	34.0	124.0	27	NA	90	Moderate
Sri Lanka (1976)	13.9	NA	NA	11.5[g]	NA	13	90+	Strong

SOURCES: UNCTC, 1981; UNCTAD, 1977a, 1977b, 1980; Trythall, 1977; Paredes López, 1977: 938.

NOTE: NA = not available.

[a] The percentages refer to finished drugs (including formulations) and not to their imported inputs.

[b] This refers to the sales turnover of foreign subsidiaries, including locally manufactured drugs and imported products.

[c] This refers to the number of large-scale pharmaceutical firms (i.e., 10 million rupees in plant and equipment, plus an industrial license) in India in 1972. In that same year, there were an additional 2,324 small-scale units (see UNCTAD, 1977a: 2–4).

[d] 1970.

[e] 1973.

[f] Costa Rica produced $21 million in pharmaceuticals in 1977, but one-half of this total was manufactured by two TNC subsidiaries for export to the Central American Common Market.

[g] This amount represents the total net sales of the State Pharmaceuticals Corporation (SPC) in 1975. The SPC was the sole buying and distribution agency for drugs in Sri Lanka from 1971 to 1977.

(primarily of active ingredients),[24] and control based on the presence of TNC manufacturing subsidiaries producing for the domestic market. On most measures the more-developed periphery falls somewhere between the semiperiphery and the less-developed periphery. It should be noted that there is no discernible pattern in Table 7.2 in the per capita consumption of pharmaceuticals. This is because the level of drug production tells us little or nothing about whether these countries are striving to reduce their great social inequalities. To get a sense of what, if anything, is being done about social inequality, we need to look toward the state.

The relative strength of the state sector is a key variable in understanding the pharmaceutical industry in these countries. Argentina has the smallest public sector in the semiperiphery, limited mainly to the purchase and distribution of drugs to public health institutions, while Egypt has the largest. Production from Egypt's public sector supplied 70 percent of national needs in 1980, the remainder of drugs consumed coming from imports and four private sector joint ventures involving TNCs.[25] In Mexico, Brazil, and India drug production by state enterprises covers 6.7, 4.3, and 1.3 percent of the market, respectively (UNCTC, 1981: 9). Public sector production is only a partial indicator of the state's importance in these countries, however. Equally significant are the relatively high levels of state activity in purchasing and distributing pharmaceuticals and in regulating TNCs and sometimes the locally owned private drug firms as well.

The countries of the more-developed periphery—Colombia, Indonesia, and Thailand—have moderately strong state sectors with regard to pharmaceuticals. Colombia and Thailand use centralized procurement or the tender system on a

---

[24] In the mid-1970s Brazil imported 70 percent of its pharmaceutical raw materials and Mexico imported 54 percent. Corresponding figures for Colombia and all of Central America are 75 percent and 90 percent, respectively (Paredes López, 1977: 938).

[25] The four TNCs represented in Egypt are Hoechst, Pfizer, Swisspharma Company (a consortium), and Squibb.

limited basis for their small public health sectors. In Colombia licensing agreements since the late 1960s are subject to government control, and common regulations adopted by countries of the Andean Pact (of which Colombia is a member) limit royalty payments by TNC subsidiaries to their parent companies and disallow most restrictive clauses in contracts between foreign and local firms. In Thailand the Government Pharmaceutical Organization founded in 1964 is the country's largest supplier of drugs, combining the functions of manufacturing, quality and price controls, promotion of research into the use of local materials, and distribution of drugs to public institutions. The state in Indonesia has sought to encourage the local production of pharmaceuticals by requiring TNCs to begin basic manufacture of at least one substance within five years of starting commercial operations. In order to control the number of medicines on the market firms have to reregister their products every two years. The government is also pressuring TNCs to divest 51 percent of their equity to Indonesian nationals.

The countries of the less-developed periphery vary considerably in the nature of their state sectors. Tanzania and Sri Lanka both installed socialist governments in 1967 and 1970, respectively. The two countries import practically all of the drugs they require. The main role of the state, therefore, is in the centralized purchasing, distribution, and selling of pharmaceuticals used nationally. There are two agencies in Tanzania that import and sell drugs: Central Medical Stores (CMS) and the National Pharmaceutical Company (NAPCO). The Ministry of Health runs CMS, which sells approximately 90 percent of its medicines to government hospitals and health units. NAPCO is also government controlled but sells over 90 percent of its drugs to private institutions (shops, private hospitals, pharmacies) and mission hospitals. In Sri Lanka the State Pharmaceuticals Corporation (SPC) was in charge of the import, export, purchase, sale, and distribution of drugs from 1971 to 1977. The SPC initiated sweeping reforms in the Sri Lankan pharmaceutical industry that in large

215

part were reversed following the election of a nonsocialist government in 1977.

Costa Rica has established centralized purchasing of bulk drugs through its social security agency that uses the public tender system, limits its purchases to a list of essential pharmaceutical products,[26] and also turns to generic drugs whenever possible. The social security agency's role was further strengthened by the government's new patent law (adopted in 1978) that favors importing less expensive drugs if patented ones are more costly. These measures have led to substantial savings, estimated at $32 million (U.S.) in 1978 (UNCTC, 1981: 23). The Costa Rican government also has tightened up the registration procedure for both existing and new pharmaceutical products. By 1979 the number of registered drugs had dropped from some 25,000 to 5,911 (UNCTC, 1981: 32).

Although about three-quarters of Malaysia's pharmaceutical needs are covered by imports, the state sector produces 26 percent of the total drug output that is manufactured locally. Domestic private firms account for 9 percent of local production and TNC subsidiaries for the remaining 65 percent (UNCTC, 1981: 50). Malaysia's regulatory environment regarding TNCs is more flexible than Costa Rica's. Emphasis in the country's development plan for 1976–1980 was on expansion of production in the public sector, increasing the share of equity held by Malaysian nationals in foreign firms,[27] and providing more training for pharmacists.

Sierra Leone has left imports of drugs largely unregulated and in private hands. Importers and suppliers freely bring into the country and sell whatever the market demands. The severe shortage of trained personnel and financial resources in Sierra Leone has prevented the private and public sectors

[26] Costa Rica's national list of essential drugs includes 850 pharmaceutical items (including dosage forms) and meets the needs of 80 percent of the population served by the social security system.

[27] The target set for 1990 is 70 percent Malaysian participation in the equity of foreign enterprises.

from establishing local production units.[28] A recently accepted new health program calls for the adoption of a list of essential drugs, presumably to better serve the needs of all income groups by assigning priorities to drug imports. In Kenya, where imports cover three-fourths of local consumption, the Central Medical Stores (CMS) acquire drugs for the public sector through an open tender system. Because of deficiencies in the system, high-priced brand-named pharmaceutical products continue to occupy a large share of public supplies and nearly the entire private sector. Kenya would like to strengthen the local production of pharmaceuticals through the CMS and the Central Public Health Laboratories. Like Sierra Leone, it has moved to adopt an essential drugs list.

Given the diversity of experiences represented among these fourteen countries, it seems advisable to look more closely at several of the cases. Special attention will be given below to all five of the semiperipheral nations and to Indonesia and Sri Lanka from the periphery.

India

The most vertically integrated of all third world countries in the pharmaceutical industry is India (see Lall, 1979b: 237–238). The government of India has traditionally placed a heavy emphasis on import substitution in all phases of drug manufacture, down to the production of fine chemicals. With respect to self-sufficiency attention has centered on the 117 "essential drugs" listed in the official Hathi Committee Report on the industry issued in 1975. The total value of India's pharmaceutical output in 1976 to 1977 stood at $980 million (U.S.) of which bulk drugs accounted for 18 percent and formulations for 82 percent;[29] in 1977 to 1978 production rose to

[28] Sierra Leone's one formulation plant is a small foreign subsidiary that manufactures a limited number of the parent firm's specialties.

[29] Of the total bulk drug sales 33 percent was produced by two public-sector units, 60 percent by large private companies, and 7 percent by

217

a level of $1.3 billion, an increase of more than 30 percent over the previous year. However, the Indian government has identified the nonavailability of certain technologies as a major barrier to a fuller development of the industry in the future. The Hathi Committee's recommendation on gradual abolition of brand names has been accepted, although in the teeth of vehement industry opposition it will be implemented initially on only five drugs.

India's pharmaceutical exports are increasing as rapidly as its output. In a three-year period (March 1975 to March 1978) the exports of bulk drugs and formulations doubled. Total exports now yield approximately 80 to 90 million dollars on an annual basis. Most are directed at the United States, Eastern Europe, Japan, and the Soviet Union, although the government's current export drive emphasizes bulk drug sales to Europe and to developing regions. A planned project of special interest is "offshore formulation" of Russian bulk drugs for re-export to the Soviet Union and other countries. This is apparently the first time such activity, common in electronics and transport equipment, has been found to be economical in pharmaceuticals. India has also set up its own "mini-multinationals" for the export of pharmaceutical technology to neighboring Asian and other third world nations. Indian Drugs and Pharmaceuticals Ltd., a large public-sector enterprise, is selling turn-key plant technical assistance and training services to Arab countries, Sri Lanka, and Bangladesh; Sarabhai Chemicals (a private firm) is setting up a turn-key multipurpose plant in Cuba under a contract awarded by UNIDO; and several possibilities of technical cooperation with Latin America are being explored, again under UNIDO auspices (Lall, 1979b: 238).

Given the impressive achievements of the Indian pharmaceutical industry it is important to know the degree to which

---

small-scale firms. The production breakdown for sales of formulations in 1976 to 1977 was as follows: 7 percent public sector, 76 percent large private enterprises, and 17 percent small-scale firms (SCRIP, June 17, 1978, p. 16).

these beneficial effects are attributable to the performance of TNCs or to domestic firms. Deolalikar's (1980) evidence supports the conclusion that, despite India's continued heavy dependence on foreign know-how for its pharmaceutical production,[30] the use of foreign technology by local enterprises generally results in societal consequences that are more desirable than those produced when foreign technology is used by TNCs. Domestic firms do a better job of developing and adapting the technology they import from abroad. Their profits are more "reasonable" than those of foreign firms, and they have been more successful in reducing their intake of external know-how over time. Local companies also tend to produce more bulk drugs (relative to formulations) and more generic products (relative to brand-name products) than do TNCs.[31] All of these trends conform to India's stated development objectives.

There is one area in which both local and foreign enterprises behave very similarly, but unfortunately this behavior subverts the goal of social equity. The product mix of both kinds of firms tends not to reflect social priorities. Attention is focused on remedies for diseases that afflict the middle-income and rich consumers, and diseases affecting the vast majority of the population (like leprosy and tuberculosis) are ignored.

One of the most serious problems India faces in its domestic pharmaceutical industry is poor quality control and lack of adequate testing and inspection facilities in certain parts of the country. One estimate puts the incidence of substandard drugs on the Indian market as high as 20 percent (Lall, 1979b: 243). Foreign firms have excellent records in this regard, as do most of the large local enterprises. The difficulties tend to

[30] It is estimated that over 90 percent of India's technological requirements in pharmaceuticals each year are acquired from external sources. Moreover, TNCs account for about 70 percent of the total sales turnover of drugs in the country (Deolalikar, 1980: 12, 20).

[31] Local firms concentrate on bulk drugs and generic products because the absence of heavy promotional expenditures and established brand names makes it easier to compete with TNCs.

arise among the myriad small firms, especially formulators. Efforts to eradicate those small-scale companies that are incompetent, ill-equipped, or simply corrupt have so far not met with much success.

Argentina

Argentina is one of the most advanced countries in the third world in the manufacture of drugs, it has an important number of TNCs operating in the industry, and it has a relatively strong domestic pharmaceutical sector (Chudnovsky, 1979; Katz, 1974). As a result, it should be possible to observe the differences between domestic drug firms and the TNCs and highlight the social implications that can be derived from these differences.

With regard to the structure of the Argentine pharmaceutical industry the leading company in terms of sales in 1972 (Laboratorios Bagó) was domestically owned, as were 3 of the top 5 firms and 6 of the top 15 companies.[32] Nonetheless, TNCs were dominant overall: in 1972 they controlled 57 percent of the total internal market for finished drugs, 65 percent of the market for active ingredients, and 98 percent of drug exports from Argentina. In a variety of areas, however, Argentina's domestic enterprises appear to have outperformed their TNC rivals. Nationally owned pharmaceutical companies are more diversified across twenty-four industry submarkets or therapeutic classes than foreign-owned firms[33] (8.2 therapeutic classes on the average for the former as compared with 6.5 for the latter); nationally owned companies are more diversified in terms of the number of products sold per firm than foreign-owned enterprises (44 drugs per firm and 35

[32] The data in this section are from Chudnovsky (1979).

[33] When the degree of submarket diversification is weighted by the share of that submarket in the whole pharmaceutical industry in terms of sales, foreign firms in Argentina are in a better position than domestic ones for the sample of seventy-six companies for which information was available.

drugs per firm, respectively); and the average nationally owned company introduced more "new" drugs each year than the average subsidiary of a TNC (4.3 new drugs as against 3.1 new drugs). The difference between national and foreign firms on this latter dimension is much more pronounced among the 15 largest pharmaceutical enterprises in Argentina. The 6 biggest local companies launched more than twice as many "new" drugs on average as the 9 largest foreign firms (7.5 versus 3.5 new products, respectively).[34] The greater innovative activity of Argentine companies is also reflected in sales figures; "new" products account for 13 percent of the total sales of the 6 largest local laboratories and for only 6.4 percent of the sales of the 9 major TNC subsidiaries.

A number of factors help explain the relative success of domestic enterprises in challenging TNC domination of the Argentine pharmaceutical industry. The conditions that have worked in favor of local firms are: first, the reduced rate of innovation of the 1960s and 1970s in the drug industry worldwide, and second, the general lack of interest of all TNCs in the Argentine market, especially in the early 1970s.[35] The success of Argentina's drug firms cannot be attributed to these factors alone, however, because the global reduction in the rate of innovation has not led to an improved performance by local companies in the other LDCs, nor has the lack of interest in the Argentine market brought parallel results in other TNC-dominated industries in the country. That domestic pharmaceutical companies in Argentina have done so well is due in large part to their distinctive strategy, which is made up of the following elements: an emphasis on marketing skills in product differentiation activities; the use of licenses to gain access to difficult submarkets; opposition to a strong patent

---

[34] Laboratorios Bagó, the leading domestic company, participated in 19 of 24 pharmaceutical submarkets in 1972, introduced 16 new drugs, and sold a total of 80 different products, making it by far the most diversified and innovative drug firm in Argentina.

[35] In 1962, for example, Argentina represented 5.9 percent of the U.S. overseas manufacturing investment; in 1975 it was only 0.7 percent of that investment (U.S. Department of Commerce, *Survey of Current Business*).

system in order to obtain active ingredients from nonpatented sources;[36] and a certain degree of local generation of technology (Chudnovsky, 1979: 52).

What are the implications of these differences in business performance between domestic and foreign enterprises in Argentina? From the point of view of the consumer of drugs one is led by the evidence to conclude that *no* tangible benefits have been achieved to date from the effort made by large domestic firms to challenge TNC domination of the local pharmaceutical industry, and in some cases the consumer is worse off. With respect to the average wholesale prices of finished pharmaceutical products in Argentina in 1972 two main findings stand out: first, big companies charge higher average prices for their drug products than smaller firms do, and second, among the leading fifteen enterprises in the industry the prices charged by domestic companies are higher than the prices quoted by foreign firms. Thus, the consumer in Argentina benefits from domestic control only when purchasing drugs from medium- and small-sized local companies. If the declared pre-tax rate of profit on net worth is considered, domestic companies are shown to be more profitable than their foreign rivals as well—the rates averaging 18 percent and 12 percent, respectively[37] (Chudnovsky, 1979: 53–54). The higher profits for local firms are consistent with their higher prices for finished drugs. High prices for foreign and large domestic enterprises alike are a direct consequence of the type of promotion-based competition prevailing in the industry.

A somewhat different assessment of the Argentine situation could be given from the perspective of national (rather than consumer) welfare. Until recently domestic companies had been reversing the denationalization process in the Argentine

[36] In Argentina product patents for pharmaceutical substances are not recognized, nor can process patents be used to prevent imports of products or ingredients made under that process in other countries.

[37] Unfortunately, the information is not available for a proper estimate of the overinvoicing of imports by TNCs, a factor that would very likely raise the profit levels of foreign firms.

pharmaceutical industry,[38] and they are taking strides toward becoming technologically autonomous. High prices of drugs thus may be viewed as an acceptable trade-off for the consolidation of a local industrial bourgeoisie, which is often considered an essential step in achieving some form of nondependent development. Nonetheless, subsidizing domestic firms through high drug prices is a very regressive type of subsidy. In a country with almost no assistance from the state in meeting the cost of pharmaceutical purchases, and with drugs accounting for about 40 percent of the personal health budget, a uniformly high price for pharmaceuticals is a burden that falls heavily indeed on the poorer sectors of the population.

Mexico

In Mexico, where drug sales totaled over one billion U.S. dollars in 1980 (75 percent in the private sector and 25 percent in the public sector), local consumption of finished pharmaceuticals was almost fully met by local production. Over half of the raw materials used are still imported, however, and TNCs account for about 85 percent of total sales[39] and an even larger share of Mexico's pharmaceutical exports (see Gereffi, 1982). Despite the fact that Mexico is one of the leading third world exporters of pharmaceutical products, the absolute level of its drug imports greatly exceeds drug exports,

[38] The market share of local drug firms in Argentina increased relative to that of TNCs between 1962 and 1970 (Katz, 1974: 62–63). Local Argentinian companies have begun to lose ground in recent years, however. By 1980 their share of the market had declined to 47 percent (*SCRIP,* Dec. 24, 1981, p. 11). Some factors that might help account for this relative slump in the performance of Argentina's domestic firms include: more stringent requirements regarding quality control, the abolition of legislation that had limited royalty payments to foreign firms and regulated restrictive business practices in the transfer of technology, an increase in the prices of imported chemical intermediates, and alleged dumping by pharmaceutical TNCs (UNCTC, 1981: 41).

[39] Thirty-eight of the forty largest pharmaceutical companies in Mexico are foreign owned.

and thus the country has experienced a steadily growing negative trade balance in the pharmaceutical sector.[40]

In response to this high level of TNC dominance the Mexican government has taken a series of measures between 1972 and 1982 to try to reduce the impact of foreign subsidiaries and increase domestic control of the industry. These include three new laws,[41] the creation of two state-owned enterprises (Proquivemex and Vitrium) to control the commercialization of barbasco and the manufacture and distribution of basic pharmaceutical products,[42] the formation of an Intersecretarial Commission for the Pharmaceutical Industry as a technical coordinating organism for public sector activities,[43] and the establishment and initial implementation of an essential drug list to standardize public sector purchases of basic medicines according to their generic names and in the dosages and presentational forms (tablets, capsules, injectable solutions, etc.) most often used.[44]

Of the three laws the 1972 Technology Transfer Law is generally considered to be the most successful. It established a National Registry of Technology Transfer to review all agreements in which a foreign company charges a Mexican

[40] Mexico's drug imports exceeded its drug exports by P $501 million in 1970. By 1975 this deficit had risen to P $1,035 million, a growth rate of 16 percent annually (de María y Campos, 1977: 898).

[41] These are the Law on the Transfer of Technology (1972), the Law to Promote Mexican Investment and Regulate Foreign Investment (1973), and the Law on Inventions and Trademarks (1976).

[42] See Chapter 5 on Proquivemex.

[43] This commission was established in Mexico by executive decree on November 17, 1978. It is composed of representatives from five ministries (Treasury, Commerce, Health, Patrimony and Industrial Development, and Agriculture), the Mexican Institute of Social Security (IMSS), and the Institute of Social Security and Services for Government Workers (ISSSTE).

[44] The Essential Drug List ("Cuadro básico de medicamentos del sector público") was published in Mexico's *Diario oficial* on March 28, 1978. It includes a total of 614 pharmaceutical preparations derived from 426 different generic medicines. It is estimated that the present essential drug list covers about 95 percent of all pharmaceutical sales to the public sector in Mexico.

company for technological and marketing know-how. If an agreement is judged too harsh in terms of price, duration, export restrictions, purchase requirements, etc., it is denied registration. Most of the proposed agreements that have been rejected are redrawn and submitted on terms more favorable to Mexico. The 1973 Foreign Investment Law required that all new foreign enterprises have at least 51 percent Mexican capital irrespective of activity. Despite the intent of this law, however, the vast majority of pharmaceutical firms in Mexico remained wholly owned by foreigners as late as 1977 (see Gereffi, 1982: Tables 5 and 6). This apparent anomaly is explained by a "grandfather clause" in the 1973 law stipulating that companies established prior to the law will not be affected by the "Mexicanization" requirement unless and until they decide to expand their operations. This expansion will be treated as a new investment, which means that it will be approved only if the foreign enterprise sells a majority share of its stock to Mexicans. Since almost all of the principal pharmaceutical firms in Mexico were set up before 1973, the original owners still can retain full control of their company. The Mexican market for drugs is growing rapidly, though, and existing TNCs will be forced to increase the size and scope of their activities just to keep pace. Sooner or later they will have to give up their long-standing resistance to Mexicanization or withdraw from the market altogether.

The 1976 Law on Inventions and Trademarks is a very ambitious piece of legislation that reduces the period of patent protection in Mexico from fifteen to ten years and requires that patents be exploited within four years of the date they are issued or they will expire and fall into the public domain.[45] Under the 1976 law, trademarks will be registered for five-year periods. Registered trademarks may be renewed indefinitely every five years provided that it can be shown they have been in use in the previous period. If a trademark has not been in effective use, or if it has become converted into a

[45] In the Mexican pharmaceutical industry TNCs hold 85 to 90 percent of all patents granted (de María y Campos, 1977: 897).

generic name, then it will be considered to have expired and to be within the public domain. Perhaps the most controversial aspect of the 1976 Law on Inventions and Trademarks is the stipulation that each foreign trademark (i.e., those originally registered abroad or whose titleholders are not Mexican) must be linked with a Mexican trademark (i.e., one originally registered in Mexico). Of particular interest to government officials, according to a wide variety of sources, are products in the pharmaceutical and food-processing industries. Not surprisingly, this aspect of the law has raised the ire of the TNCs, which have steadfastly refused to give up the tremendous marketing advantages associated with foreign trademarks by gratuitously linking them to Mexican names or symbols.

By 1982 much in the 1976 Law on Inventions and Trademarks still had not been implemented. In the face of strong opposition by the TNCs Mexico has indefinitely postponed applying that part of the law which requires foreign and national trademarks to be linked. Most people in both the public and private sectors feel that this aspect of the law will never be applied. The underlying problem is a political one. The 1976 law came at the end of Luis Echeverría's six-year term as president of Mexico. It is thought by many to epitomize Echeverría's hostile and at times oversimplified view of TNCs. The succeeding administration of José López Portillo, anxious to restore investor confidence in Mexico and to stabilize the country economically, was reluctant to fully implement a law it did not consider its own, especially if it incurred high political costs and uncertain gains in the short run.

Although its ostensible objective is to "promote and regulate the pharmaceutical industry so that its development contributes at a national level to the solution of the problem of health," the Intersecretarial Commission for the Pharmaceutical Industry in fact represents the first governmental body entrusted with formulating policy for the industry as a whole in Mexico. The main lines of policy developed and supported by the Intersecretarial Commission are found in the "Program to Promote the Pharmaceutical Industry" ("El programa de fomento a la industria farmacéutica"), published in Mexico's *Diario oficial* on April 25, 1980.[46] This program sets forth objectives for the period 1980 to 1983.[47] While the program is quite comprehensive, its main goals can be summarized as follows: to increase the annual output of pharmaceutical firms at a rate of 15 to 20 percent and to export between 5 and 20 percent of this output;[48] to keep imports of finished drugs at the present level of 3 percent of local consumption and restrict the importation of raw materials; to increase the market share of Mexican firms from 30 to 50 percent, and to increase the local equity share of Mexican capital from its current level of 28 percent to at least 51 percent; to raise the share of local inputs to at least 50 percent of the total production cost of pharmaceuticals; to limit royalty payments to a range of 0.5 percent to 3 percent depending on the type of product and the percentage of equity held by foreign firms; to standardize public-sector purchases through use of the essential drug list;[49] and to divide the Mexican market for pharmaceutical products into three types—private, public, and social-interest—with lower prices for identical drugs in the latter two markets.[50]

[46] Officially, this program was issued by the Ministry of Patrimony and Industrial Development in Mexico. It is widely acknowledged, however, to be the product of the Intersecretarial Commission.

[47] José López Portillo's term as president of Mexico ended in 1982. That the objectives of the "Program to Promote the Pharmaceutical Industry" extend to 1983 was apparently an effort on the part of the planners to overcome the lack of political continuity that frequently characterizes the transition from one six-year presidential administration to the next.

[48] With respect to both output and exports the lower percentage refers to finished drugs and the higher percentage to active ingredients.

[49] This is related to a program sponsored by the Mexican government called COPLAMAR ("Coordinación de los planes para los marginados"), which concentrates on a subset of about sixty products from the essential drug list for free distribution to the rural poor.

[50] In the private market all pharmaceutical products registered in Mexico can be sold, in the public sector market those products from the essential drug list can be sold, and in the social interest market a selected num-

In order to help implement this sectoral program, the Mexican government announced in 1981 that it was setting up a second state pharmaceutical company called Vitrium (*Diario oficial*, October 27, 1981). Vitrium is, in a number of respects, a far bolder initiative than Proquivemex, whose primary function was to control barbasco supply. Capitalized at P $30 million (U.S. $1.2 million), Vitrium will be 75 percent owned by the Mexican government and 25 percent owned by a Swedish state pharmaceutical enterprise, KabiVitrium. The new Mexican firm will be responsible for the manufacture, import, and distribution of basic pharmaceutical products. The decision to create Vitrium was based in part on the findings of a study of pharmaceutical production and demand in Mexico over the 1979–1986 period. The study estimated that pharmaceutical consumption in the public sector will grow at twice the rate of that for the private sector and that current installed capacity in the country is insufficient to meet the 1986 demand for drugs. No new investment was foreseen in the private sector (*SCRIP*, November 23, 1981, p. 7).

It is hoped that Vitrium will ensure the availability of imported raw materials at fair prices by acting as a clearinghouse for the import of active ingredients. The company will try to foster the development of local research and technology and reduce royalty and technical assistance payments to foreign countries. One of Vitrium's biggest goals is to lower pharmaceutical prices to consumers through direct manufacture and distribution. This will involve an increase in the local manufacture of active ingredients. The leading pharmaceutical products in Mexico (accounting for two-thirds of the country's drug consumption) are based on 223 active ingredients, of which only 80 are made locally. The government

---

ber of products from the essential drug list receives top priority. Each pharmaceutical firm is encouraged to participate in each of these three markets. It is expected (although not formally stated) that the prices for identical medicines will be lower in the public sector market than in the private sector market, and lower still in the social interest market (i.e., poor individuals who neither work for the government nor are covered by social security) than in either of the first two.

has already asked for and received tenders for the local manufacture of 22 additional active ingredients (*SCRIP*, November 23, 1981, p. 7). Mexican production of these 22 raw materials was scheduled to start in 1982 or 1983.

Brazil

The Brazilian pharmaceutical industry went through a major
period of denationalization between 1957 and 1977 when
thirty-four of the largest domestic firms were acquired by
TNCs. In the hope of increasing the competitiveness of local
firms vis-à-vis their foreign rivals Brazil completely abolished
patent protection for pharmaceuticals in 1969. A decade after
the introduction of the ban the ten largest national drug
companies had increased their share of the market by close to
10 percent. This trend was broken, however, when two of the
firms were acquired by TNCs in 1978 and 1979. It is interesting to note that despite the ban on patents foreign investment
in the pharmaceutical sector rose from 113 million U.S. dollars in 1971 to 646 million dollars in 1979, one of the highest
growth rates of any industry in Brazil. This seems to contradict the argument of those who contend that the absence
of patents will keep foreign investors away. In the area of
trademarks Brazil tried to prohibit brand names from being
used for drugs containing a single active ingredient. The
legal challenge to this measure by TNCs was upheld in the
courts, and the Brazilian Parliament subsequently enacted a
less restrictive bill on trade names in 1977 (UNCTC, 1981:
41–42).

The Brazilian "triple alliance" (see Evans, 1979*a*) between
TNCs, the state, and local private capital has led to an unusual compromise arrangement between a rationalized drug
list and free market forces involving the state-owned enterprise Central de Medicamentos (CEME) (Evans, 1976:
133–136; Ledogar, 1975: 61–67). CEME was created in 1971
by a nationalist faction within the Brazilian military elite,
under the direct responsibility of the president of the republic. CEME's role was elaborated in the four-volume *Plano*

diretor de medicamentos (Master Plan for Pharmaceuticals).

In order to satisfy its original objective of social service for the poor majority in Brazil, CEME set out to rationalize the procurement of medicines for the hospitals and clinics associated with Brazil's system of state medical assistance, the Instituto Nacional de Previdência Social (INPS), and to provide free prescription drugs to the poorest of the INPS's clients. In addition, the Master Plan proposed reviving approximately twenty state-owned laboratories and giving preferential treatment to local companies, with the ultimate goal of having the country manufacture most of its own pharmaceutical raw materials by the end of the decade. Other provisions in the plan included tight controls on the sale and promotion of drugs, regulations on the content of drug package inserts, and restrictions on the distribution of free drug samples.

Only part of the Master Plan was ever put into effect, and it was done in a way that did not threaten the dominant position or continued growth of private (and especially foreign) drug firms. In 1973 CEME distributed medications to nine million people. Its target group consisted of those people receiving the official minimum wage or less—in other words, exactly that segment of the population which is normally excluded from the commercial market for medicines. Thus, CEME was not likely to take any customers away from private firms; on the contrary, its activities probably stimulated the expansion of the commercial market. A large share of the medications distributed by CEME were not produced by public laboratories but purchased from private companies, many of them foreign owned. In 1973 CEME increased private-sector sales by a total of 3.5 million U.S. dollars (Evans, 1976: 135). Furthermore, whereas the logic of profitability for private firms lies in maximizing product differentiation, CEME's strategy was quite the opposite: to limit the number of medicines it deals with, concentrating on those needed for the diseases most prevalent among the population it serves. The Master Plan contains a list of 134 pharmaceutical products accounting for about three-fourths of the cost of national drug imports in 1971. To the extent that CEME might try to manufacture these products domestically through its system of public laboratories, the only private enterprises likely to suffer would be locally owned ones whose output is less technologically advanced and not the foreign subsidiaries of TNCs.

CEME's hopes of leading Brazil to raw material self-sufficiency and greater technological autonomy in the pharmaceutical sector appear to have been thwarted by changes in government policy. In 1975 it suddenly found itself removed from the Office of the Presidency; its research functions were transferred to the Ministry of Industry and Commerce, and its responsibility for distributing free medicines to the poor was placed under the control of the Ministry of Welfare (Ledogar, 1975: 69–70). Although CEME is still supposed to encourage and coordinate the production of basic medicines, the list of essential drugs has been reduced in number and lessened in status to a mere guideline. CEME and other government institutions that distribute drugs to the poor can substitute for the generic-named drugs on the list any similar differentiated product on the market, much to the delight of the private-sector enterprises which specialize in promoting many versions of the same product.

A different kind of basic drugs/free market compromise has been proposed by a group of West German, Swiss, and French pharmaceutical TNCs who are offering to provide about twenty-five "basic drugs" at cost to the poorest of the LDCs using governmental rather than commercial distribution channels. In return the TNCs want unregulated markets in new drugs and the acceptance of drug patents and trademarks by the LDCs that would benefit from the scheme. Both WHO's Director-General, Dr. Halfdan Mahler, and U.S. Senator Edward Kennedy expressed their support for such a proposal (*SCRIP*, May 14, 1977). Opposition has come from TNCs who resist the idea of setting preferential prices for LDCs, particularly when developed country authorities keep a careful watch on international price differences and when antitrust issues (especially in the United States) may be involved.

Egypt

Prior to 1952 Egypt depended on imports to meet 90 percent of its pharmaceutical supply requirements.[51] In the absence of any overall government policy on drugs or regulatory control for consumer protection there were some twenty thousand pharmaceutical preparations on the market, and TNCs dominated. The three local drug firms then in existence had no real impact. When Egypt broke with monarchic rule in 1952, profit margins on imported pharmaceuticals were reduced and two new organizations were established to handle public and private sector drug distribution.[52] Between 1952 and 1963 the government was able to increase the domestic industry's contribution from 10 percent to 53 percent of Egypt's total demand for drugs.

All local pharmaceutical plants were nationalized in 1963. At the same time the government established three joint ventures with well-known pharmaceutical TNCs: Hoechst, Pfizer, and Swisspharma (a consortium made up of Ciba, Sandoz, and Wander).[53] The Egyptian General Organisation for Pharmaceutical Chemicals and Medical Appliances (EGOPCA) was established to manage the planning, importation, exportation, and distribution of drugs and to control pharmaceutical prices. A Drug Research and Control Centre was also set up to control drug quality and to do production-related research. By 1965 the Egyptian pharmaceutical industry had ten formulation plants (seven state-owned companies and the three TNC joint ventures), one public sector bulk pharmaceutical plant, and one public sector factory to make packaging materials.

[51] This section on Egypt draws from UNCTC (1981: 39–40) and from an unpublished manuscript by Mr. Hailu Guadey, a consultant for the United Nations Centre on Transnational Corporations.

[52] These distribution agencies were called the Supreme Organisation for Drugs (public sector) and the Egyptian General Organisation for Drug Distribution and Trading (private sector).

[53] A fourth joint venture was formed in 1978 with Squibb.

Since 1973 the government has shifted to a more liberal "open-door" policy toward foreign investment. This strategy involves revitalization of the private sector, incentives to beneficial foreign investment,[54] and improved efficiency in public sector activities. Pursuant to this policy, the EGOPCA was abolished in 1975 and replaced by an interministerial committee on drugs (The Technical Secretariat for Drugs) chaired by the Minister of Health. The Technical Secretariat includes representation by the domestic industry and is responsible for overall control of the pharmaceutical sector. Presently Egypt's drug industry is able to meet 83 percent of the country's total demand for pharmaceuticals (69 percent attributable to the output of national firms and 14 percent to TNCs). The country has succeeded in achieving complete self-reliance in immunological preparations and is even able to export some of these products. Some of the larger national companies (such as Memphis, El Nil, and C.I.D.) are extracting active ingredients from local herbs as well as processing them into dosage forms and placing them on the market. Production of bulk drugs is still limited to a few essential products, however, with the major bulk inputs for pharmaceutical manufacture being imported. Transnationals from outside of Egypt also supply a large portion of the machinery, equipment, and packaging materials used in the industry because output from the only two national firms competing in these fields (El Nasr and Pharmaceutical Packaging Company) is insufficient to meet domestic needs. In order to strengthen the local pharmaceutical industry further Egypt will have to increase its capabilities in the chemical and petrochemical sectors.

In actuality Egypt has enjoyed a relatively strong bargaining position with regard to TNCs since the industry was nationalized in the early 1960s. Because the public sector did not have to fight a protracted battle against TNCs within the

[54] Special tax concessions may be granted to private investors (foreign or indigenous) who establish enterprises designed to use domestic resources or to promote exports. Tax holidays of five to ten years are offered, and the repatriation of profits is unrestricted.

framework of market forces in order to enlarge its role, the state may have found it easier to negotiate licensing agreements and joint ventures with TNCs on terms that were generally favorable to the local industry. On the other hand, the government has accepted patent and trademark protection of branded drugs. Given the large and increasing size of the public sector market, however, foreign brand names are not a very effective instrument for TNCs to use to curtail the growth of local firms.

Indonesia

Indonesia is a nation of great contrasts.[55] Its oil production and membership in OPEC and its relative political stability have given the country increasing importance recently in Southeast Asia. Its population of 130 million is scattered over a vast area with considerable distribution and communication problems, however, and it is wracked by severe disparities in income and access to basic goods and services. The market for brand-named drugs, for example, is confined to about 10 percent of the population. Throughout Indonesia there is an average of one doctor for every 20,000 people, and one pharmacist (or chemist) serves about 115,000 people. The actual distribution is sharply distorted in favor of the capital, Jakarta.[56] There the ratios drop to 1 to 3,200 for doctors and 1 to 20,000 for pharmacists.

Indonesia has two hundred pharmaceutical firms, about forty of which are foreign owned or have some sort of foreign involvement. There are thirty TNCs with wholly or majority-owned pharmaceutical subsidiaries. Another ten TNCs have entered contract (or toll) manufacturing agreements with indigenous companies whereby the foreign enterprise licenses the technology and supplies the active ingredient for one or more of its specialty items and the Indonesian firm carries out

[55] My discussion of Indonesia is based on Trythall (1977).

[56] Jakarta's population is about 5.2 million, or 4 percent of the national total.

local production. With but one exception,[57] there are no joint ventures where the TNC has a minority interest. Overall, indigenous drug companies supply 50 percent of the medicines produced locally, TNC subsidiaries 44 percent, and TNCs utilizing domestic contract manufacturers 6 percent.

In the late 1960s the Indonesian government began to pursue a policy of achieving domestic self-sufficiency in finished pharmaceutical products. Initially there were broad hints to TNCs that unless they invested in plants in Indonesia they would be excluded from importing and marketing their products locally. This was followed in 1974 by a regulation banning, for the most part, drugs that are not manufactured within the country's borders. Transnationals complain that the government's emphasis on basic manufacture (which includes a commitment from foreign firms to begin local production within five years of starting commercial operations) has led to substantial overcapacity in the industry. The poverty of many Indonesians affords them very limited purchasing power. In addition, Indonesia has a serious smuggling problem caused by the high prices of local products and aggravated by widespread corruption. It is estimated that 20 percent of the pharmaceuticals available in Indonesia are illegally imported, despite official figures claiming that local factories meet nearly all of the country's drug needs. Another way the government has tried to protect the indigenous sector is through its unwillingness to accept pharmaceutical patents in any form. The government contends that, at least in the beginning, local research and development can survive only through its ability to copy products. Original research is so far away that patent protection is meaningless as an advantage to research and development efforts in the domestic industry.

At least some TNCs claim they are thinking about withdrawing from the Indonesian market, and a few have already left. Other TNCs remain convinced that the pharmaceutical

[57] One TNC entered Indonesia by contributing 20 percent of the authorized capital of a local firm.

industry in Indonesia has a promising future if the government can achieve a more even distribution of wealth. The government definitely supports the private sector in the industry, and there appears to be no pressure for nationalization of drug firms. Nor is there any official concern expressed about restricting the use of brand names in promoting pharmaceuticals or mandating generics. Indonesia, in short, is both pro-private sector and very nationalistic, a combination that TNCs are learning to live with.

Sri Lanka

Sri Lanka is an example of a far-reaching attempt by a small import-dependent third world nation to implement major reforms in the areas of drug importation and distribution. In 1971 Sri Lanka set up the State Pharmaceuticals Corporation (SPC) with the following objectives: 1) to centralize all imports, replacing the 134 private importers that had previously done this, 2) to economize on the costs of drug purchase by buying in bulk, by buying generically, and by "shopping around" world markets, and 3) to switch from the sale and use of drugs by brand names to generic names (Bibile, 1977; Lall and Bibile, 1977; Lall, 1979b). The results of the Sri Lankan experience have been mixed and offer some valuable lessons to developing countries considering similarly comprehensive changes.

First, the SPC reduced the number of drugs imported into Sri Lanka from 2,100 (3,000 dosage forms) to 600 (1,000 dosage forms). The pharmaceutical products eliminated by this rationalization were: imitative drugs, needless fixed-combination products (so judged when a flexible use of single drugs would do), and drugs without clear therapeutic value or with high toxicity.[58] Second, brand-named products were almost

---

[58] Among the exceptionally toxic drugs that had been banned in the United States or Europe yet were being promoted and sold without proper warning in Sri Lanka are dipyrone, dithiazanine iodide, and long-acting sulfonamides (Lall and Bibile, 1977: 693).

completely abolished from the import list and replaced by cheaper generic substitutes. In an effort to ensure high quality the SPC did not import any drugs that did not carry quality certificates from abroad; imports were also tested locally in the Ministry of Health's quality control laboratory. There were potential problems of bioequivalence but only for twenty-five of the drugs on the rationalized import list.[59] These continued to be imported from so-called "traditional sources" (i.e., pre-SPC suppliers of these drugs, which were usually TNCs) until bioequivalence testing could guarantee that cheaper products were therapeutically identical to those they replaced (Lall and Bibile, 1977: 689). Third, the SPC greatly reduced the prices of Sri Lankan pharmaceutical imports by instituting a national system of worldwide tenders. Under this tender system a number of drugs were still purchased from the TNCs that had traditionally supplied Sri Lanka; in many other cases, however, TNCs were replaced by small companies in developed countries and by manufacturers from Eastern Europe and the third world (mainly India). The savings achieved in 1972, the first year of SPC operations, were over 40 percent. Consumers benefited in terms of lower drug prices. The savings were spent partly in increasing the quantity of drugs purchased and partly in providing foreign exchange for other purposes (Lall, 1978b: 15–18; 1979b: 239). Illustrative figures for imports of ten pharmaceutical products by SPC in 1974 show savings of 65 percent when compared with the price offered that year by the traditional suppliers of these drugs (Lall, 1978a: 11).

Notwithstanding these accomplishments, Sri Lanka encountered serious obstacles in its attempted program of reforms. For one thing, it proved far easier to rationalize the imports of finished drugs than those of intermediate products

---

[59] Even though two products are chemically identical with respect to active ingredients, their effectiveness or absorption into the body (i.e., bioavailability) may differ as a result of other factors (including the nature of the inert ingredients and particle size and shape). Chemically equivalent drugs, in other words, may not be bioequivalent.

(i.e., pharmaceutical chemicals for local formulation). The SPC's objective was not just to reduce the cost of imported chemicals but also to increase the local processing of drugs by requiring the pharmaceutical manufacturers in Sri Lanka to formulate intermediate chemicals imported by the SPC. Whereas the seven small local producers responded favorably to this policy, the five TNC subsidiaries (three British and two from the United States) showed resistance. The reason why is easy to understand: the requirement to purchase intermediate chemicals from the state interfered with the ability of TNCs to increase their net income through transfer pricing, which is based on their control over the import and export prices of those products moving through their intrafirm trade channels. It is to the advantage of local firms, on the other hand, to buy intermediate materials at the lowest possible world-market price, which is what the SPC hoped to attain.[60]

In general, there were a series of forces that combined to mitigate, and eventually overturn, the sweeping reforms the pharmaceutical industry pursued in Sri Lanka from 1972 to 1977 (see Lall and Bibile, 1977). First, the TNCs brought several sorts of pressure to bear on the Sri Lankan government: they used threats and persuasion from abroad; they got home government support when nationalization seemed imminent; they threatened to restrict future investments and technology transfer; and they used their powerful alliance with the local medical profession. Second, doctors were reluctant to accept the change from brand to generic names for pharmaceutical products. The promotional system of the large companies is so strong in most countries that doctors are virtually dependent on the drug producers themselves for information about new therapies, and they become convinced of the superiority

---

[60] Pfizer, for example, was buying tetracycline from its parent at a price of $99 (U.S.) per kilogram when the same material of equivalent quality was being offered by Hoechst to the SPC at $20 per kilogram. Glaxo, a TNC from the United Kingdom, was involved in an identical practice: its chlorpheniramine imports cost $411 per kilogram from the parent company and $53 from Halewood, a small British firm (Lall and Bibile, 1977: 686).

of branded products. Generally they remain unaware of the economics of prescribing. Whereas in developed countries this situation has begun to change, in the third world belief in international brand names remains very strong, official attempts to provide objective information are weak, and "consumerism" is nascent. Despite the SPC's measures to ensure that drug imports were of adequate quality and volume, there were occasional reports of substandard products and of interruptions in the supply of drugs. These instances were highly publicized by those opposed to reform in an effort to discredit the entire SPC program.[61]

Finally, the fortunes of the SPC and its reform program cannot be dissociated from the overall political direction of Sri Lanka during this period. In 1970 a socialist government was installed in a landslide electoral victory. The SPC made its major achievements before 1975, when the government had a unified socialist ideology. From 1975 onwards the government began to shift its course to the right, which slowed down or halted the pace of reform in the pharmaceutical industry and elsewhere in the economy. Local and foreign vested interests pushed for a reversion to the old system of TNC-dominated drug provision. Under a new, nonsocialist government elected in 1977 the following changes in drug industry policies were instituted: 1) restrictions on importations of pharmaceutical raw materials (mainly intermediate chemicals) by the private sector were largely abolished; 2) since January 1978 the private sector has been permitted to import finished drugs in competition with the SPC; 3) the SPC's "34 Drug Programme" to increase local manufacture of key pharmaceuticals has been terminated; and 4) controls over

---

[61] Problems of quality, bioequivalence, and doctor and patient acceptance are particularly severe in many developing nations. Pakistan's hasty and ill-planned move in the early 1970s to abolish brand names and thus promote indigenous producers may have served only to retard genuine progress: poor quality drugs flooded the market; the market share of TNCs, with their justifiable reputation for excellent quality control, rose rather than fell; prices did not decline; and the plan had to be substantially altered.

the selling prices of drugs have been modified to allow increases reflecting cost inflation and the devaluation of the Sri Lankan rupee.

Some Generalizations

These seven country profiles suggest some generalizations about the performance of the pharmaceutical industry in a third world context. First, domestic private firms tend to contribute more to societal goals of resource efficiency and equity than TNCs do. The motives underlying this socially desirable behavior are not altruistic, however. It just so happens that the self-interest of local firms and national development objectives often overlap. The tendency of local companies to reduce their reliance on foreign know-how because it compromises their management control coincides with the third world country's interest in technological independence. And whereas domestic enterprises favor bulk drug and generic product manufacture because the absence of heavy promotion and established brand names makes competition with TNCs easier, peripheral and semiperipheral nations prefer this strategy too because it leads to increased vertical integration and lower drug prices, especially for essential items required by the poor. If the transfer pricing behavior of TNCs, to take a final example, tends to lessen a host country's foreign exchange and tax revenues, the profit incentive that leads indigenous entrepreneurs to set up rival local production facilities may also counteract this national problem by generating alternative cost figures through which overinvoicing may come to light.

The main reason why the divergence between private interests and social interests will be narrower for domestic firms than for TNCs lies in the latter's transnational decision-making framework. Transnationals have a global perspective and seek to maximize their global profits, while the production and research functions of these enterprises are often centralized in their home countries. This situation frequently leads to conflicts between the TNC's goal of global efficiency and a third world country's desire for increased national autonomy. Since the domestic firm's decisions are made in a milieu affected by local scarcities and local values, its performance is more likely to reflect these social realities.

There are significant exceptions to the coincidence between local private and societal interests. One such area forms the basis for a second generalization. Neither indigenous nor foreign pharmaceutical firms can be regarded as having a more socially desirable combination of finished products than the other. In countries such as India, Argentina, Brazil, and Tanzania there is evidence that TNCs and local companies alike directed their manufacturing efforts overwhelmingly toward drugs desired by upper-income consumers and disregarded products needed by the poor majority of the population.

The third generalization relates to the second. Because the private sector as a whole is frequently unresponsive to important social needs, especially with regard to the poor, a wide variety of third world nations has decided to rely on state-owned enterprises in the pharmaceutical sector. Proquivemex in Mexico, CEME in Brazil, the State Pharmaceuticals Corporation in Sri Lanka, the Memphis and El Nasr companies in Egypt, and Hindustan Antibiotics Ltd. (HAL) and Indian Drugs and Pharmaceuticals Ltd. (IDPL) in India are all state firms that have played important roles in both the distribution and production of drugs. A number of other government agencies have substantially lowered the price of medicines through bulk buying. The private sector, as a rule, tends to protest the state's entry into drug manufacture far more vehemently than it does state involvement in the purchasing or distribution of pharmaceuticals.

Fourth, all of the countries in the semiperiphery and a number in the more-developed periphery want pharmaceutical TNCs to expand their local production of active ingredients. Some of the TNCs actually agree, quietly if not publicly, that their own interests in the long run would be best served by more involvement in active ingredient manufacture. They feel that in the area of finished drugs, government preference for local firms in public sector sales will steadily reduce the TNCs' share of the market.[62]

Fifth, in the countries where the private sector is predominant (e.g., Argentina, Brazil, Indonesia) product differentiation and promotional expenses tend to be greater than in countries with large public sectors (such as Egypt or Sri Lanka in the mid-1970s). The price of drug products could be lowered and the position of local firms in the industry improved if some of the more pernicious aspects of pharmaceutical marketing were better regulated. Two priority areas can be singled out here. One is the mandatory use of generic names in advertising and prescribing pharmaceutical products. The institutionalization of essential drug lists, which many third world nations are adopting (see WHO, 1976), should greatly help generic names to become more widely accepted and used. The other area is the excessive use of free samples by detail men in promoting their company's products. For instance, the usual practice when introducing a new drug into the Mexican market is to give away an average of four capsules for each capsule sold in the first year, three capsules for each capsule sold in the second year, and so on until a level of one to one is reached (de María y Campos, 1977: 901). This heavy reliance on free samples, which usually originates with the TNCs, multiplies the promotional costs for local firms to successfully enter the market. If such practices were restricted, competition would increase and the cost of many drugs would come down.

Sixth, adequate quality control in pharmaceutical production continues to be one of the biggest problems plaguing many third world drug industries. This is also an area in which the TNCs excel. Stricter quality control for drugs, whether this is taken to mean better manufacturing practices

[62] In a country like Mexico where the public sector market is growing about twice as fast as the private market state preference for locally owned companies is a potent policy instrument indeed.

or more stringent labeling and advertising control, is generally more expensive for everyone. Since TNCs can meet higher costs more easily than can most of the beleaguered local firms, stricter quality control in third world countries usually makes it more difficult for domestic pharmaceutical companies to compete, thus leading some to charge that higher quality favors the foreign firms.[63] Transnational corporations, on the other hand, are also prone to want to relax quality standards when these relate to the excessive claims or suppressed warnings for some of their prescription drugs no longer approved in their countries of origin. Lack of state action in the quality control area may at times reflect, therefore, the political influence of drug producers (local and/or foreign) rather than governmental ignorance of the facts.

Finally, successful pharmaceutical industry reforms require continued governmental support. In the cases of Sri Lanka, Brazil, and Mexico major reform attempts were overturned or vitiated because of shifting political circumstances and the withdrawal of regime support. The TNCs, local private laboratories, and the local medical profession generally banded together to preserve the status quo, irrespective of the varying kinds of reform being promoted. Effective change in the industry thus requires not only technological and organizational capability but a strong political will.

WHITHER DEPENDENCY?

In the first chapter of this book the dependency perspective toward third world development problems was outlined. It asserted that underdevelopment results, to a large degree, from dependency relationships created by the global expansion of capitalism. Whereas center countries are industrially advanced and develop according to their internal needs, peripheral nations are far less autonomous and frequently adopt an imitative or stunted pattern of growth that serves the economic interests of center countries and TNCs better than the

[63] See the comment by a Brazilian doctor in Ledogar (1975: 18).

CROSS-NATIONAL DEPENDENCY ANALYSIS

, needs of their own people. The cross-national look at the international pharmaceutical industry presented in Chapters 6 and 7 provides a test of this proposition.

Countries in the core, semiperiphery, and more-developed and less-developed peripheries of the world system offer a full panoply of development experiences in the drug industry, ranging from virtual self-sufficiency to utter dependency. Transnationals based in the center countries do, in fact, dominate the international pharmaceutical industry. They are not only leaders at the level of total world supply; they are, in addition, usually the major firms within each national market. Dependency in this industry is social and knowledge-based as well as economic. Prescribing doctors and pharmacists are key intermediaries in the promotion-oriented drug distribution system. Without the university infrastructure and financial resources needed to generate new drugs, the vast majority of third world countries find themselves locked into the role of patent licensors rather than patent producers. Trademarked brand names, which are inevitably tied to patented drugs, allow TNC pharmaceutical manufacturers to extend their hold on the market well beyond the limited period of formal patent protection.

According to their position in the world system each set of countries has distinctive concerns about how to maintain or increase their autonomy in the pharmaceutical industry. For center countries the main objective has been to assure a continued high rate of pharmaceutical innovation. In the 1960s and 1970s there was plenty of cause for worry, as the rate at which new drugs were introduced onto the market in the United States and elsewhere declined abruptly. The case of the United States is particularly well documented. In 1957–1961 there were 233 new pharmaceutical products (i.e., new chemical entities or NCEs) introduced in the U.S. market by the drug industry. In the 1962–1966 period the number of NCEs shrank to 93, and by 1967–1971 the appearance of new drugs in the United States had dropped further still to a total of just 76. It is interesting to note that while the rate of U.S.

244

innovation declined, the extent of innovational concentration increased sharply. The four-firm concentration ratio of innovational output rose from a level of 46 percent of all NCEs in 1957–1961 to 54 percent in 1962–1966 and 61 percent in 1967–1971. The leading innovative enterprises, in other words, enlarged their share of total innovations in successive periods. Finally, innovation has also become more concentrated in the biggest pharmaceutical companies in terms of sales. While the four largest drug firms' share of total ethical pharmaceutical sales in the United States remained stable at around 25 percent during the three periods under consideration, these same four companies' share of the industry's innovational output *doubled*, going from 24 percent of NCEs in 1957–1961 and 25 percent in 1962–1966 to 49 percent in 1967–1971 (see Grabowski and Vernon, 1977: 361). Firm size and innovational activities, then, are becoming more closely linked.

Available evidence supports a dual explanation of these trends. On the one hand, the decline in the amount of pharmaceutical innovation carried out in the post–1962 period, and its concentration in fewer and larger firms, appears to be linked to more stringent regulatory controls for drugs in the United States—in particular, the 1962 Kefauver-Harris Amendments[64] (see Peltzman, 1974). On the other hand, an alternate explanation for the decline in new drug discovery is that the underlying stock of research opportunities in the

[64] The 1962 Kefauver-Harris Amendments to the U.S. Food, Drug and Cosmetic Act of 1938 extended the mandate and regulatory control of the Food and Drug Administration (FDA) in several ways. First, they required companies to provide documented scientific evidence on a new drug's *efficacy* in addition to the proof of *safety* required by the 1938 act, generally leading to a substantial increase in the number of tests called for. Second, for the first time the amendments gave the FDA discretionary authority over the clinical research process. Third, firms had to restrict advertising claims in labeling and package inserts to those accepted by the FDA in order to receive approval for the new drug application (NDA) required for product marketing. Finally, FDA regulatory reviews of drug safety became tighter in the post-amendment period than they were before (Grabowski, 1976: 15).

pharmaceutical industry was depleted by the rapid rate of innovation that occurred in the early part of the post–World War II era. According to this argument, the pharmaceutical industry in the 1960s and early 1970s found itself at least temporarily on a "knowledge plateau" (see Grabowski, 1976: 19–24; Schnee and Caglarcan, 1976: 33; Cohen et al., 1975: 18–26). In their comparative study of the United States and the United Kingdom over the pre– and post–1962 amendment periods, Grabowski, Vernon, and Thomas (1976: 64–65, 77) found, in accordance with this dual explanation, that U.S. research and development productivity declined by about sixfold between 1960–1961 and 1966–1970,[65] whereas the corresponding decrease in the United Kingdom was only about threefold. Clearly some worldwide phenomenon, which might be labeled a "depletion of research opportunities," had reduced innovative pharmaceutical output in both countries during this period. Yet the fact that research and development productivity in the United States dropped twice as much as it did in the United Kingdom also gives support to the hypothesis that more stringent regulation in the U.S. drug industry is an additional and important factor causing innovative decline.

One final aspect of innovational concentration in the ethical drug industry should be mentioned. The most innovative firms in the pharmaceutical industry are not only large in terms of sales and based in the center countries, they also tend to be strongly transnational in character. The eight leading innovative firms in the United States in the 1967–1971 period (accounting for over 80 percent of innovative output) were all

[65] Nineteen sixty was the earliest date for which the authors were able to obtain appropriate data on U.K. drug introductions. Nineteen seventy-one was selected as the terminal year to avoid confounding the results with stricter regulatory requirements in the United Kingdom after 1971 due to the implementation of the Medicines Act, which mandated for the first time in that country proof-of-efficacy standards for drugs and made compulsory the investigational new drug (IND) procedure giving the government power of review over the clinical research process. Both measures had been adopted in the United States in 1962.

TNCs, each with manufacturing plants in at least eight foreign countries and seven of them with foreign sales in excess of $100 million (U.S.) in 1970 (Grabowski and Vernon, 1977: 362). This transnational orientation of the most innovative drug companies offers them significant advantages in dealing with the stringent regulatory situations that have evolved in the United States and elsewhere. United States TNCs, for example, can introduce new drug products into foreign markets where regulatory conditions are less stringent prior to (or instead of) introduction in the United States. They thus can gain both knowledge and sales revenues while a new drug compound remains under regulatory review and development in their "home" country. In addition, TNCs can perform certain research and development activities in foreign countries in order to reduce time delays and the overall development costs of new products.

There is an important and recent set of developments in the pharmaceutical industry in center countries that deserves special mention. In the past few years a rash of exciting and potentially revolutionary drug products has been introduced onto the market by pharmaceutical manufacturers, leading many to claim that the industry is on the threshold of a new "golden age of research productivity"[66] (see *Dun's Review,*

---

[66] What is so significant about these recent drug products is that they seem to reflect a series of breakthroughs at the level of basic research—i.e., new knowledge about how the body functions, how disease is caused, and what chemicals interfere with physiological processes. Perhaps the most revolutionary characteristic of many of the new drugs is that instead of simply treating symptoms they have a direct effect on the causes of disease. Up to now, pharmaceutical products have treated arthritis by reducing pain, ulcers mainly by coating the stomach with antacids, allergies by constricting nasal passages, and hypertension by flushing the body of water to reduce blood pressure. Now, equipped with a better understanding of the body's immune-response system and such natural substances as interferon, beta blockers, and prostaglandins, researchers are able to concoct tailor-made pharmaceutical agents to stop the body from overproducing damaging products. Tagamet, for example, counteracts the production of H_2 histamines, which increase the amounts of gastric acid in the stomach. Since the overproduction of acid leads to an ulcer, an agent that

1979; *Newsweek,* 1979*a* and 1979*b*; *Business Week,* 1979).
The star performer of the decade was SmithKline's Tagamet,
an antiulcer drug that was approved by the U.S. FDA in nine
months (instead of the normal two years) and netted for
SmithKline $275 million in sales in 1978, its first full year on
the U.S. market. It generates about one-third of SmithKline's
earnings and helped increase its company's sales by 60 percent and net income by more than 100 percent in two years.
All in all, the U.S. FDA approved the introduction of twenty-
three new compounds in 1978, the most in any year since
1967 (*Business Week,* 1979: 134).

While the pharmaceutical industry may indeed be on the
threshold of a second "golden age" in drug discovery, the
commercial benefits of these scientific advances are likely to
remain highly concentrated. Merck & Co., the biggest U.S.
pharmaceutical TNC, increased its sales by 15 percent and its
net income by 11 percent in 1978 largely on the basis of the
five new drugs it marketed in that year, more than any other
company. Eli Lilly's boom in performance—a sales jump of
19 percent and a 24 percent rise in net income in 1978—was
also closely tied to its research productivity, which led to the
introduction of three major pharmaceuticals in a ten-month
period (*Business Week,* 1979: 134, 137). But for those companies that are lagging behind in the new products race (such
as Richardson-Merrell, G.D. Searle, and Squibb) the economic prospects in the industry's innovative track seem

---

blocks the histamine stops the ulcer from forming. Closely linked to their
revolutionary mode of therapeutic action is a profound change in the
strategy used to develop these new drugs. The traditional method has
been to screen at random thousands of compounds, both synthetic chemicals and natural substances, to discover pharmaceutical products that
have significant medical activity and are safe. More and more, however,
the development job is done today by specifying in advance the characteristics desired in a new drug. This is fundamentally a biological approach,
since the molecules of the chemical compound are designed, atom by
atom, to alter a pretargeted physiological process in the body. The chemists thus must create compounds with the emphasis on effect rather than
chemical structure, which is the reverse of the traditional process.

248

bleak. Few drugmakers can maintain the kind of research and development program that Merck supported, for example, when during a recent ten-year period it spent about $750 million without producing a single important drug for the market. The probable outcome is that the TNCs who reduce their research and development efforts will come to dominate the generic sector of the drug industry (see Frost and Sullivan, Inc., 1976), leaving less and less room for the most price-conscious manufacturers: the smaller-sized national suppliers.

Semiperipheral countries in the pharmaceutical industry have tried to reduce their dependency (or, conversely, increase their autonomy) by increasing the production of active ingredients and their own intermediate chemicals. This is viewed as particularly advantageous because the specialized chemicals used as pharmaceutical inputs are the products most often subject to transfer pricing. One interesting development in this area is that some of the smaller TNCs in the advanced countries have started to demonstrate a strong interest in helping third world nations industrialize, particularly through the mechanism of technology transfer. Swedish firms appear to have taken a lead in this area. Astra, a Swedish drug company that already has manufacturing facilities in Argentina, Brazil, and Mexico, has proposed to be a 26 percent joint owner with both an Indian pharmaceutical company and Nitro-Nobel, another Swedish firm, in order to manufacture clofazimine (a leprosy treatment) in India. When Ciba-Geigy, which holds the patents on clofazimine, refused to transfer its rights or knowledge, Astra offered to help develop a production method based on know-how that bypasses the restrictive patents. The project may take one or two years with an annual cost of about $1 million (U.S.) (Developing World Industry and Technology, Inc., 1979: 23). SweDrug Consulting, a Swedish state-owned company, also provides developing countries with know-how on the manufacture of drugs. While TNCs normally transfer technology only on the basis of wholly owned subsidiaries or majority-owned joint ventures, SweDrug Consulting has been willing to go in on a minority basis or even to accept a lump-sum payment. The company is currently involved in several projects in Cuba and the Arab countries (Agarwal, 1978: 49–50). The Swedish health ministry is trying to set up another enterprise to assist with organizational know-how for third world drug supply systems, including distribution, administration, and plant inspection.

On the whole, pharmaceutical TNCs in semiperipheral countries have made a very limited contribution to local industrialization efforts. There are signs that this is changing, however, as smaller firms from the developed countries have begun accommodating third world demands for increased production capacity. In the larger countries, where packaging and chemical industries are already well established, there is a move to begin local production of the equipment and machinery used by the pharmaceutical industry. Manufacturers in Argentina, Brazil, Egypt, India, and Mexico are willing to sell pharmaceutical plants to other third world nations (UNCTC, 1979: 91). India is on the forefront of this movement. It has begun to concentrate on producing plants of small-scale capacity (less than one ton per day) that can make a variety of chemically related synthetic drugs on a batch basis.

For countries in the periphery local production is far less advanced (if indeed it is carried out at all), the resources made available for health care from the national budget are very limited, and there is a serious shortage of trained personnel. Most of these countries have small national markets, imports are unrestricted, and the proliferation of different brand-named products is great. Pharmaceutical procurement generally is not centralized, and national policy with regard to the drug industry is lacking. For the more-developed nations of the periphery engaged in the packaging and formulation of pharmaceutical products, the prices of imported bulk drugs and raw materials are often considered too high. Many countries also have had difficulty obtaining suitable formulation technology on reasonable terms. This latter problem is manageable, however, since the technology for formulation is relatively simple and can be acquired from a number of third world nations—such as Algeria, Argentina, Brazil, Egypt, India, Mexico, and Pakistan—where the similarity of environment and available infrastructure make it easily adaptable to other developing countries.

The main problems peripheral nations confront are monitoring and controlling the prices of imported finished and semifinished drugs and trying to guarantee that the products actually brought into the country are those most needed by the population. In an effort to reduce the prices of imported pharmaceutical products the state throughout the third world has assumed a more active role in the industry. A basic strategy for the state—endorsed by WHO, UNIDO, and UNCTAD—has been to rationalize the procurement of pharmaceuticals to include only those drugs that, tested for quality and safety, meet the broadest range of health needs in the most economical fashion possible. Such an approach, which is predicated on drawing up a "rationalized" or essential drug list, allocates different priorities to different kinds of drugs based on the incidence of illness, therapeutic efficacy, available resources, and cost. All of the pharmaceutical products contained in such a list would be provided nationally. First-line (or basic) drugs are those that are needed by the primary health-care units of the country, are effective against widely prevalent diseases, and are required for preventive care. Such drugs would probably number no more than fifty to sixty, yet they would meet 80 to 90 percent of total third world health needs. Many of these first-line products are unpatented and fairly standard and thus could be produced by a variety of developing nations. Second-line drugs would be available at regional hospitals to be used for severe cases that do not respond to the first-line drugs and for less prevalent conditions. Third-line drugs would be available only for specialized care (Lall, 1978a: 31). India, Brazil, and Sri Lanka have already introduced reduced lists of drugs in the last decade, following the WHO model list.[67]

One of the main attractions of a rationalized drug list is that it combines the functions of 1) a drug-screening and registration authority, 2) a centralized buying and price control office, and 3) a generic-promotion and information regulation agency (Lall, 1979c). The coordination and implementation of these activities raise a number of practical problems, however, and consequently many states that have set out to reduce pharmaceutical costs have limited themselves to establishing a national drug-purchasing agency. Those third world countries that have initiated a central procurement system for drugs include: Algeria, Brazil, Chad, Egypt, Ethiopia, Guinea, India, Iraq, Rwanda, South Pacific countries (or areas), Sri Lanka, the Syrian Arab Republic, Uganda, the United Republic of Tanzania, and Zambia (UNCTC, 1979: 88–89; Fattorusso, 1979: 253–254). Centralized buying can be instituted for the total drug demand of a country or, alternatively, for only a section (e.g., the public sector or the clients of national health insurance). The economic advantages of a national drug-buying agency apply to purchases of domestic output as well as imports. The benefits of this kind of arrangement include: 1) better market information (from worldwide "shopping around"); 2) better product information (by choosing the most economical of differentiated but therapeutically identical drugs); 3) bulk purchase; and 4) bargaining. There are economies of scale with each of these factors so that the larger the buying agency, the cheaper it is to collect information and assure safety, the more it can buy at low bulk rates, and the better it can bargain. Neighboring small countries,

---

[67] The government of India, for example, has drawn up a list of 117 essential medicines, while the state pharmaceutical firm Central de Medicamentos (CEME) in Brazil has a list of 108 drugs, of which 52 are classified as essential. In 1976 WHO issued a preliminary listing of about 150 pharmaceutical products for developing nations, which was divided into two categories corresponding to first-line and second-line drugs on WHO's priority list (see *SCRIP*, June 11, 1977).

such as the Central American Common Market, the Andean Group, and the Caribbean Centre for Pharmaceuticals, have been able to achieve economies of scale by pooling their drug purchases (see UNCTC, 1981: 51–52; Agarwal, 1978: 36–37). Pooled purchasing eventually could lead to joint manufacture.

Dependency as manifested in the pharmaceutical industry thus takes different forms according to a third world country's level of development. In all cases TNCs are involved. This is true for capitalist as well as socialist third world nations, which must deal with pharmaceutical TNCs as importers, local producers, or licensors of technology. In their quest for greater autonomy, developing nations have turned inward to domestic institutions like the state while simultaneously trying to modify their links with the external world. The continuing dilemmas of development must be understood, then, as generating not just constraints but also opportunities for national actors.

Bibliography

Agarwal, Anil. 1978. *Drugs and the Third World*. London: Earthscan.

Alfaro Lara, Carlos; Calderón Rodríguez, Carlos; and Alfaro Lara, Gerardo. 1977. "Las transnacionales y el costo de los medicamentos en Costa Rica." *Comercio exterior* 27, no. 8 (August): 945–950.

Almond, Gabriel A., and Coleman, James S., eds. 1960. *The Politics of the Developing Areas*. Princeton, N.J.: Princeton University Press.

Amin, Samir. [1970], 1974. *Accumulation on a World Scale*. 2 vols. New York: Monthly Review Press.

———. [1973a], 1976. *Unequal Development: An Essay on the Social Formations of Peripheral Capitalism*. New York: Monthly Review Press.

———. 1973b. "Underdevelopment and Dependence in Black Africa—Their Historical Origins and Contemporary Forms." *Social and Economic Studies* 22, no. 1 (March): 177–196.

Applezweig, Norman. 1953. "Steroid Hormone Products: A Key to the Future." *Drug and Cosmetic Industry* 73, no. 6 (December): 754–755, 851–857.

———. 1959. "The Big Steroid Treasure Hunt." *Chemical Week* (January 31): 38–52.

———. 1962. *Steroid Drugs*. New York: McGraw-Hill.

———. 1969. "Steroids." *Chemical Week* (May 17): 58–68.

Aron, Raymond. [1962], 1967. *18 Lectures on Industrial Society*. London: Weidenfeld and Nicolson.

Asociación latinoamericana de industrias farmacéuticas (ALIFAR). 1982. "Industria farmacéutica latinoamericana." 28 pp. Buenos Aires, April.

Bachrach, Peter, and Baratz, Morton S. 1962. "The Two Faces of Power." *American Political Science Review* 56, no. 4 (December): 947–952.

———, and Baratz, Morton S. 1963. "Decisions and Nondecisions: An Analytical Framework." *American Political Science Review* 57, no. 3 (September): 632–642.

Balandier, Georges. 1955. *The Sociology of Black Africa: Social Dynamics in Central Africa.* New York: Praeger.

Bambirra, Vania. 1974. *El capitalismo dependiente latinoamericano.* Mexico, D.F.: Siglo XXI.

Baran, Paul A. [1957], 1968. *The Political Economy of Growth.* New York: Monthly Review Press.

Bell, Daniel. [1973], 1976. *The Coming of Post-Industrial Society: A Venture in Social Forecasting.* New York: Basic Books.

Bell, Wendell. 1974. "A Conceptual Analysis of Equality and Equity in Evolutionary Perspective." *American Behavioral Scientist* 18, no. 1 (September–October): 8–35.

Bendix, Reinhard. 1963. "Concepts and Generalizations in Comparative Sociological Studies." *American Sociological Review* 28, no. 4 (August): 532–539.

Bennett, Douglas; Blachman, Morris J.; and Sharpe, Kenneth. 1978. "Mexico and Multinational Corporations: An Explanation of State Action." In *Latin America and World Economy: A Changing International Order,* edited by Joseph Grunwald, pp. 257–282. Beverly Hills, Ca.: Sage Publications.

———, and Sharpe, Kenneth. 1979. "Agenda Setting and Bargaining Power: The Mexican State Versus Transnational Automobile Corporations." *World Politics* 32, no. 1 (October): 57–89.

———, and Sharpe, Kenneth. 1980. "The State as Banker and Entrepreneur: The Last-Resort Character of the Mexican State's Economic Intervention, 1917–1976." *Comparative Politics* 12, no. 2 (January): 165–189.

Bertero, Carlos O. 1973. "Drugs and Dependency in Brazil: An Empirical Study of Dependency Theory, the Case of

the Pharmaceutical Industry." Latin American Studies
Program Dissertation Series, no. 36, Cornell University,
Ithaca, N.Y.

Bibile, Senaka. 1977. "Case Studies in Transfer of Technol-
ogy: Pharmaceutical Policies in Sri Lanka." Geneva:
United Nations Conference on Trade and Development.
(TD/ B/ C.6/ 21).

Biersteker, Thomas J. 1979. *Distortion or Development? Contending Perspectives on the Multinational Corporation.*
Cambridge, Mass.: MIT Press.

Black, Cyril E. 1966. *The Dynamics of Modernization: A
Study in Comparative History.* New York: Harper &
Row.

Bodenheimer, Susanne J. 1970. "The Ideology of Develop-
mentalism: American Political Science's Paradigm-Sur-
rogate for Latin American Studies." *Berkeley Journal of
Sociology* 15: 95–137.

———. 1971. "Dependency and Imperialism: The Roots of
Latin American Underdevelopment." In *Readings in
U.S. Imperialism,* edited by K. T. Fann and Donald C.
Hodges, pp. 155–181. Boston: Porter Sargent.

Booth, David. 1975. "Andre Gunder Frank: An Introduction
and Appreciation." In *Beyond the Sociology of Development: Economy and Society in Latin America and
Africa,* edited by Ivar Oxaal, Tony Barnett, and David
Booth, pp. 50–85. London: Routledge and Kegan Paul.

Borkin, Joseph. 1978. *The Crime and Punishment of I. G. Farben.* New York: Free Press.

Bremer, Quintana, Vaca, Rocha, Obregon y Mancera (law
firm). 1976. "El problema del precio del barbasco en la
industria mexicana de productos esteroides." Mimeograph. 37 pp. Mexico, D.F.: February 25.

Brooke, Paul A. 1975. *Resistant Prices: A Study of Competitive Strains in the Antibiotic Markets.* New York: Council
on Economic Priorities.

Bruchey, Stuart. [1965], 1968. *The Roots of American Eco-*

BIBLIOGRAPHY

nomic Growth, 1607–1861: An Essay in Social Causation. New York: Harper & Row.

Brzezinski, Zbigniew. 1970. Between Two Ages: America's Role in the Technetronic Era. New York: Viking.

Business Latin America (New York, N.Y.).

Business Week. 1974. "The Drug Industry's Clouded Future." November 23: 64–73.

———. 1979. "Eli Lilly: New Life in the Drug Industry." October 29: 134–145.

Caporaso, James A. 1978a. "Introduction: Dependence and Dependency in the Global System." International Organization 32, no. 1 (Winter): 1–12.

———. 1978b. "Dependence, Dependency, and Power in the Global System: A Structural and Behavioral Analysis." International Organization 32, no. 1 (Winter): 13–43.

Cardoso, Fernando Henrique. 1971. Ideologías de la burguesía industrial en sociedades dependientes (Argentina y Brasil). Mexico, D.F.: Siglo XXI.

———. 1972a. "Dependency and Development in Latin America." New Left Review 74 (July–August): 83–95.

———. 1972b. "Notas sobre el estado actual de los estudios sobre dependencia." Revista latinoamericana de ciencias sociales, no. 4 (December): 3–31.

———. 1973. "Associated-Dependent Development: Theoretical and Practical Implications." In Authoritarian Brazil: Origins, Policies, and Future, edited by Alfred Stepan, pp. 142–176. New Haven, Conn.: Yale University Press.

———. 1974. "Las contradicciones del desarrollo asociado." Desarrollo económico 14, no. 53 (April–June): 3–32.

———. 1977. "The Consumption of Dependency Theory in the United States." Latin American Research Review 12, no. 3: 7–24.

———. 1979. "On the Characterization of Authoritarian Regimes in Latin America." In The New Authoritarianism in Latin America, edited by David Collier, pp. 33–57. Princeton, N.J.: Princeton University Press.

————, and Faletto, Enzo. [1969], 1979. *Dependency and Development in Latin America.* Expanded and emended edition. Berkeley, Ca.: University of California Press.

Chilcote, Ronald H. 1974. "Dependency: A Critical Synthesis of the Literature." *Latin American Perspectives* 1, no. 1 (Spring): 4–29.

————. 1978. "A Question of Dependency." *Latin American Research Review* 13, no. 2: 55–58.

————, and Edelstein, Joel C., eds. 1974. *Latin America: The Struggle with Dependency and Beyond.* Cambridge, Mass.: Schenkman.

Chudnovsky, Daniel. 1979. "The Challenge by Domestic Enterprises to the Transnational Corporations' Domination: A Case Study of the Argentine Pharmaceutical Industry." *World Development* 7, no. 1 (January): 45–58.

Clarkson, Kenneth W. 1977. *Intangible Capital and Rates of Return: Effects of Research and Promotion on Profitability.* Washington, D.C.: American Enterprise Institute for Public Policy Research.

Clymer, Harold A. 1975. "The Economic and Regulatory Climate: U.S. and Overseas Trends." In *Drug Development and Marketing,* edited by Robert B. Helms, pp. 137–154. Washington, D.C.: American Enterprise Institute for Public Policy Research.

Cohen, Benjamin I.; Katz, Jorge; and Beck, William T. 1975. "Innovation and Foreign Investment Behavior of the U.S. Pharmaceutical Industry." National Bureau of Economic Research, Working Paper no. 101. New York.

Collier, David, ed. 1979. *The New Authoritarianism in Latin America.* Princeton, N.J.: Princeton University Press.

Cooper, Joseph D. 1970. "The Sources of Innovation." In *The Economics of Drug Innovation,* edited by Joseph D. Cooper, pp. 41–54. Washington, D.C.: The American University.

Crenson, Matthew A. 1971. *The Un-Politics of Air Pollution: A Study in Non-Decisionmaking in the Cities.* Baltimore, Md.: Johns Hopkins Press.

BIBLIOGRAPHY

Cueva, Agustin. 1976. "A Summary of 'Problems and Perspectives of Dependency Theory'." *Latin American Perspectives* 3, no. 4 (Fall): 12–16.

Dahl, Robert A. 1961. *Who Governs? Democracy and Power in an American City.* New Haven, Conn.: Yale University Press.

Dahrendorf, Ralf. [1957], 1959. *Class and Class Conflict in Industrial Society.* Stanford, Ca.: Stanford University Press.

de María y Campos, Mauricio. 1977. "La industria farmacéutica en México." *Comercio exterior* 27, no. 8 (August): 888–912.

Deolalikar, Anil B. 1980. "Foreign Technology in the Indian Pharmaceutical Industry: Its Impact on Local Innovation and Social Equity." Mimeograph. 99 pp. Paper prepared for the Council on International and Public Affairs, New York.

de Oliveira, Francisco, and Travolo Popoutchi, María Angélica. 1979. *Transnacionales en América Latina: el complejo automotor en Brasil.* Mexico, D.F.: Editorial Nueva Imagen.

Developing World Industry and Technology, Inc. 1979. "Changes in the Terms and Conditions of Technology Transfer by the Pharmaceutical Industry to Newly Industrializing Nations: An Overview of the Past Ten Years." Mimeograph. 28 pp. Paper prepared for the U.S. Agency for International Development, Washington, D.C.

El día (Mexico City).

Diario oficial (Mexico City).

Djerassi, Carl. 1968. "A High Priority? Research Centers in Developing Nations." *Bulletin of the Atomic Scientists* 26, no. 1 (January): 22–27.

———. 1979. *The Politics of Contraception.* New York: Norton.

Dos Santos, Theotonio. 1969. "La crisis de la teoría del desarrollo y las relaciones de dependencia en América Latina." In *La dependencia político-económica en América*

Latina, edited by Hélio Jaguaribe et al., pp. 147–187. Mexico, D.F.: Siglo XXI.

————. 1970. "The Structure of Dependence." *American Economic Review* 60, no. 9 (May): 231–236.

————. 1972. *Socialismo o fascismo: el nuevo carácter de la dependencia y el dilemma latinoamericano.* Santiago, Chile: Editorial Prensa Latinoamericana S.A.

Dun's Review. 1979. "Prescription for Profits." January: 39–41.

Durkheim, Emile. [1893], 1964. *The Division of Labor in Society.* New York: Free Press.

Eckstein, Harry. 1975. "Case Study and Theory in Political Science." In *Handbook of Political Science, Vol. 7: Strategies of Inquiry,* edited by Fred I. Greenstein and Nelson W. Polsby, pp. 79–137. Reading, Mass.: Addison-Wesley.

Erickson, Kenneth Paul, and Peppe, Patrick V. 1976. "Dependent Capitalist Development, U.S. Foreign Policy, and Repression of the Working Class in Chile and Brazil." *Latin American Perspectives* 3, no. 1 (Winter): 19–44.

Evans, Peter B. 1971. "National Autonomy and Economic Development: Critical Perspectives on Multinational Corporations in Poor Countries." In *Transnational Relations and World Politics,* edited by Robert O. Keohane and Joseph S. Nye, pp. 325–342. Cambridge, Mass.: Harvard University Press.

————. 1976. "Foreign Investment and Industrial Transformation: A Brazilian Case Study." *Journal of Development Economics* 3: 119–139.

————. 1977. "Multinationals, State-Owned Corporations, and the Transformation of Imperialism: A Brazilian Case Study." *Economic Development and Cultural Change* 26, no. 1 (October): 43–64.

————. 1979a. *Dependent Development: The Alliance of Multinational, State, and Local Capital in Brazil.* Princeton, N.J.: Princeton University Press.

————. 1979b. "Beyond Center and Periphery: A Comment

on the Contribution of the World System Approach to the Study of Development." *Sociological Inquiry* 49, no. 4: 15–20.

————, and Gereffi, Gary. 1980. "Inversión extranjera y desarrollo dependiente: una comparación entre Brasil y México." *Revista mexicana de sociología* 42, no. 1 (January–March): 9–70.

————, and Gereffi, Gary. 1982. "Foreign Investment and Dependent Development: Comparing Brazil and Mexico." In *Brazil and Mexico: Patterns in Late Development*, edited by Sylvia Hewlett and Richard Weinert, pp. 111–168. Philadelphia, Pa.: Institute for the Study of Human Issues.

Excelsior (Mexico City).

Fajnzylber, Fernando, and Martínez Tarragó, Trinidad. 1976. *Las empresas transnacionales: expansión a nivel mundial y proyección en la industria mexicana.* Mexico, D.F.: Fondo de Cultura Económica.

Faria, Vilmar. 1976. "Urban Marginality as a Structural Phenomenon: An Overview of the Literature." Ph.D. dissertation, Harvard University, Cambridge, Mass.

Fattorusso, Vittorio. 1979. "Developing Country Perspectives—An Overview." In *Pharmaceuticals for Developing Countries*, the Institute of Medicine, pp. 250–259. Washington, D.C.: United States National Academy of Sciences.

Fieldhouse, D. K., ed. 1967. *The Theory of Capitalist Imperialism.* New York: Barnes & Noble.

Fogel, Robert W. 1964. *Railroads and American Economic Growth: Essays in Econometric History.* Baltimore, Md.: Johns Hopkins Press.

Foster-Carter, Aidan. 1978. "The Modes of Production Controversy." *New Left Review*, no. 107 (January–February): 47–77.

Frank, Andre Gunder. 1967a. *Capitalism and Underdevelopment in Latin America: Historical Studies in Chile and Brazil.* New York: Monthly Review Press.

────. 1967b. "Sociology of Development and Underdevelopment of Sociology." *Catalyst,* no. 3 (Summer): 20–73. (Reprinted in Frank, 1969.)

────. 1969. *Latin America: Underdevelopment or Revolution.* New York: Monthly Review Press.

────. 1972. *Lumpenbourgeoisie: Lumpendevelopment.* New York: Monthly Review Press.

────. 1978. *World Accumulation, 1492–1789.* New York: Monthly Review Press.

Frost & Sullivan, Inc. 1976. "The U.S. Generic Drug Market." New York: Frost & Sullivan, Inc.

Furtado, Celso. [1959], 1971. *The Economic Growth of Brazil: A Survey from Colonial to Modern Times.* Berkeley, Ca.: University of California Press.

────. [1970], 1978. *Economic Development of Latin America: Historical Background and Contemporary Problems.* 2d ed. Cambridge, Eng.: Cambridge University Press.

Galtung, Johan. 1980. "The Politics of Self-Reliance." In *Self-Reliance: A Strategy for Development,* edited by Johan Galtung, Peter O'Brien, and Roy Preiswerk, pp. 355–383. London: Bogle-L'Ouverture Publications.

Gereffi, Gary. 1970. "Dimensions of Community Power: A Study of an Unincorporated Town." *Sociological Focus* 3, no. 4 (Summer): 43–64.

────. 1977. "Los oligopolios internacionales, el estado y el desarrollo industrial en México: el caso de la industria de hormonas esteroides." *Foro internacional* 17, no. 4 (April–June): 490–541.

────. 1978. "Drug Firms and Dependency in Mexico: The Case of the Steroid Hormone Industry." *International Organization* 32, no. 1 (Winter): 237–286.

────. 1980. " 'Wonder Drugs' and Transnational Corporations in Mexico: An Elaboration and Limiting-Case Test of Dependency Theory." Ph.D. dissertation, Yale University, New Haven, Conn.

────. 1982. "Transnational Corporations and the Pharmaceutical Industry in Mexico." Mimeograph. 42 pp. Paper prepared for the United Nations Centre on Transnational Corporations, New York.

————. 1983. "The Global Pharmaceutical Industry and Its Impact in Latin America." In *International Oligopolies and Development*, edited by Richard S. Newfarmer. University of Notre Dame Press, forthcoming.

————, and Evans, Peter. 1981. "Transnational Corporations, Dependent Development, and State Policy in the Semiperiphery: A Comparison of Brazil and Mexico." *Latin American Research Review* 16, no. 3: 31–64.

————, and Newfarmer, Richard. 1982. "The State and International Oligopolies: Some Patterns of Response to Uneven Development in Latin America." Mimeograph. 75 pp. Paper presented at the annual meeting of the American Political Science Association, Denver, September.

Gilbert, Guy J. 1974. "Socialism and Dependency." *Latin American Perspectives* 1, no. 1 (Spring): 107–123.

Ginsberg, Chaim. 1972. "An Historical Analysis of the Multinationalization Process of the U.S. Pharmaceutical Industry." Ph.D. dissertation, New School for Social Research, New York.

Goodman, Louis Wolf. 1976. "The Social Organization of Decision-Making in the Multinational Corporation." In *The Multinational Corporation and Social Change*, edited by David E. Apter and Louis Wolf Goodman, pp. 63–95. New York: Praeger.

Goodsell, Charles. 1974. *American Corporations and Peruvian Politics*. Cambridge, Mass.: Harvard University Press.

Grabowski, Henry G. 1976. *Drug Regulation and Innovation: Empirical Evidence and Policy Options*. Washington, D.C.: American Enterprise Institute for Public Policy Research.

————, and Vernon, John M. 1977. "Innovation and Invention: Consumer Protection Regulation in Ethical Drugs." *American Economic Review* 67, no. 1 (February): 359–364.

————; Vernon, John M.; and Thomas, Lacy Glen. 1976. "The Effects of Regulatory Policy on the Incentives to Innovate: An International Comparative Analysis." In *Impact of Public Policy on Drug Innovation and Pricing*, edited by Samuel A. Mitchell and Emery A. Link, pp. 47–82. Washington, D.C.: American Enterprise Institute for Public Policy Research.

Gusfield, Joseph R. 1967. "Tradition and Modernity: Misplaced Polarities in the Study of Social Change." *American Journal of Sociology* 72, no. 4 (January): 351–362.

Hagen, Everett E. 1962. *On the Theory of Social Change: How Economic Growth Begins*. Homewood, Il.: Dorsey.

Halperin-Donghi, Tulio. 1982. " 'Dependency Theory' and Latin American Historiography." *Latin American Research Review* 17, no. 1: 115–130.

Hamilton, Nora. 1975a. "Dependent Capitalism and the State: The Case of Mexico." *Kapitalistate*, no. 3 (Spring): 72–82.

————. 1975b. "Mexico: The Limits of State Autonomy." *Latin American Perspectives* 2, no. 2 (Summer): 81–108.

Hansen, Roger D. 1971. *The Politics of Mexican Development*. Baltimore, Md.: Johns Hopkins Press.

Harding, Timothy F. 1976. "Dependency, Nationalism, and the State in Latin America." *Latin American Perspectives* 3, no. 4 (Fall): 3–11.

Heilbroner, Robert L. 1980. *An Inquiry into the Human Prospect: Updated and Reconsidered for the 1980s*. New York: Norton.

El heraldo (Mexico City).

Hirschman, Albert O. 1978. "Beyond Asymmetry: Critical Notes on Myself as a Young Man and on Some Other Old Friends." *International Organization* 32, no. 1 (Winter): 45–50.

Hoselitz, Bert F. 1960. *Sociological Aspects of Economic Growth*. Glencoe, Il.: Free Press.

Huntington, Samuel P. 1971. "The Change to Change: Modernization, Development, and Politics." *Comparative Politics* 3, no. 3 (April): 283–322.

Illich, Ivan. 1976. *Medical Nemesis: The Expropriation of Health.* New York: Bantam Books.

IMSworld Publications Ltd. 1979. "Health, Pharmaceutical and Development Indicators World-Wide: A Statistical Survey." London: IMSworld Publications Ltd. (Prepared as a supplement to Tiefenbacher, 1979.)

Inkeles, Alex. 1969. "Making Men Modern: On the Causes and Consequences of Individual Change in Six Countries." *American Journal of Sociology* 75, no. 2 (September): 208–225.

Jaguaribe, Hélio. 1969. "Dependencia y autonomía en América Latina." In *La dependencia político-económica de América Latina,* edited by Hélio Jaguaribe et al., pp. 1–85. Mexico, D.F.: Siglo XXI.

James, Barrie G. 1977. *The Future of the Multinational Pharmaceutical Industry to 1990.* New York: Halsted Press.

Jenkins, Rhys Owen. 1977. *Dependent Industrialization in Latin America: The Automotive Industry in Argentina, Chile, and Mexico.* New York: Praeger.

Kahl, Joseph A. 1976. *Modernization, Exploitation and Dependency in Latin America: Germani, González Casanova, and Cardoso.* New Brunswick, N.J.: Transaction Books.

Katz, Jorge M. 1974. *Oligopolio, firmas nacionales y empresas multinacionales: la industria farmacéutica argentina.* Buenos Aires: Siglo XXI.

―――. 1981. "Estudios de desarrollo e industria químico-farmacéutica." *Cuadernos médico sociales* (Argentina), vol. 18 (October): 53–75.

Kefauver, Estes (with the assistance of Irene Till). 1965. *In a Few Hands: Monopoly Power in America.* New York: Pantheon Books.

Kerr, Clark; Dunlop, John T.; Harbison, Frederick; and Myers, Charles A. 1960. *Industrialism and Industrial Man: The Problems of Labor and Management in Economic Growth.* Cambridge, Mass.: Harvard University Press.

Kindleberger, Charles P. 1969. *American Business Abroad: Six Lectures on Direct Investment.* New Haven, Conn.: Yale University Press.

———. 1973. *The World in Depression, 1929–1939.* Berkeley, Ca.: University of California Press.

———, and Herrick, Bruce. 1977. *Economic Development.* 3d ed. New York: McGraw-Hill.

Knickerbocker, Frederick T. 1973. *Oligopolistic Reaction and Multinational Enterprise.* Boston: Division of Research, Graduate School of Business Administration, Harvard University.

Krasner, Stephen D. 1973. "Manipulating International Commodity Markets: Brazilian Coffee Policy, 1906 to 1962." *Public Policy* 21, no. 4 (Fall): 493–523.

Krieger, Mario, and Prieto, Norma. 1977. "Comercio exterior, sustitución de importaciones y tecnología en la industria farmacéutica argentina." *Desarrollo económico* 17, no. 65 (July–September): 179–210.

Labastida M. del Campo, Julio. 1975. "Nacionalismo reformista en México." *Cuadernos políticos,* no. 3 (January–March): 33–51.

Lall, Sanjaya. 1973. "Transfer-Pricing by Multinational Manufacturing Firms." *Oxford Bulletin of Economics and Statistics* 35, no. 3 (August): 173–195.

———. 1974. "Less-Developed Countries and Private Foreign Direct Investment: A Review Article." *World Development* 2, nos. 4 & 5 (April–May): 43–48.

———. 1975a. "Major Issues in Transfer of Technology to Developing Countries: A Case Study of the Pharmaceutical Industry." Geneva: United Nations Conference on Trade and Development. (TD/ B/ C.6/4).

———. 1975b. "Is 'Dependence' a Useful Concept in Analysing Underdevelopment?" *World Development* 3, nos. 11 & 12 (November–December): 799–810.

———. 1978a. "Growth of the Pharmaceutical Industry in Developing Countries: Problems and Prospects." Vienna: United Nations Industrial Development Organization. (United Nations publication, Sales No. E.78.II.B.4).

———. 1978*b*. "Price Competition and the International Pharmaceutical Industry." *Oxford Bulletin of Economics and Statistics* 40, no. 1 (February): 9–21.

———. 1979*a*. "Transfer Pricing and Developing Countries: Some Problems of Investigation." *World Development* 7, no. 1 (January): 59–71.

———. 1979*b*. "Problems of Distribution, Availability, and Utilization of Agents in Developing Countries: An Asian Perspective." In *Pharmaceuticals for Developing Countries*, the Institute of Medicine, pp. 236–249. Washington, D.C.: United States National Academy of Sciences.

———. 1979*c*. "Emerging Trends and Future Prospects in the Less Developed Countries." In *Medicines for the Year 2000*, edited by George Teeling-Smith, pp. 100–109. London: Office of Health Economics.

———, and Bibile, Senaka. 1977. "The Political Economy of Controlling Transnationals: The Pharmaceutical Industry in Sri Lanka (1972–1976)." *World Development* 5, no. 8 (August): 677–697.

Ledogar, Robert J. 1975. *Hungry for Profits: U.S. Food & Drug Multinationals in Latin America*. New York: IDOC/ North America.

Lehmann, Pedro A.; Bolivar G., Antonio; and Quintero R., Rodolfo. 1973. "Russell Marker: Pioneer of the Mexican Steroid Industry." *Journal of Chemical Education* 50, no. 3 (March): 195–199.

Lenin, Vladimir I. [1899], 1956. *The Development of Capitalism in Russia*. Moscow: Foreign Languages Publishing House.

———. [1916], 1971. "Imperialism, the Highest Stage of Capitalism." In *V. I. Lenin: Selected Works*, pp. 169–263. New York: International Publishers.

Lerner, Daniel. [1958], 1964. *The Passing of Traditional Society: Modernizing the Middle East*. New York: Free Press.

Leys, Colin. 1974. *Underdevelopment in Kenya: The Political Economy of Neocolonialism, 1964–1971*. Berkeley, Ca.: University of California Press.

Lukes, Steven. 1974. *Power: A Radical View*. London: Macmillan.

McClelland, David C. 1961. *The Achieving Society*. New York: Van Nostrand.

McClelland, Peter D. 1975. *Causal Explanation and Model Building in History, Economics, and the New Economic History*. Ithaca, N.Y.: Cornell University Press.

McDermott, Walsh. 1980. "Pharmaceuticals: Their Role in Developing Societies." *Science* 209, no. 4453 (July): 240–245.

McDonough, Peter. 1981. *Power and Ideology in Brazil*. Princeton, N.J.: Princeton University Press.

McGreevey, William Paul. 1971. *An Economic History of Colombia, 1845–1930*. Cambridge, Eng.: Cambridge University Press.

Maine, Sir Henry. [1861], 1965. *Ancient Law: Its Connection with the Early History of Society and Its Relation to Modern Ideas*. New York: Dutton.

Mandelbaum, Maurice. 1971. *History, Man, and Reason: A Study in Nineteenth-Century Thought*. Baltimore, Md.: Johns Hopkins Press.

Marini, Ruy Mauro. 1972. "Brazilian Sub-Imperialism." *Monthly Review* 9 (February): 14–24.

————. 1973. *Dialéctica de la dependencia*. Mexico, D.F.: Ediciones Era.

Marx, Karl. [1867], 1967. *Capital: A Critique of Political Economy*. Vol. 1. New York: International Publishers.

Measday, Walter S. 1977. "The Pharmaceutical Industry." In *The Structure of American Industry*, edited by Walter Adams, pp. 250–284. New York: Macmillan.

Mendelsohn, Robert S. 1979. *Confessions of a Medical Heretic*. Chicago: Contemporary Books.

El mercado de valores (Mexico City).

México. Secretaría de Industria y Comercio. Dirección General de Estadística. 1966–1977. *Anuario estadístico del comercio exterior.* Mexico, D.F.

Michels, Robert. [1911], 1968. *Political Parties: A Sociological Study of the Oligarchical Tendencies of Modern Democracy.* New York: Free Press.

Miliband, Ralph. 1969. *The State in Capitalist Society.* New York: Basic Books.

Moran, Theodore H. 1973. "Foreign Expansion as an 'Institutional Necessity' for U.S. Corporate Capitalism: The Search for a Radical Model." *World Politics* 25, no. 3 (April): 369–386.

———. 1974a. *Multinational Corporations and the Politics of Dependence: Copper in Chile.* Princeton, N.J.: Princeton University Press.

———. 1974b. "The Theory of International Exploitation in Large Natural Resource Investments." In *Testing Theories of Economic Imperialism,* edited by Steven Rosen and James Kurth, pp. 163–181. New York: Heath.

———. 1978. "Multinational Corporations and Dependency: A Dialogue for Dependentistas and Non-Dependentistas." *International Organization* 32, no. 1 (Winter): 79–100.

Newfarmer, Richard S. 1980a. *Transnational Conglomerates and the Economics of Dependent Development.* Greenwich, Conn.: JAI Press.

———. 1980b. "State Elites in Power: State Control of the Electric Power Industry in Latin America." Mimeograph. 309 pp. Mexico City: ILET (DEE/D/50/I).

———, ed. 1983. *International Oligopoly and Development.* University of Notre Dame Press, forthcoming.

———, and Mueller, Willard F. 1975. *Multinational Corporations in Brazil and Mexico: Structural Sources of Economic and Noneconomic Power.* Report to the Subcommittee on Multinational Corporations, Committee on Foreign Relations, U.S. Senate. Washington, D.C.: Government Printing Office.

Newsweek. 1979a. "Relief from Migraine." September 10: 69.

————. 1979b. "Drugs and Psychiatry: A New Era." November 12: 98–104.

New York Times. 1976. "Drugs in Europe: Collision of Interests." March 21, sec. 3, pp. 1, 6.

————. 1978. "European Drug Companies on a U.S. Buying Spree." January 22, sec. F, p. 3.

Niehans, Jürg. 1977. "Benefits of Multinational Firms for a Small Parent Economy: The Case of Switzerland." In *Multinationals from Small Countries,* edited by Tamir Agmon and Charles P. Kindleberger, pp. 1–39. Cambridge, Mass.: MIT Press.

Nisbet, Robert A. 1969. *Social Change and History: Aspects of the Western Theory of Development.* New York: Oxford University Press.

North, Douglas C. 1966. *Growth and Welfare in the American Past.* Englewood Cliffs, N.J.: Prentice-Hall.

Novedades (Mexico City).

O'Brien, Peter. 1977. "Trademarks, the International Pharmaceutical Industry, and the Developing Countries." The Hague: Institute of Social Studies Occasional Papers, no. 63.

O'Donnell, Guillermo A. 1973. *Modernization and Bureaucratic-Authoritarianism: Studies in South American Politics.* Berkeley, Ca.: Institute of International Studies, University of California.

————. 1978. "Reflections on the Patterns of Change in the Bureaucratic-Authoritarian State." *Latin American Research Review* 13, no. 1: 3–38.

————, and Linck, Delfina. 1973. *Dependencia y autonomía: formas de dependencia y estratégias de liberación.* Buenos Aires: Amorrortu Editores.

Olizar, Marynka. 1975–1976. *Guía de los mercados de México.* 8th ed. Mexico, D.F.: Marynka Olizar.

Organization for Economic Co-operation and Development (OECD). 1977. "Impact of Multinational Enterprises on National Scientific and Technical Capacities: Pharmaceutical Industry." Paris: OECD. (DSTI/ SPR/ 77.34).

Packenham, Robert A. 1974. "Latin American Dependency Theories: Strengths and Weaknesses." Mimeograph. 62 pp. Paper presented at the Harvard-M.I.T. Joint Seminar on Political Development, Cambridge, Mass., February 6.

————. 1978. "The New Utopianism: Political Development Ideas in the Dependency Literature." Mimeograph. 40 pp. Paper presented at the annual meeting of the American Political Science Association, New York, September.

————. 1982. "Plus ça Change . . . : The English Edition of Cardoso and Faletto's *Dependencia y Desarrollo en América Latina.*" *Latin American Research Review* 17, no. 1: 131–151.

Palma, Gabriel. 1978. "Dependency: A Formal Theory of Underdevelopment or a Methodology for the Analysis of Concrete Situations of Underdevelopment?" *World Development* 6, nos. 7 & 8 (July–August): 881–924.

Paredes López, Octavio. 1977. "Consideraciones sobre la actividad de las empresas farmacéuticas en México." *Comercio exterior* 27, no. 8 (August): 932–941.

Parsons, Talcott. [1951], 1964. *The Social System.* New York: Free Press.

Peltzman, Sam. 1974. *Regulation of Pharmaceutical Innovation: The 1962 Amendments.* Washington, D.C.: American Enterprise Institute for Public Policy Research.

Pharmaceutical Manufacturers Association (PMA). 1976. "The Economic and Social Contributions of the U.S. Multinational Pharmaceutical Industry." Washington, D.C.

————. 1978. "Annual Survey Report: Ethical Pharmaceutical Industry Operations 1977–1978." Washington, D.C.

Pinto, Aníbal, and Kñakal, Jan. 1973. "The Centre-Periphery System Twenty Years Later." *Social and Economic Studies* 22, no. 1 (March): 34–89.

Portes, Alejandro. 1973. "Modernity and Development: A Critique." *Studies in Comparative International Development* 8, no. 3 (Fall): 247–279.

———. 1976. "On the Sociology of National Development: Theories and Issues." *American Journal of Sociology* 82, no. 1 (July): 55–85.

———. 1980. "Convergencies Between Conflicting Theoretical Perspectives in National Development." In *Sociological Theory and Research: A Critical Appraisal*, edited by Hubert M. Blalock, Jr., pp. 220–227. New York: Free Press.

Prebisch, Raúl. 1950. *The Economic Development of Latin America and Its Principal Problems*. New York: United Nations.

Productos Químicos Vegetales Mexicanos, S.A. de C.V. (Proquivemex). 1976. "Informe al honorable consejo de administración." Mexico, D.F.: January 16.

Quijano, Aníbal. 1971. "Nationalism and Capitalism in Peru: A Study in Neoimperialism." *Monthly Review* 23 (July–August): 1–122.

Ray, David. 1973. "The Dependency Model of Latin American Underdevelopment: Three Basic Fallacies." *Journal of Interamerican Studies and World Affairs* 15, no. 1 (February): 4–20.

Renaud, Marc. 1975. "On the Structural Constraints to State Intervention in Health." *International Journal of Health Services* 5, no. 4: 559–571.

Rostow, Walt W. [1960], 1971. *The Stages of Economic Growth: A Non-Communist Manifesto*. 2d. ed. Cambridge, Eng.: Cambridge University Press.

Roxborough, Ian. 1976. "Dependency Theory in the Sociology of Development: Some Theoretical Problems." *West African Journal of Sociology and Political Science* 1, no. 2 (January): 116–133.

Rustow, Dankwart A. 1967. *A World of Nations: Problems of Political Modernization*. Washington, D.C.: The Brookings Institution.

Sarett, Lewis H. 1979. "Current Programs for Development of Pharmaceuticals: The United States Pharmaceutical Industry." In *Pharmaceuticals for Developing Countries*, the Institute of Medicine, pp. 130–135. Washington, D.C.: United States National Academy of Sciences.

Schaumann, Leif. 1976. "Pharmaceutical Industry Dynamics and Outlook to 1985." Menlo Park, Ca.: Stanford Research Institute.

Schnee, Jerome, and Caglarcan, Erol. 1976. "The Changing Pharmaceutical R & D Environment." *Business Economics* 11, no. 3 (May): 31–38.

Schwartzman, David. 1976. *Innovation in the Pharmaceutical Industry.* Baltimore, Md.: Johns Hopkins Press.

SCRIP (Richmond, Surrey, England).

Silverman, Milton. 1976. *The Drugging of the Americas: How Multinational Drug Companies Say One Thing About Their Products to Physicians in the United States, and Another Thing to Physicians in Latin America.* Berkeley, Ca.: University of California Press.

———. 1977. "The Epidemiology of Drug Promotion." *International Journal of Health Services* 7, no. 2: 157–166.

———, and Lee, Philip R. 1974. *Pills, Profits, and Politics.* Berkeley, Ca.: University of California Press.

Slatter, Stuart St. P. 1977. *Competition and Marketing Strategies in the Pharmaceutical Industry.* London: Croom Helm.

Smith, Tony. 1979. "The Underdevelopment of Development Literature: The Case of Dependency Theory." *World Politics* 31, no. 2 (January): 247–288.

El sol de México (Mexico City).

Spalding, Hobart A., Jr. 1977. *Organized Labor in Latin America: Historical Case Studies of Workers in Dependent Societies.* New York: New York University Press.

Spencer, Herbert. [1850], 1893. *Social Statics, or the Conditions Essential to Human Happiness.* New York: Appleton.

Starr, Paul. 1976. "The Politics of Therapeutic Nihilism." *Hastings Center Report* 6, no. 5 (October): 24–30.

Stauffer, Thomas R. 1975. "Profitability Measures in the Pharmaceutical Industry." In *Drug Development and*

Marketing, edited by Robert B. Helms, pp. 97–119. Washington, D.C.: American Enterprise Institute for Public Policy Research.

Stepan, Alfred. 1978. *The State and Society: Peru in Comparative Perspective.* Princeton, N.J.: Princeton University Press.

Stocking, George W., and Watkins, Myron W. 1947. *Cartels in Action: Case Studies in International Business Diplomacy.* New York: The Twentieth Century Fund.

Stopford, John M., and Wells, Louis T., Jr. 1972. *Managing the Multinational Enterprise: Organization of the Firm and Ownership of the Subsidiaries.* New York: Basic Books.

Sunkel, Osvaldo. 1969. "National Development Policy and External Dependence in Latin America." *Journal of Development Studies* 6, no. 1 (October): 23–48.

————. 1973. "Transnational Capitalism and National Disintegration in Latin America." *Social and Economic Studies* 22, no. 1 (March): 132–176.

Syntex Laboratories, Inc. 1966. *A Corporation and a Molecule: The Story of Research at Syntex.* Palo Alto, Ca.: Syntex Laboratories, Inc.

Temin, Peter. 1979a. "The Origin of Compulsory Drug Prescriptions." *Journal of Law and Economics* 22, no. 1 (April): 91–105.

————. 1979b. "Technology, Regulation, and Market Structure in the Modern Pharmaceutical Industry." *Bell Journal of Economics* 10, no. 2 (Autumn): 429–446.

Thomas, Clive Y. 1974. *Dependence and Transformation: The Economics of the Transition to Socialism.* New York: Monthly Review Press.

Tiefenbacher, Max P. 1979. "Problems of Distribution, Availability, and Utilization of Agents in Developing Countries: Industry Perspectives." In *Pharmaceuticals for Developing Countries,* the Institute of Medicine, pp. 211–227. Washington, D.C.: United States National Academy of Sciences.

Tipps, Dean C. 1973. "Modernization Theory and the Comparative Study of Societies: A Critical Perspective." *Comparative Studies in Society and History* 15, no. 2 (March): 199–226.

Toennies, Ferdinand. [1887], 1957. *Community and Society.* East Lansing, Mi.: Michigan State University Press.

Touraine, Alain. [1969], 1971. *The Post-Industrial Society.* New York: Random House.

Trythall, I. R. 1977. "The Drug Industry in Indonesia." *Drug and Cosmetic Industry* 120, no. 4 (April): 38–42, 124–127.

Tugwell, Franklin. 1975. *The Politics of Oil in Venezuela.* Stanford, Ca.: Stanford University Press.

United Nations Centre on Transnational Corporations (UNCTC). 1979. "Transnational Corporations and the Pharmaceutical Industry." New York: UNCTC. (United Nations publication, Sales No. E.79.II.A.3).

————. 1981. "Transnational Corporations in the Pharmaceutical Industry of Developing Countries." New York: UNCTC. (E/ C.10/85).

————. 1983. "Transnational Corporations in the Pharmaceutical Industry of Developing Countries: A Technical Study." New York: UNCTC.

United Nations Conference on Trade and Development (UNCTAD). 1975. See Lall (1975a).

————. 1977a. "Case Studies in the Transfer of Technology: The Pharmaceutical Industry in India." Geneva: UNCTAD. (TD/ B/ C.6/ 20).

————. 1977b. "The Impact of Trade Marks on the Development Process of Developing Countries." Geneva: UNCTAD. (TD/ B/ C.6/AC.3/ 3).

————. 1977c. See Bibile (1977).

————. 1980. "Technology Policies in the Pharmaceutical Sector in the United Republic of Tanzania." Geneva: UNCTAD. (UNCTAD/ TT/ 35).

United Nations Economic Commission for Europe (UNECE). 1975. *Annual Bulletin of Exports of Chemical Prod-*

ucts, 1973. (United Nations publication, Sales No. E.75.II.E.10).

United Nations Industrial Development Organization (UNIDO). 1978*a.* See Lall (1978*a*).

——. 1978*b.* "The Steps Involved in Establishing a Pharmaceutical Industry in Developing Countries." Vienna: UNIDO. (ID/ WG.267/ 3).

——. 1979. "The Cairo Declaration." Vienna: UNIDO. (ID/ WG.292/ 3/ Rev. 1).

——. 1980. "Global Study of the Pharmaceutical Industry." Vienna: UNIDO. (ID/ WG.331/ 6).

El universal (Mexico City).

U.S. Congress, Senate, Committee on Military Affairs, Subcommittee on War Mobilization. 1944. *Scientific and Technical Mobilization Hearings—Monopoly and Cartel Practices: The Hormone Cartel.* 78th Cong., 1st Sess., December 9, 1943. Washington, D.C.: Government Printing Office.

U.S. Congress, Senate, Committee on the Judiciary, Subcommittee on Patents, Trademarks, and Copyrights. 1957. *Wonder Drugs Hearings.* 84th Cong., 2d Sess., July 5 & 6, 1956. Washington, D.C.: Government Printing Office.

Vaitsos, Constantine. 1974. *Intercountry Income Distribution and Transnational Enterprises.* Oxford: Clarendon Press.

Valenzuela, J. Samuel, and Valenzuela, Arturo. 1978. "Modernization and Dependency: Alternative Perspectives in the Study of Latin American Underdevelopment." *Comparative Politics* 10, no. 4 (July): 535–557.

Vernon, Raymond. 1967. "Long-Run Trends in Concession Contracts." *Proceedings of the American Society of International Law,* 61st annual meeting (April): 81–89.

——. 1971. *Sovereignty at Bay: The Multinational Spread of U.S. Enterprises.* New York: Basic Books.

——. 1976*a.* "Multinational Enterprises in Developing Countries: Issues in Dependency and Interdependence." In *The Multinational Corporation and Social Change,* edited by David E. Apter and Louis Wolf Goodman, pp. 40–62. New York: Praeger.

———. 1976*b*. "A Decade of Studying Multinational Enterprises." *Harvard Business School Bulletin*, no. 5 (September–October): 24–28.

———. 1977. *Storm Over the Multinationals: The Real Issues.* Cambridge, Mass.: Harvard University Press.

Wallerstein, Immanuel. 1974*a*. "Dependence in an Interdependent World: The Limited Possibilities of Transformation Within the Capitalist World Economy." *African Studies Review* 17, no. 1 (April): 1–26.

———. 1974*b*. "The Rise and Future Demise of the World Capitalist System: Concepts for Comparative Analysis." *Comparative Studies in Society and History* 16, no. 4 (September): 387–415.

———. 1976. "Semi-Peripheral Countries and the Contemporary World Crisis." *Theory and Society* 3, no. 4: 461–484.

Wall Street Journal (New York, N.Y.).

Warren, Bill. 1973. "Imperialism and Capitalist Industrialization." *New Left Review*, no. 81 (September–October): 3–44.

Weber, Max. [1922], 1964. *The Theory of Social and Economic Organization.* New York: Free Press.

Wells, Louis T., Jr. 1969. "The Evolution of Concession Agreements." Economic Development Reports, no. 117. Cambridge, Mass.: Harvard Development Advisory Service.

Wescoe, W. Clarke. 1979. "Constraints on Expanding the Role of the U.S. Pharmaceutical Industry: United States Industry Perspective." In *Pharmaceuticals for Developing Countries,* the Institute of Medicine, pp. 179–186. Washington, D.C.: United States National Academy of Sciences.

Whyte, William Foote. [1943], 1967. *Street Corner Society: The Social Structure of an Italian Slum.* Chicago: University of Chicago Press.

Wionczek, Miguel S. 1964. "Electric Power: The Uneasy Partnership." In *Public Policy and Private Enterprise in Mexico*, edited by Raymond Vernon, pp. 19–110. Cambridge, Mass.: Harvard University Press.

————. 1967. "La explotación del azufre, 1910–1966." In *El nacionalismo mexicano y la inversión extranjera*, edited by Miguel S. Wionczek, pp. 169–314. Mexico, D.F.: Siglo XXI.

World Health Organization (WHO). 1976. "Consultation on Drug Policies." Geneva: WHO. (PDT:29.11.76).

Yudkin, John S. 1980. "The Economics of Pharmaceutical Supply in Tanzania." *International Journal of Health Services* 10, no. 3: 455–477.

Index

in Egypt, 233–234; in Mexico, 57n, 121, 128–130, 151, 162
BASF, 174n
Bayer, 174
Beecham, 191
Beisa, 90, 95, 97, 159
Belgium, 200, 207–208
Bell, Daniel, 5n
Bell, Wendell, 68n
Bendix, Reinhard, 40–41
Bennett, Douglas, 39, 47–48, 74, 77n, 159n
Bibile, Senaka, 236–238
Biersteker, Thomas J., 39, 42–43, 56n
bilaterial monopoly, 69, 108
bile acid, as pharmaceutical raw material, 85–86, 88, 104–105
bioequivalence, 237
Black, Cyril, 4, 10n
Bodenheimer, Susanne J., 23n
Boehringer Ingelheim, 174n
Boehringer Mannheim, 174n
Bolivia, 20
Boots (United Kingdom), 191
bourgeoisie, 9, 20, 33–34, 38, 97, 223; state bourgeoisie, 34, 163
brand-named drugs, 48, 107, 120, 194n, 207–208, 219, 229, 234, 236, 239, 244, 250
Brazil, 12n, 19–21, 30, 33–34, 44, 46–48, 58n, 66, 179; drug prices in, 193, 196–197; pharmaceutical industry in, 181–182, 188, 199, 203–204, 207, 209, 214, 229–232, 243, 249–252. See also Central de Medicamentos (CEME)
Bristol-Myers (Bristol), 107n, 136n, 173, 193
Brooke, Paul A., 194n, 207
Brzezinski, Zbigniew, 5n

cabeza de negro, 82, 84–85
caciques, 140

campesinos, see peasants
Canada, 81n, 179, 193, 195n, 207, 208
cancer, 201
capitalism, 7, 10, 15, 21n–22n, 25, 29, 32, 41, 46. *See also* world system
Caporaso, James A., 24n, 26, 73n, 74
Cardoso, Fernando Henrique, 6, 11, 12n–14n, 18–21, 23–26, 29–30, 32, 34–36, 38, 44, 46, 58
Caribbean Centre for Pharmaceuticals, 253
Caribbean countries, 46
cartels, 31n, 81, 84, 93, 102, 107n, 118, 170
Central America, 20, 46, 214n
Central American Common Market, 253
central countries, *see* core countries
Central de Medicamentos (CEME), 162, 229–231, 241, 252n
centralized procurement of drugs, 214–217, 252–253; in Brazil, 162, 230; in the United Kingdom, 194–195
Chad, 252
chemical industry, 54, 129, 173, 174n, 233, 250
Chilcote, Ronald H., 7n, 22, 23n, 44
Chile, 20, 38, 44, 47, 65
China, People's Republic of, 30, 135n, 153, 181, 199
chloramphenicol, 209n, 210
cholesterol, 80–82, 86–87, 89, 104
Chudnovsky, Daniel, 220–222
Ciba (Ciba-Geigy), 81, 83n, 87, 92n, 102, 111, 113, 173, 193, 232, 249
Collier, David, 39

Productos Químicos Naturales
(Proquina), 111n, 114n
profits: in pharmaceutical industry, 112, 115, 119–120, 124, 170,
190–192, 195n–196n; of transnational corporations compared to
local private firms, 106, 119,
219, 222, 240
progesterone, 80, 82–88, 123,
145–146
Prontosil (sulfanilimide), 107n,
174n
Proquivemex (Productos Químicos
Vegetales Mexicanos), 132, 224,
241; defense of natural resources, 138, 141; diosgenin
manufacturing plants, 141;
prices for barbasco sold to
transnational corporations,
137–138, 142–143, 151; promotion of peasant welfare,
138–141; toll manufacturing for,
138, 144n, 150, 151
Protex, 91–92, 97n, 104, 114n
Puerto Rico, 55, 106, 110

quality control, 219, 237, 239,
242–243
Quijano, Aníbal, 44

Rank Xerox, 191
reform, of pharmaceutical industry, 117, 133, 152, 211, 224,
230–231, 238–239, 243
regulation, of pharmaceutical industry, 167, 169, 187, 189;
country differences, 210–211;
effect on innovation, 245–247;
voluntary, by manufacturers,
211
replacement therapy, 80
research and development, in
pharmaceutical industry, 107,
169, 187–189, 192n, 201, 228

retrospective fallacy, 72n
Richardson-Merrell, 248
Rosenkranz, George, 83–84
Rostow, Walt W., 4, 10n
Roussel (France), 105
Royal Netherlands Yeast and Al-
cohol Factory, 124
royalties, 107n, 215, 227, 228
Rustow, Dankwart A., 4, 10n
Ruzicka, Leopold, 83n
Rwanda, 252

Sandoz (Sandoz-Wander), 173, 232
sapogenins, 82
Sarabhai Chemicals, 203, 218
Sarett, Lewis H., 201
Schaumann, Leif, 169
Schering A.G. (Germany), 81, 84,
87, 93, 102, 105, 111, 114n, 124,
174n
Schering Corporation (Schering-
Plough), 102, 119–120, 124,
158–159, 173, 193
Schwartzman, David, 191n–192n
Searle (G.D. Searle & Company),
59n, 92n, 102, 173, 248
sedatives, 192n, 200n
"self-medication," 205
semiperiphery, 9n, 46, 183,
187–189, 212, 240–241, 249–250
Serenace, 200n
Serpasil, 193
serums, 188, 196
sex hormones, 79–81
Sharpe, Kenneth, 39, 47–48, 74,
77n, 159n
Sierra Leone, 216–217
Silverman, Milton, 191, 193, 199,
209–211
Singapore, 188n
Smith, Kline & French Laboratories (SmithKline), 102, 112,
114n, 173, 248
Smith, Tony, 14n

social classes, role in development, 15, 20, 21n–22n, 35–38, 155
socialism, as opposite of dependency, 14–15, 17–18, 22–30, 32–33, 35, 61
socialist governments, policies towards pharmaceutical industry, 215–216, 239
Social Science Research Council, project on transnational corporations, 46n–47n
socio-historical configurations, 40–41, 43
Somlo, Emeric, 83, 93, 109, 129n
South Africa, 183, 208
South Pacific countries, 252
Soviet Union, 30, 181, 218
Spain, 210
Spencer, Herbert, 4n
spironolactone, 152
Squibb, 105n, 107n, 111, 173, 232n, 248
Sri Lanka, 200n, 203, 215, 218, 236–243, 251–252
Starr, Paul, 202n
state: autonomy of, 154–163; democratic, 35; repressive, 22n, 23–24; role in development, 8–9, 21–24, 46, 65–67, 154–163, 214–217; theories of, 38–39
state-owned enterprises, 34, 121, 161–163, 189, 214, 241
State Pharmaceuticals Corporation (Sri Lanka), 215, 236–239, 241
Stepan, Alfred, 44, 48, 155–160
steroid hormones, 79–80; as bulk intermediate products, 86–87, 89, 95, 98, 110, 117, 122, 152; demand for, 59n–60n, 87–88, 103, 122, 133; raw materials for, 80–83, 104–105; world retail sales, 54
stigmasterol, 86, 105, 134

Stopford, John M., 105
streptomycin, 107n
structural-functionalism, 5
sulfanilimide, see Prontosil
Sunkel, Osvaldo, 24n, 44
Sweden, 183, 208, 228, 249–250
SweDrug Consulting, 249–250
Swisspharma, 214n, 232
Switzerland: drug prices in, 193, 195; as home country of transnational corporations, 116n, 146, 174, 176, 178, 183, 191, 195n–196n, 209, 231; pharmaceutical industry in, 173, 179n, 187–188
Synalar, 59n, 111
Syntex (Mexico): founding of, 83, 97n; relations with European pharmaceutical corporations, 84, 87–88, 111n; relations with United States pharmaceutical corporations, 84, 88, 90–93; sales, 111–112, 117
Syntex (United States), 109–112, 135n
synthesis, of pharmaceutical products, 80–81, 105, 188
Syrian Arab Republic, 252

Tabacos Mexicanos (Tabamex), 162n
Tagamet, 247–248
Tanzania, 30, 200n, 210n, 215, 241, 252
tax fraud, 145–147
tax havens, 106, 108, 110
technology: appropriateness of, 198, 202–204, 219; entrenched, 104; transfer of, 202, 218–219, 224–225, 249–251; technological autonomy, 203–204, 223, 231, 240; technological dependence, 141, 153, 159, 244
Temin, Peter, 107n, 169

testosterone, 87
tetracycline, 107n, 207n, 209n, 238n
Thailand, 214–215
therapeutic nihilism, 202n
thiacetazone, 201
third world, *see* periphery; semi-periphery
Thomas, Lacy Glen, 246
Tiefenbacher, Max P., 200
Toennies, Ferdinand, 4n
Touraine, Alain, 5n
trademarks, 225–226, 231. *See also* brand-named drugs
tradition, contrasted with modernity, 4–5, 10
transfer pricing, 98–99, 106, 192n, 195–198, 249; in Mexico, 55, 124, 145–146; in Sri Lanka, 238
transnational corporations (TNCs), 56–58, 95–96; compared with local private firms, 114–121, 240–243; dominance in third world countries, 42–43, 181–183, 188–189, 244; industrialization in the periphery, role in, 24, 33–34, 250; international expansion in pharmaceutical industry, 169–181
triple alliance, 8, 34, 229
Trythall, I. R., 234n
tuberculosis, 200–201, 219
Tugwell, Franklin, 39
Turkey, 208

Uganda, 252
United Kingdom: drug prices in, 193–194, 195n–196n; as home country of transnational corporations, 174n, 176, 183, 238; pharmaceutical industry in, 178n, 179, 187–188, 191, 207–208, 246

United Nations Conference on Trade and Development (UNCTAD), 251
United Nations Industrial Development Organization (UNIDO), 203, 218, 251
United States: drug prices in, 107n, 193, 194n, 195; Food and Drug Administration (FDA), 110, 210–211, 245n, 248; government antitrust measures, 81n, 93, 116n, 195n, 232; as home country of transnational corporations, 134, 170, 173–174, 176, 178–179, 181, 183; marketing of pharmaceutical products in, 199, 207–209; pharmaceutical industry profits in, 190–191
Upjohn, 86–88, 92, 105n, 107n, 120, 123, 134, 173
Uruguay, 20, 47n

vaccines, 188
Vaitsos, Constantine, 99, 146
Valenzuela, J. Samuel and Arturo, 4n, 10n
Valium, 194–196, 200n
Venezuela, 20, 47, 65, 68, 199
Vernon, John M., 245–247
Vernon, Raymond, 43n, 60n, 73, 95–96, 105n
vertical integration, 104–105, 127–128, 142, 152, 182, 217, 240
vitamins, 196, 199–201
Vitrium, 224, 228

Wallerstein, Immanuel, 8n–9n, 183, 187
Wander (Sandoz-Wander), 173, 232
Warner-lambert, 173
Warren, Bill, 24n

INDEX

Weber, Max, 4n, 32, 43
Wellcome, 174n
Wells, Louis T., Jr., 73, 105
Wescoe, W. Clarke, 201
Whyte, William Foote, 64
Wionczek, Miguel S., 47, 57n
working class, 8, 23, 32, 38
World Health Organization
(WHO), 201n, 231, 251–252

world system, pharmaceutical industry in, 183, 187–189
World War II, 3, 16, 33, 68, 84,
125, 169, 174N

Yudkin, John S., 200n, 201n, 210n
Yugoslavia, 30

Zambia, 252

Library of Congress Cataloging in Publication Data

Gereffi, Gary, 1948–
The pharmaceutical industry and
dependency in the Third World.

Bibliography: p.   Includes index.
1. Steroid hormone industry—Mexico
2. Mexico—Dependency of foreign countries.
3. International business enterprises.
4. Underdeveloped areas—Drug trade.
5. Dependency. I. Title.
[DNLM: 1. Developing countries. 2. Drug industry.
3. Political systems.
QV 736 G367p]
HD9675.S833M623   1983   338.4'76153660972   83-42560
ISBN 0-691-09401-2
ISBN 0-691-02828-1 (pbk.)

Gary Gereffi is Assistant Professor of Sociology
at Duke University.